Disability and Passing

Disability
and Passing

Blurring the Lines of Identity

EDITED BY

Jeffrey A. Brune
Daniel J. Wilson

TEMPLE UNIVERSITY PRESS
Philadelphia

TEMPLE UNIVERSITY PRESS
Philadelphia, Pennsylvania 19122
www.temple.edu/tempress

Library of Congress Cataloging-in-Publication Data

Disability and passing : blurring the lines of identity / edited by
Jeffrey A. Brune and Daniel J. Wilson.
     pages cm
Includes bibliographical references and index.
ISBN 978-1-4399-0979-9 (cloth : alk. paper)
ISBN 978-1-4399-0980-5 (pbk. : alk. paper)
ISBN 978-1-4399-0981-2 (e-book)
1. People with disabilities. 2. Discrimination against people with
disabilities 3. Sociology of disability. 4. Group identity. I. Brune,
Jeffrey A., 1972– II. Wilson, Daniel J., 1949–

√HV1568.D5634 2013
  305.9'08—dc23   2012042290

Printed in the United States of America

070113P

◆ Contents

Acknowledgments   vii

1   Introduction   1
Jeffrey A. Brune and Daniel J. Wilson

2   Passing in the Shadow of FDR: Polio Survivors,
Passing, and the Negotiation of Disability   13
Daniel J. Wilson

3   The Multiple Layers of Disability Passing in Life,
Literature, and Public Discourse   36
Jeffrey A. Brune

4   The Menstrual Masquerade   58
David Linton

5   "I Made Up My Mind to Act Both Deaf and Dumb":
Displays of Disability and Slave Resistance in the
Antebellum American South   71
Dea H. Boster

6   Passing as Sane, or How to Get People to
Sit Next to You on the Bus   99
Peta Cox

7 Athlete First: A Note on Passing, Disability, and Sport   111
    Michael A. Rembis

8 The Sociopolitical Contexts of Passing and
    Intellectual Disability   142
    Allison C. Carey

9 Growing Up to Become Hearing:
    Dreams of Passing in Oral Deaf Education   167
    Kristen C. Harmon

    Contributors   199
    Index   201

Acknowledgments

HE EDITORS THANK the contributors for their hard work and high-quality essays. All of them demonstrated a commitment to the project and worked hard to advance our understanding of this important topic. Our appreciation also goes to Craig Royal for allowing us to use his artwork on the cover. Janet Francendese at Temple University Press was a most reliable editor and kept things moving. Finally, we especially thank Kim Nielsen, who played a key role in the early phases of the project and helped get it off the ground. Although her name does not appear elsewhere in the book, she deserves much credit for making it happen.

Disability and Passing

 **Introduction**

JEFFREY A. BRUNE AND
DANIEL J. WILSON

D ISABILITY PASSING is a complex and wide-ranging topic. Most often, the term refers to the way people conceal social markers of impairment to avoid the stigma of disability and pass as "normal."[1] However, it also applies to other ways people manage their identities, which can include exaggerating a condition to get some type of benefit or care. Going further, disability passing encompasses the ways that others impose, intentionally or not, a specific disability or non-disability identity on a person. It even provides a framework for understanding how the topic of disability is ignored in texts and conversations.

The topic of disability passing reveals the dynamic nature of disability and identity and provides insight into what is at stake when it comes to disability and nondisability identification. Nearly all disabled people confront, often routinely, the choice of hiding their disability or drawing attention to it and the question of what to do when others overlook it. Going to the root of a disability identity, their decisions weigh issues of stigma, pride, prejudice, discrimination, and privilege but rarely put the matter to rest. Even those who choose not to pass still must decide what to do when others fail to recognize or intentionally overlook their disability. Furthermore, the importance of passing extends well beyond the individual and has larger social, cultural, and political implications. Quite simply, it is hard to understand disability and identity in modern America without examining issues of passing.

Passing is an act that blurs the lines between disability and normality, but those lines were not always sharp to begin with. As the field of disability studies has shown, minds and bodies are better understood in terms of variance than as deviation from a fixed norm. This in part accounts for many disabled people's ability to pass so often and so easily. Rather than assume a dichotomy between disability and normality, an examination of passing from a disability perspective reveals how the social construction of disability remains fluid. It also informs our understanding of what constitutes "normal," since passing expresses, reifies, and helps create concepts of normality.

Despite its importance, disability passing has received inadequate attention from scholars until now. Almost all studies of passing focus on race, gender, or sexuality and fail to account for disability as a fundamental, destabilizing component of a person's identity.[2] This reflects a more widespread reluctance among mainstream scholars to consider disability as an analytic category alongside the others. By the same token, within disability studies passing has received relatively little attention, despite acknowledgment of its importance.[3] This book is an effort to address that neglect.

In addition to exploring the topic of disability passing, this interdisciplinary anthology aims to avoid the trap of sequestering disability, race, class, gender, and sexuality from one another. Intersectionality, which considers how all those categories interact and affect one another, provides a more nuanced and accurate understanding of identity. Passing as a disabled or nondisabled person will have a different meaning depending on specific contexts of race, gender, class, and sexuality. What disability passing meant for an enslaved African American woman in the antebellum South is far different from what it meant for an educated white man in the post–World War II era. Disability can destabilize gender and race, and vice versa. The focus on intersectionality that many of these chapters share should also make this book useful to people interested primarily in identity issues other than disability. However, readers will notice a more thorough treatment of gender and sexuality than of race. This unfortunate circumstance is one we had hoped to avoid but in the end could not. We will note that this shortcoming still reflects a general tendency within disability studies to focus more on gender and sexuality than on race.

The act of passing occurs on an intimate, interpersonal level and often relates to issues of stigma. Our discussion of passing builds on, but also differs significantly from, a classic work that remains seminal and is often cited in disability studies: Erving Goffman's *Stigma*.[4] Given that the work was written fifty years ago, before disability studies existed as a recognized field of study, it is remarkable that it still holds such sway. This anthology, serendipitously published during the year of *Stigma*'s fiftieth anniversary, offers an ideal opportunity to reexamine one of the most enduring works in the field.

Many within the field of disability studies continue to use *Stigma* and cite it without criticism, but a few serious critiques deserve attention. One has to do with the sites Goffman chose for understanding disability. To approach the issue of stigma, Goffman focused on personal encounters—what he called "the primal scene of sociology"—arguing that they are the locations where stigma is created and learned. The Marxist geographer Brendan Gleeson offers a brief but searing critique of Goffman for ignoring the larger structural forces that shape notions of disability. To Gleeson, personal encounters represent merely the outcome of powerful social, economic, and political forces. Upset that disability studies continues to embrace Goffman's approach, Gleeson suggests completely doing away with Goffman's "interactionist fallacy."[5]

This materialist critique has merit and deserves more attention than it has received, but it should not provoke us to completely jettison an examination of passing and identity on an interpersonal level. As many chapters in this volume show, a synthesis in which we understand passing and identity on both a micro and a macro scale is possible. Larger social, political, economic, and cultural forces create contexts and conditions that affect passing and identity, but they are not completely deterministic and do not reveal the individual consequences of disability issues.

Another criticism of Goffman's work is that he approached disability only from the perspective of normality, positioning himself and his reader as "normals" and disabled people as "others."[6] This serious problem, however, is not difficult to rectify. The chapters in this anthology examine stigma but privilege a disabled perspective. Ours is by no means an original contribution, since one of the main emphases of disability studies has been to center a disabled perspective. This approach is also more useful for understanding the social construction of normality, which expands the range of disability studies.

This anthology offers another correction to Goffman's assumptions about disability, using history to counter his essentialist assumptions.

4 ◆ Jeffrey A. Brune and Daniel J. Wilson

These essays seek to historicize passing and, by extension, stigma. Stigma is not fixed, natural, essential, or transhistorical; rather, it changes over time and varies across regions, cultures, and other contexts. Goffman, by contrast, sought to make claims about the universal production and function of stigma. His universalist assumptions are not surprising, given the trends within his discipline at the time and that his "primal scene of sociology" uses terminology that comes directly from Freud. However, as Gelya Frank points out, Goffman's study of stigma was rooted in the 1950s and would not account for the vast changes that came soon after with the disability rights movement and disability pride.[7] Frank could have added that Goffman's generalizations about stigma also did not account for some 1950s disability activists, including many within the National Federation of the Blind, as well as earlier examples. This anthology examines stigma, which Goffman originally explained in universalist terms, and shows how the issue changes over time and across spaces and (sub)cultures. It is our hope that this volume will further the project of understanding disability according to historical context rather than universalist assumptions and explanations. Within disability studies there is still a disagreement, not made explicit enough, between those who imply universalist or essentialist explanations of disability and those who historicize issues of disability. Readers should take note of this debate and locate this anthology in the latter camp.

The anthology takes a scholarly approach to passing, but like most of disability studies, it also aims to effect political and personal transformation. Passing becomes a site of conflict between those who derive power from defining the boundaries of normality and those who lose rights and privileges when they are labeled deviant. This scholarship on passing can and should have an impact on nonacademic audiences. It can affect the way people deal with disability on a personal and political level.

We hope this anthology does not lead to condemnation of those who pass and that readers will recognize that the political, personal, and moral issues that relate to passing are not always as simple as they appear. Some of these essays draw attention to the costs of passing that disabled people might want to consider as they grapple with their own identity issues. Passing can take a psychological toll and can also reinforce—or, at least, fail to challenge—the stigma of disability. However, the meaning, costs, and morality of passing are not clear-cut. For all marginalized peoples who pass, "The allure of rewriting identity cannot be disconnected from the very real emotional and material advantages of doing so."[8] Passing can be more complicated than simply an acceptance or internalization of the stigma of disability. The meaning of passing varies widely according to context and can represent a challenge to power rather than simply an acceptance of oppression and stigma. Furthermore, as Linda Schlossberg points out when writing about passing in the context of race, religion, and sexuality, "Passing is not simply about erasure or denial, as it is often castigated but, rather, about the creation and establishment of an alternative set of narratives. It becomes a way of creating new stories out of unusable ones, or from personal narratives seemingly in conflict with other aspects of self-presentation."[9] Even when passing seems to reinforce the stigma of disability, it is more productive, and more just, to challenge the ableism that compels people to pass rather than blame the individuals who choose to do so.

Disability and Passing brings together eight essays that explore the diverse ways in which passing occurs. The essays describe ways to pass with a variety of disabilities, including blindness, deafness, physical impairments, mental illness, intellectual and cognitive disabilities, and menstruation, and the way that disability passes out of texts and public discourse. Since passing is an unstable condition, the authors also discuss the ways in which passing changes over time. A changing social environment, such as that which followed the passage of the Americans with Disabilities Act in 1990, could make it advantageous to come out as disabled to benefit from newly available services. Or bodily changes associated with aging could necessitate adopting new and more obvious assistive devices that made passing impossible. In still other cases, adopting a disabled identity and taking up advocacy on behalf of individuals with disabilities warranted abandoning the effort to pass as normal. The decision to try to pass or not was and is difficult and complex, and the authors of these essays have acknowledged the complexities associated with trying to appear normal.

Visible physical impairments often come to mind when people think of disability. Individuals using a wheelchair or scooter for mobility, reliant on crutches or canes to walk, and supported by braces appear visibly and obviously disabled. It is often difficult, if not impossible, to disguise the visual evidence of physical impairments. For individuals with such disabilities, passing often meant passing in plain sight. In other words, they had to develop strategies that suggested to others that the individual was not, after all, really disabled. Two of the essays, Daniel J. Wilson's "Passing in the Shadow of FDR: Polio Survivors, Passing, and the Negotiation of Disability" (Chapter 2) and Michael A. Rembis's "Athlete First: A Note on Passing, Disability, and Sport" (Chapter 7), address the ways in which individuals with obvious physical disabilities negotiated their way into the mainstream.

Wilson's "Passing in the Shadow of FDR" explores how polio survivors used the example of President Franklin D. Roosevelt's public image as a recovered and cured polio patient as inspiration for their own efforts to pass as normal. Many polio survivors succeeded to a large extent in passing into the mainstream of American life in the second half of the twentieth century, although the effort was not without psychological and physical consequences. Passing meant many different things to polio survivors. Many first had to convince themselves that they were not disabled, that like the president they could do whatever they wanted. As with FDR, walking—or at least seeming to walk—was often the key to passing successfully, even if that meant walking with obvious braces and crutches. Polio survivors developed a variety of strategies to deflect attention from their withered limbs, unusual gaits, and necessary assistive devices to be accepted as "normal." However, they discovered that their efforts to pass by pushing their bodies and ignoring pain gave rise to post-polio syndrome some thirty to forty years after they had polio. Post-polio syndrome challenged anew their ability to pass and often reawakened psychological issues. These late effects of polio have forced many survivors to renegotiate their relationship to disability and to society, and many have concluded that passing is simply too costly, both physically and psychologically.

Rembis's "Athlete First" deals with the post–World War II rise of disabled athletics first as part of the rehabilitation of injured veterans and then as physical activity available to a much wider range of individuals with mainly physical impairments. Rembis picks up some of the themes developed in Wilson's essay, especially the need to pass in plain sight and be accepted as normal despite obvious disabilities and assistive devices—to be accepted as an athlete first and not simply as a disabled athlete. Rembis argues that these athletes do not need to conceal their impairments to pass if they can approximate social, cultural, and athletic norms in their appearance, behavior, competitiveness, and performance. He focuses most of his essay on two contemporary disabled athletes, Mark Zupan and Aimee Mullins. After an automobile accident, Zupan became a quadriplegic and played wheelchair rugby at its highest levels, winning the gold medal in the 2008 Paralympic Games. Mullins is a double below-the-knee amputee as the result of a birth defect who pursued a career in track and worked as a fashion model and film actor. Rembis explores how these two individuals negotiate their relationship to their disability and their athletic success. The chapter concludes with thoughts on overcoming and passing that are applicable not only to disabled athletes but to anyone attempting to succeed in today's culture.

Expanding the range of the topic, the chapters by Dea H. Boster, Jeffrey A. Brune, and David Linton examine passing in the context of the removal of disability issues from texts and public discourse, the ways that the advertising of feminine hygiene products has played on notions of disability passing, and slave malingering. Boster's "'I Made Up My Mind to Act Both Deaf and Dumb': Displays of Disability and Slave Resistance in the Antebellum American South" (Chapter 5), an account of how slaves used disability to mitigate some of the consequences of slavery, explores how slaves tried to pass as disabled to prevent a sale or modify and lessen their work obligations. She discusses how and why passing as disabled enabled some slaves to assert some control over their bodies and to resist the authority of their masters. As she writes, "Performing disability—a condition normally associated with dependence and powerlessness—and forcing white authority figures to contend with their conditions could allow slaves to achieve a degree of independence and control in many different situations." By taking on the stigmatized condition of disability, these slaves were able to negotiate with their masters an altered status. Boster examines a number of cases from plantation and court records of slaves who feigned illness, often epileptic fits or mental illness, and who in some cases "intentionally disabled themselves as a form of sabotage." Boster's essay insightfully explores the benefits and costs of passing at the nexus of race and disability and raises interesting questions about the stability of these categories of race and disability, especially when they are performed together.

While Boster examines the issue of passing as disabled, Brune studies how the topic of disability passes out of texts and public discourse. "The Multiple Layers of Disability Passing in Life, Literature, and Public Discourse" (Chapter 3) focuses on John Howard Griffin and his famous book *Black Like Me* (1961). Chronicling the author's experience passing as an African American in the Jim Crow South, the book shaped many white people's views of black civil rights for decades. However, Brune notes that this was not Griffin's first experience with passing. Wounded in World War II, Griffin slowly lost his vision but attempted to pass as sighted for a number of years before embracing an empowered blind identity. Then, unexpectedly, he regained his sight in 1957 and seemed to have left the disabled world behind, just two years before conducting his famous racial experiment. Nonetheless, Brune's reading of *Black Like Me* reveals the ways in which Griffin's earlier experience of disability influenced his writing of the book. Curiously, Griffin avoids the topic of disability that left such a mark on him and his later work. The essay explores how Griffin erased the experience of disability from his text on racial passing and how disability has also passed from subsequent discussions of the work and the author. The chapter concludes with thoughts about how disability becomes a marginalized topic in modern American texts and discourses.

Further expanding the topic of disability passing, Linton's "The Menstrual Masquerade" (Chapter 4) examines how the promotion of modern feminine hygiene products has played on intersecting notions of gender and disability. In a fascinating analysis of the language and imagery of ads for sanitary napkins in the 1920s, Linton shows how companies such as Kotex used notions of disability and passing as nondisabled to educate women to pass as non-menstruators. He then attempts to examine attitudes about menstruation both before and since that era. Exploring further the relationship between gender and disability, Linton concludes with speculation about how current notions of menstruation and passing may be starting to change.

Two of the anthology's chapters focus on the role that institutions, including families, play in disability passing. Kristen C. Harmon's "Growing Up to Become Hearing: Dreams of Passing in Oral Deaf Education" (Chapter 9) focuses on the role that families and deaf educational institutions play in compelling children to pass as normal. Harmon begins with a brief discussion of her own experience going through the "pure oral method" of deaf education and discovering as an adult the limitations of trying to pass for hearing. She focuses on a series of films produced by the Oberkotter Foundation that promote oral deaf education for young deaf children. In her careful study of both the imagery and the scripts of these films, Harmon explores the ways in which they play on the parents' desires for their child and their family to be perceived as normal—having a child pass as nondisabled becomes a means for the family to pass as normal. What these films do not show, as Harmon points out, are the consequences when the children reach adolescence and adulthood. By analyzing parental roles, Harmon emphasizes that passing is not a singular performance. She also reminds us that where young children are concerned, it is the parents who make the initial decision whether or not their child will attempt to pass.

Another chapter that examines power and institutional interests in relation to passing is Allison C. Carey's "The Sociopolitical Contexts of Passing and Intellectual Disability" (Chapter 8). Carey's broad historical analysis begins with early-twentieth-century eugenic concerns about feeblemindedness. Fears that "feebleminded" individuals might pass as normal, marry, and pass on their defective genes led to systems to diagnose, register, sequester, and sometimes sterilize such individuals. After World War II, however, parents and professionals took a different approach. They softened category boundaries and began to develop services and resources to allow individuals with intellectual disabilities to pass into the mainstream of American society. As with Harmon's essay on deaf education, this chapter also explores family involvement in disability passing. Many families sought to reduce the stigma not only for the individual but for the family as well. Carey also discusses recent developments in this history, as disability pride and advocacy have become more prominent since the 1990s even as issues of stigma persist. Self-advocates and allies have argued for a blurring of the lines between abled and disabled, for respecting the individual regardless of his or her impairment. At the same time, the need to be seen as disabled to secure certain rights and benefits has further complicated these issues of passing related to intellectual disability.

Using postmodern theory to delve further into cognitive disabilities, Peta Cox's essay, "Passing as Sane, or How to Get People to Sit Next to You on the Bus" (Chapter 6), draws on theories of performativity and performance to understand sanity and mental illness. Issues of passing are central to how we define and perceive sanity and mental illness, and the complex act of passing, which can either increase or decrease an individual's distress, affects how people experience mental issues. Cox draws on Judith Butler's theories of performativity but also notes the important ways in which the differences between gender and mental illness limit the usefulness of Butler's theories in analyzing passing as (in)sane. Cox interrogates the goals of therapy—whether they are designed to reduce the actual impairment or to modify the external symptoms so the individual can pass as sane. She also examines how strategies for passing and notions of sanity vary according to other social identities, such as gender, sexuality, class, and race.

In addition to the chapters, the cover art for this volume merits explanation. On the most obvious level, its overlapping and blurred lines offer a literal representation of how passing blurs the lines between disability and normality. Going further, the production of this art adds layers to its significance. While the photograph ostensibly does not appear to be about disability, the photographer, Craig Royal, is blind, which blurs the distinction between disability and nondisability art. Moreover, the very idea of "blind photography" challenges the opposition between blindness and visual art that most people take for granted. On a variety of levels, this image encapsulates the blurred boundaries between disability and normality.

We hope readers will recognize that these essays by no means exhaust the topic and will choose to pursue more studies of disability and passing. As mentioned previously, there is more possibility for integrating race into this discussion. Another topic ripe for study is the exhibition of disability pride, including the adornment of various technologies that serve as disability markers. Various chapters touch on this issue, but none make it their main focus. There are also many time periods, places, and (sub)cultures, as well as disabilities and impairments, that do not appear in these pages.

As the essays in this volume make clear, passing has been and continues to be a complex psychological and physical performance that can only be understood when situated in a particular historical and social context. The issues differ somewhat depending on the disability. Physical impairments require different kinds of decisions and actions from less visible impairments, such as intellectual disabilities, that may be evident only in particular settings. These essays also remind us that while disability passing shares some features with gender and racial passing, it has its own particular characteristics. There is no better example than Boster's essay, which describes how slaves took on the mantle of disability to mitigate the harshness of racial slavery and even to escape it. Eight essays on disability and passing by no means exhaust the subject, but we hope this anthology demonstrates what is possible through a close study of passing and disability and encourages other scholars to explore the subject further.

Notes

1. Throughout the anthology, the authors undermine notions of "normal" and "normality" and see them as social constructions. With this understanding, the editors have decided it is not necessary to put quotes around the words every time, although there are cases in which the extra emphasis is warranted.

2. Leading studies of passing include Elaine K. Ginsberg, ed., *Passing and the Fictions of Identity* (Durham, N.C.: Duke University Press, 1996); Gerald Horne, *The Color of Fascism: Lawrence Dennis, Racial Passing, and the Rise of Right-Wing Extremism in the United States,* annotated ed. (New York: New York University Press, 2006); Joanne J. Meyerowitz, *How Sex Changed: A History of Transsexuality in the United States* (Cambridge, Mass.: Harvard University Press, 2002); James M. O'Toole, *Passing for White: Race, Religion, and the Healy Family, 1820–1920* (Amherst: University of Massachusetts Press, 2003); María Carla Sánchez and Linda Schlossberg, eds., *Passing: Identity and Interpretation in Sexuality, Race, and Religion* (New York: New York University Press, 2001); Martha A. Sandweiss, *Passing Strange: A Gilded Age Tale of Love and Deception across the Color Line* (New York: Penguin, 2009); Eve Kosofsky Sedgwick, *Epistemology of the Closet* (Berkeley: University of California Press, 1990); Werner Sollors, *Neither Black nor White yet Both: Thematic Explorations of Interracial Literature* (New York: Oxford University Press, 1997); Gayle Freda Wald, *Crossing the Line: Racial Passing in Twentieth-Century U.S. Literature and Culture* (Durham, N.C.: Duke University Press, 2000).

3. Thus far, there has been no major, book-length study of disability passing, although one article has received much attention and is referenced often in these chapters: Tobin Siebers, "Disability as Masquerade," *Literature and Medicine* 23, no. 1 (Spring 2004): 1–22. Other works that address disability passing include Brenda Jo Brueggemann, "On (Almost) Passing," *College English* 59, no. 6 (1997): 647–660; Georgina Kleege, *Sight Unseen* (New Haven, Conn.: Yale University Press, 1999), chap. 1; Ellen Jean Samuels, "My Body, My Closet: Invisible Disability and the Limits of Coming-Out Discourse," *GLQ: A Journal of Lesbian and Gay Studies* 9, no. 1 (2003): 233–255; Tanya Titchkosky, *Disability, Self, and Society* (Toronto: University of Toronto Press, 2003), chaps. 3, 6.

4. Erving Goffman, *Stigma: Notes on the Management of Spoiled Identity* (New York: Simon and Schuster, 1963).

5. Brendan Gleeson, *Geographies of Disability* (London: Routledge, 1999), 17.

6. Those who have made this critique include Gelya Frank, "Beyond Stigma: Visibility and Self-Empowerment for Persons with Congenital Limb Deficiencies," *Journal of Social Issues* 44, no. 1 (1988): 106; Grace M. Mest, "With a Little Help from Their Friends: Use of Social Support Systems by Persons with Retardation," *Journal of Social Issues* 44, no. 1 (1988): 117–125; Tanya Titchkosky, "Disability Studies: The Old and the New," *Canadian Journal of Sociology/Cahiers Canadiens de Sociologie* 25, no. 2 (April 2000): 204.

7. Frank, "Beyond Stigma," 97. Others have made the same critique, including Karen Hirsch, "Culture and Disability: The Role of Oral History," *Oral History Review* 22, no. 1 (1995): 10.

8. Linda Schlossberg, "Introduction: Rites of Passing," in Sánchez and Schlossberg, *Passing,* 4.

9. Ibid.

2 Passing in the Shadow of FDR

Polio Survivors, Passing, and the Negotiation of Disability

DANIEL J. WILSON

THE AMERICAN WRITER and novelist Wilfred Sheed spent many years following his case of polio attempting to disguise the fact that he was disabled. He noted that most individuals with handicaps "find themselves faced as one with the same task," which is to "make the world, and ourselves, forget for as long and as often as possible that there has ever been anything wrong with us: to be, in other words, 'great pitchers,' and not just 'great one-armed pitchers.'"[1] Some forty years after his illness, when post-polio syndrome created new disabilities, Sheed came to the recognition that his efforts to pass, to conceal his disability all those years, probably had not been as complete as he had convinced himself: "The truth is I was probably always a lot more handicapped than I let on, either to myself or others. My knacks were all geared to the same end, a massive cover-up, a downright Watergate of the nerves and muscles, in order to pass inspection."[2]

In seeking to "pass inspection," Sheed, like many polio survivors, sought to emulate Franklin D. Roosevelt, who successfully cultivated the image of a healthy man who had recovered from polio with no significant permanent disability. Roosevelt's carefully constructed image posed significant challenges for polio survivors. With the aid of advisers and a complicit press, Roosevelt passed as a man recovered from polio who could walk and stand and was thus fit to hold high political office. In fact, FDR walked and stood with great difficulty and spent most of his time in a wheelchair or otherwise sitting. Polio survivors from the late 1920s on were urged by their doctors, families, and friends to emulate Roosevelt and become whatever they wished, regardless of their impairments caused by polio. Many sought to follow FDR's example, in spite of considerable physical and psychological pain. Others eventually came to the conclusion that it was futile to try to emulate the "passer-in-chief" without the resources available to a wealthy man who was also the governor of New York and then the president of the United States.

Since the physical disabilities characteristic of polio and the assistive devices used to compensate (braces, crutches, and wheelchairs) were impossible to hide, polio survivors developed strategies to "pass" even when evidence of their disability was in plain sight. As FDR demonstrated, walking, or simulating walking and being upright, was a common way to pass. But other strategies came into play, as well. These "knacks," as Sheed called them, included not asking for accommodations but finding a way to do the required tasks; gaining additional education so as not to be reliant on physical strength for employment; and scoring high on civil service exams before revealing disability to potential employers. An important step to passing in the world of normals was first to "pass" in one's own thinking. Many polio survivors did not consider themselves disabled; they were only inconvenienced by their physical impairments. This gave them the confidence to perform as if they were not disabled and thus "pass" in both their own estimation and in the minds of others.

When post-polio syndrome struck some thirty to forty years after the initial illness, passing suddenly become more difficult. Post-polio syndrome brought an end to the deception. Many survivors had to reconsider their disability and recognize that they were not simply inconvenienced. They were, in fact, disabled. When that happened, some abandoned the role of "super-crip," and others realized that FDR might not have been an appropriate role model after all. In attempting to pass as FDR had done, they had only deceived themselves at considerable physical and psychological cost. These survivors found they had to renegotiate their relationship with their disability and, often, with family, friends, co-workers, and colleagues.[3]

Roosevelt's appeal as a role model and inspiration to polio survivors drew on his own experience and on the public presentation of him as a recovered cripple. Roosevelt and his family and associates deceived the public regarding his condition from the beginning of his illness in

August 1921. They downplayed the severity of the initial illness and the extent of his paralysis. The earliest press reports of FDR's illness in the *New York Times* following his transfer to a New York hospital stated "he will definitely not be crippled." As Hugh Gallagher wrote in his study of FDR's deceptions, at the time of his hospital admission Roosevelt was still very weak, various muscles were atrophying, and "his body below the waist was paralyzed."[4] Throughout his long recovery and rehabilitation, Roosevelt, his wife, and his advisers, especially Louis Howe, all sought to minimize public knowledge about the extent of permanent paralysis and disability.[5] Roosevelt never denied that he had had polio, and after he began creating the polio rehabilitation facility at Warm Springs, Georgia, his name became permanently linked with the disease. Still, Roosevelt's goal was to convince himself and others that he was a "cured cripple."[6]

The ability to stand and walk—or, at least, to appear to walk—was crucial to FDR's goal of convincing others, especially other politicians and potential voters, that he was no longer disabled by polio-paralyzed muscles. Not just any walking would do. Roosevelt was determined to learn to walk without crutches, for crutches were a "universal symbol of the cripple" and aroused "fear, revulsion, and pity—emotions quite opposite to those a leader would wish to stir."[7] While working with Helena Mahoney, a physical therapist at Warm Springs, FDR described what he hoped to gain through rehabilitation: "I'll walk without crutches. . . . I'll walk into a room without scaring everybody half to death. I'll stand easily enough in front of people so that they'll forget I'm a cripple."[8]

The first very public tests of Roosevelt's ability to convince observers that he had fully recovered from polio came at the Democratic National Conventions of 1924 and 1928. In 1924, Al Smith, then the governor of New York, asked Roosevelt to place his name in nomination as a candidate for president of the United States. The Smith campaign thought that Roosevelt's Protestant and patrician background would somewhat offset Smith's Catholic and Irish heritage. Roosevelt was determined not to be wheeled to his seat on the convention floor. He had developed with his son James a way to walk while holding tightly to James's arm with his left hand while using a crutch under his right arm. Using this technique, the pair slowly made their way to FDR's sturdy aisle seat before most of the delegates had arrived. They bantered with each other and nodded and smiled, "locking eyes with onlookers to take their attention from their slow, hitching progress." After most had left, FDR and his son slowly made the long trek back to the waiting wheelchair just off the convention floor.[9]

When the time came for Roosevelt to give his nominating speech for Smith, he stood some fifteen feet behind the podium. After being assured that the podium was firmly fastened to the floor so he could use it to support himself during the speech, FDR took the second crutch from his son and began to "walk" stiffly and laboriously toward the podium. Once there, he flashed his famous smile to the cheers of the delegates. He stood for some thirty minutes to deliver his speech with his hands tightly gripping the podium for support. After he made his slow exit, he collapsed into his wheelchair just off-stage. As he exclaimed to a friend later that evening, "I did it!"[10] In spite of this seeming triumph, Roosevelt knew that "he would have to discover a better way to *seem* to walk than on crutches" if he was to have any kind of a career as a politician.[11]

Roosevelt discovered that better way of seeming to walk in 1928 and perfected it with the Mahoney's aid. He thought he could develop the technique of walking with one cane and with the other hand firmly grasping his son Elliot's arm. It took the two men a month to perfect this new method of walking. But FDR wanted it to appear easy and natural, even if it was not. He reminded Elliott, "As soon as you feel confident, Son, look up and around at people, the way you would do if I weren't crippled." As Hugh Gallagher observed, "This technique for walking was devised for the sake of appearance. It was not in any sense a practical means of locomotion. It was treacherous, slow, and awkward."[12] However inelegant, it worked. Roosevelt "walked" to the podium of the 1928 Democratic National Convention, where he delivered a rousing nomination address for Smith and, at the same time, convinced many delegates that Roosevelt the politician was back and cured.

Later that same year, Roosevelt, at Smith's urging, agreed to run for governor of New York on the Democratic ticket. Roosevelt carried out an active and extensive campaign across New York in part to deflect stories and rumors of his ill health. More than once he allowed himself to be carried up back stairs or fire escapes unseen by the waiting crowd to be able to "walk" into an otherwise inaccessible hall. In speech after speech across the state, FDR cracked a joke about the supposed "sick" man standing before them in what appeared to be good health.[13] The campaign and the deception worked. In November, Roosevelt was elected to the first of his two terms as governor of New York while Smith lost the presidential race to Herbert Hoover.

As governor, Roosevelt perfected the deceptions that would hide the extent of his disability from the American people for the next seventeen years. During the 1928 campaign, he had asked that no newsreel movies be taken of him being helped into or out of his car. The news photographers complied with his request, and none were taken then or during his terms as governor and president. While Roosevelt served as governor, two of his bodyguards, Gus Gennerich and Earl Miller, became adept as the strong arms he needed to "walk" with a cane. They were strong enough to lift FDR in a standing position up stairs so that it appeared as if he was climbing the stairs. During his governorship, Roosevelt made regular visits to Warm Springs, usually in the fall and spring, where he swam in the pools, exercised, had dinner with the polio patients then in residence, and used his prominent position to raise funds for the institution.[14]

The campaign tactics of minimizing and hiding his disability that had won Roosevelt two terms as governor of New York were also successful in 1932 when he defeated Hoover for the presidency. To be sure, Hoover was saddled with responsibility for the Great Depression, but Roosevelt still needed to reassure voters that he had recovered from polio and was physically fit to be president. Once in the White House, Roosevelt had the full resources of the federal government to help him maintain what Gallagher has called his "splendid deception." The Secret Service saw to it that Roosevelt was never lifted in public and that when he had to be lifted out of his car, it occurred in a garage or behind a constructed screen. The public never saw the president sitting in a wheelchair: "Either he appeared standing, leaning on the arm of an aide, or he was seated in an ordinary chair." Podiums were bolted to the floor so they would support Roosevelt when he stood to speak. When he "walked," he was usually surrounded by Secret Service and other aides who partially blocked the view of spectators. If he needed ramps to gain access to a building, the Secret Service had the ramps built. At large White House dinners, Roosevelt was always seated at the head table before the dinner guests entered.[15]

Roosevelt "walked" on public, ceremonial occasions, but he spent most of his days seated and being wheeled around the White House. The White House was accessible, and initially Roosevelt wheeled himself around, but in later years he allowed the Secret Service or a military aide to push his chair. FDR used a chair he designed that was much more maneuverable than the heavy wicker chairs of the time. It was based on a sturdy armless kitchen chair, with large front wheels and small rear ones and a small platform for his feet. The president did not spend much time in this wheelchair; it was for getting from place to place. On arriving, he usually transferred to a regular chair. In public comments, he admitted to using the wheelchair only to get around in his bedroom.[16]

Many people, including the press, Secret Service, aides, and visitors, saw Roosevelt being wheeled around the White House or lifted in and out of his car. Gallagher, however, argued that since the nation valued FDR's political skill and judgment, "an agreement was struck: the existence of FDR's handicap would simply be denied by all. The people would pretend that their leader was not crippled, and their leader would do all that he could not to let them see that he was." The accepted story on both sides was that he had had polio but had recovered and was "a bit lame." He had gotten over his paralysis and was now a "cured cripple."[17] The deception—the denial—largely worked. Roosevelt was elected president four times and led the nation through the depression and almost to the end of World War II. In surveys by historians since, Roosevelt always comes out near the top, and his paralysis and disability are mentioned only as something he overcame, if they are mentioned at all. It was not until 1994 that Gallagher, himself a polio survivor, explored in detail why and how FDR deceived the American public about the extent of his disability.

Roosevelt's apparent recovery and successful reentry into public life as governor and president set a high standard for polio survivors to emulate. Most polio patients from the 1920s on were urged by doctors, therapists, family members, and friends to follow FDR's example. During the 1930s and '40s, many polio patients and members of their families wrote to Roosevelt directly seeking support and encouragement. Roosevelt sometimes sent a brief reply, but more often a secretary replied in FDR's name. As one young polio patient wrote, "You now hold the highest office in the United States. That took fight and courage. I shan't be President but I will hold a good position."[18] Anne Finger recalls that "when you had polio it didn't matter if you were a boy or a girl: You were always being told about President Roosevelt. You were expected to be smart, to be accomplished, to make something of your life, maybe even grow up to be president."[19]

As a model for polio survivors to follow, Roosevelt posed several challenges. First, what a polio survivor could accomplish depended in part on how much damage polio had done and where. Clearly, someone who needed the respiratory assistance of an iron lung had fewer options and opportunities than someone with paralyzed legs. Second, ordinary polio survivors did not have FDR's wealth—or, later, the resources of the U.S. government—to ease reentry into society. When Roosevelt was president, the Secret Service ensured that buildings and rooms were accessible to him, and they were able to do it in ways that minimized the appearance of disability. Most polio survivors had to struggle with accessibility for much of their lives, and they found it much more difficult to hide evidence of their handicaps.[20] Still, FDR was an important model because he had an important political career after polio, because he did it by minimizing the extent of his disabilities, and because many polio survivors found that by minimizing or denying their disabilities they, too, could "pass" into society and lead relatively normal lives. Unfortunately, the physical and psychological costs of passing were not readily apparent when these polio survivors embarked on their attempt to live a normal twentieth-century American life.

In his classic study of 1963 of twelve children with polio in Baltimore, Fred Davis identified three strategies they and their families used to diminish the stigma associated with a disability. None of the children he studied was able to employ what Davis called passing. His concept of passing meant eradicating or disguising "the visible signs of impairment" so that no one would know that the individual was handicapped. Most of his subjects used what Davis called "normalization" to reduce stigma. These individuals and their families accepted the "normal standard" but developed strategies of denying the importance of the disability, of finding ways to diminish its visibility, and of avoiding situations in which the impairment was particularly obvious or disabling. These individuals believed that they were normal and thought that most others also regarded them as normal.[21]

Davis called the final approach to diminish stigma "disassociation." Disassociation involved "some significant relinquishing of the normal standard, at least with respect to actual interaction, if not always at the level of personal ideology." Individuals who practiced disassociation employed several tactics to protect themselves from harsh stares and comments of others. Some passively accepted their "exclusion from the world of 'normals' punctuated" occasionally by attempts to conform.

Others retreated "to a more or less privatized sphere of hopes and fantasies in which the harsh impress of the normal standard [was] tenuously kept at bay." Another group attempted to "recast and reformulate personal values, activities, and associations so as to avoid or remove the sting from the often negative, condescending, and depreciating attitudes of 'normals.'"[22] One's ability to employ a particular strategy was determined largely by the extent of one's impairment and its impact on appearance and the activities of daily living.

Davis made a distinction between "passing" and "normalization" that I want to collapse. Few polio survivors with the characteristic impairments of polio could meet his standards for passing. Most survivors employed what Davis called "normalization" and what I consider a form of passing. These were the men and women who found ways to live relatively normal lives following polio, even with significant handicaps. They found ways to negotiate their disability with the normal world with a minimum of stigmatization. They managed to finish their education, get a job and a career, and marry and have a family. Their disability and any necessary assistive devices might have been more or less visible, but they found ways to render them "invisible" even when they were in plain sight. In the social settings that mattered to them, they were more or less accepted as "normal."

Passing meant many different things to polio survivors. For many, the first step was to "pass" in their own minds. They had to convince themselves that they were not disabled, only inconvenienced. If they could not convince themselves, they could hardly convince others. As for Roosevelt, walking was a key skill for many attempting to pass, and the fewer assistive devices one needed, such as braces, canes, or crutches, the better. Being able to stand and to move about unassisted helped immeasurably when attempting to pass, even if the walking was not quite normal. Others found ways to pass in plain sight, even when assistive devices such as wheelchairs were used. As Roosevelt had, polio survivors found ways to deflect attention from their disability through dress, attitude, and accomplishment so that others did not think of them as disabled.

However, as Tobin Siebers has noted, "These tactics may also exact a heavy toll on individuals both mentally and physically, leading to psychological crises and secondary health problems."[23] For example, some individuals persisted in walking, despite the pain and strain on legs and arms, when it would have been safer and healthier to have used a wheelchair. Over time, others found it increasingly difficult psychologically to deny their disability, to pretend they were not disabled, to carry on as if nothing was wrong. Post-polio syndrome often brought the deception to an end. The new pain, fatigue, and muscle weakness was simply too much. The body could no longer sustain the behaviors suggestive of normality. As their bodies became more disabled, some polio survivors who had successfully passed realized how disabled they always had been and began to accept more fully a new identity as an individual with a disability. Finally, some who had sought for years to emulate FDR abandoned him as a role model. The fiction that you could be anything or do anything you wanted simply could not be sustained.

If polio survivors were going to pass as normal, they first had to convince themselves that they were not disabled. In the rehabilitation settings of the mid-twentieth century, recovering polio patients were aided in thinking of themselves as nondisabled by doctors, therapists, and family members who urged them to try harder to restore muscle function and mobility and to emulate FDR in becoming a "cured cripple." Carol Gill, for example, recalled that she had been "tutored" not to think of herself as disabled: "Although three of my limbs were paretic, my scoliosis was severe, and I practically lived in heavy leg braces, no one in my family ever uttered a word suggesting I had a disability. . . . Nothing lay beyond my abilities if I worked hard enough. I learned to see myself not as disabled but as a regular child challenged and inconvenienced by some obstacles to surmount."[24] Richard Owen remembered that for many years, he was in denial about his disability: "I didn't think there was much wrong with me. My vision of myself was of a person who was just maybe one step behind everybody else physically, but equal in every other way."[25] Like the others, Sheed minimized the impact of his disability in characteristic language: "A handicap is just a series of inconveniences to add to the normal inconveniences of life, and in no time one is handling them just as automatically."[26] In Kathryn McGowan's study of polio-related impairments, many of the upright polio survivors who were able to walk in some fashion refused to think of themselves as disabled, despite their reliance on assistive devices. As she wrote, many of these "walking" polio survivors had "managed to separate their sense of self from their bodies" and insisted "'they' were not crippled, even though their bodies might have been significantly altered and mechanically assisted."[27] One of her participants who consciously emulated FDR stressed that what mattered was "'how you hide it'; as opposed to 'how you have it.'"[28] Her study participants who used wheelchairs were much less likely to think of themselves as nondisabled and to attempt to pass. Irving Zola, writing from the perspective of finally having accepted his disability, noted that he and other individuals with disabilities who successfully passed believed that "a key element" was "the self-conception, 'I never think of myself as handicapped.'"[29]

One consequence of having convinced themselves that they were "normal" was that these polio survivors often shunned contact with other polio survivors or with individuals with other disabilities. On some level, they knew they were disabled and if they were seen in close proximity to others individuals with disabilities it would be impossible to maintain their status as "normals." Zola wrote that he had early separated himself "from the physically handicapped by refusing to attend a special residential school. Later I had simply never socialized with anyone who had a chronic disease or physical handicap. I too had been seeking to gain a different identity through my associations."[30] Gill recognized that polio survivors often resisted being identified with or joining disability groups. They viewed "themselves as different from others with disabilities. Seeking the company or support of disabled peers would mean admitting on a deep emotional level that they *had* a disability."[31] Associating with others who were disabled would inevitably call attention to their own disability, something they were trying desperately to avoid. McGowan found a similar pattern in her study participants who "walked": "upright participants rarely, if ever, socialized with other people who had polio or who had altered bodies considered disabled by the socio-cultural mainstream. To associate with other people who had polio or were disabled would weaken the uprights' ability to blend into the normal world and place their position within the social fabric of the "real" world in jeopardy." They would be unable to "deflect attention away from the braces and crutches" that allowed them to walk.[32] They, too, would become disabled instead of passing as normal.

Walking, or seeming to walk, as Roosevelt discovered, facilitated passing for many polio survivors. Finger noted the paradox that when she used her wheelchair, she was "quite mobile and independent," but when she walked with crutches, she received few offers of help, even though she needed help more than she did when she was in the wheelchair. As she reflected, "People assume that, since I'm walking on crutches—a step down in the hierarchy of orthopedic equipment—I'm therefore *less disabled*."[33] Brenda Serotte remembers the feeling in the

1950s that "the blessed walked out of the hospital on their own power; the cursed were pushed out."[34] This view that walking was key to living a normal life after polio was shared by patients and physicians alike. Sister Elizabeth Kenny, whose hot packs and stretching revolutionized polio rehabilitation, believed so deeply in the importance of walking to recovery that she titled her autobiography *And They Shall Walk*. Orthopedic surgeons such as Philip Lewin argued that most polio patients could learn to walk again through physical rehabilitation and, if necessary, surgery.[35] Like Finger and Serotte, many of the polio survivors in McGowan's study emphasized the importance of walking into normality. One of her study participants "who used braces, crutches, and a corset to stand upright explained 'I was almost normal when I was on crutches.' In other words, participants noted, one was walking ergo one was normal."[36] Another of her subjects said that "walking 'put me in line with the mainstream of life.'" For him, "'Getting back into life' meant 'walking' back into life and attempting to return to how things used to be."[37]

The "walking" of polio survivors was often distinctive, sometimes clumsy and slow, and occasionally dangerous, but they persisted because they, and the normals around them, believed that being upright and walking, no matter how difficult, brought one closer to normality. But walking by itself often was not enough; ideally, one practiced to reduce the oddness of the walk to reduce the visibility of one's disability. Even after Serotte could walk, her mother took her to doctor after doctor in New York, always with the same questions: "Would I walk normally? In other words, would I again be *exactly the same as before*? The same as *others*?" Finally, one doctor told her mother, "She is fine as she is; she may even walk better one day. *But there are no miracles!* Accept it." Her mother never really accepted it, but this was the last physician she consulted.[38] Charles Mee recalls that he worked hard learn to walk without his left leg brace until, finally, he was able to shed the brace and to "fake walking" with just his two crutches. No brace also meant no ugly shoes, and his sister gave him a pair of white bucks for Christmas, the height of fashion in the mid-1950s. Still, he felt the need to practice "standing, not just standing so I wouldn't fall over, but standing like someone who is cool, whose body has natural grace" to better disguise his disability.[39]

Still, no matter how much practice, the walking patterns of polio survivors were distinctive. The first time Dorothea Nudelman heard a tape of her walk, "It was weird hearing the rhythmic click of aluminum crutches, the slow deliberate step of my right foot and the slide-clunk sound of my braced left leg." She had not known that she "sounded like *that*" and worried how it must have come across in California, where "external conformity to physical ideals is the rule if not the obsession."[40] Siebers also had a distinctive walk, with a "trademark rhythm, rocking from side to side, like a metronome," although he tried hard to pretend that it was not unusual. However, when he resisted using a cane after post-polio struck, the therapist told him, "You're used to the way you walk and probably think a cane will make you look funny. But most people already think you look funny."[41] Sheed expressed the goal of these and many polio survivors who "walked" when he wrote that he worked on his walking "assiduously . . . not just to do it better, which is hard, but to fool people, which is surprisingly easy."[42]

Polio survivors employed techniques other than walking or faux walking to deflect attention from their disability and to pass. Recall FDR's advice to his son as he assisted his father to walk: look around, smile, make it look easy. Clothing could help disguise assistive devices and thus a disability. Barb Johnson was grateful that by the time she entered junior high school, "You didn't have to wear dresses to school anymore. Being able to wear pants to school saved me a lot of embarrassment."[43] Gail Bias hid her polio-affected legs behind "long skirts and boots." She also noted that she found acceptance with new people much more readily when they first encountered her sitting at a table. Those who first saw her walk with a limp were much more likely to be "stand-offish."[44] Nudelman recalled that as a young woman, she knew she "could be cute, and sometimes when guys would see me sitting at a table and not notice my legs and crutches, they'd flirt with me as if I weren't a cripple." That lasted until she stood up.[45] Richard Daggett was always visibly disabled, but he remembers, "Whenever I went out I wore a suit and tie. I felt I looked less disabled if I dressed well."[46]

Walking posed its own challenges to passing. At parties, Mee feared that an accidental bump could precipitate a fall. Consequently, he always picked his "way very slowly through a cocktail party, braced at all times against an inadvertent shove from any direction—trying, as I do this, to make the stately manner of my progress look intentional and dignified rather than defensive."[47] But walking as if nothing was wrong carried its own risks, as Zola recognized: "I should walk as if looking for pennies. But I resist impositions which impede social interactions.

If I am constantly looking down to where my foot or cane must be placed, then I cannot look directly at the person with whom I am conversing. And so I run the risk and pay the price, which means I trip, stumble, and fall all too often."[48]

The techniques to deflect attention from a disability, to pass as normal, varied according to the disability and the inclination of the polio survivor. Finger adopted an approach to deal with strangers she encountered: "'Hi!' I call out. I'm warm and friendly wherever I go, meeting the gazes of strangers on the street—interrupting their looks before they can become stares—offering my cheery 'Good Mornings!' and 'Hellos!' A coping strategy many of us develop."[49] For Martha Mason and many others, a key to passing as normal was not asking for assistance, even when help would have made tasks easier. As part of her denial of being disabled, Mason "refused to demand any special accommodations" other than a car with hand controls. Mason recalled her attitude as a new wife in Cambridge, Massachusetts: "I rarely thought of myself as disabled at this time. I was negotiating a two-floor apartment, taking care of housekeeping and the children, and teaching and studying. I was married. I was not alone. I was passing as able-bodied."[50] Others passed by choosing carefully the activities they took up. In high school, Stanley Lipshultz followed "mainstreaming rules to the letter. I pretended to be normal and kept up with the best of them. I couldn't play football or basketball, but neither could a lot of kids. Only my best friends in the whole world knew about my disability. I became the consummate *passer*."[51] Others passed with the aid of friends. Mee recalled that his life improved when he began dating Suzy Harvey: "She was a cheerleader, which is to say, she was not only pretty and energetic and popular, she was also the mainstream. . . . Suzy took me into the mainstream with her."[52]

As the memoirs by Mason and Mee suggest, part of passing for polio survivors was to become part of the American mainstream in the post–World War II era in which young men and women married early and had a family. In her study of sexuality, Mary Ryan noted that in this period, most "young women anticipated a future in which marriage was paramount." She also observed that "most all the men and women of this generation married and bore children."[53] Similarly, Michael Kimmel's study of masculinity revealed that in the postwar era, "Real men were breadwinning men. They were family men, too, actively involved in the raising of their children."[54] In her study of American families in the Cold War era, Elaine Tyler May concluded that "pressures and disappointments notwithstanding, postwar Americans expected to find life's satisfactions at home. They were determined to get married and *stay* married."[55] This striking consensus on marriage and family that produced the Baby Boom put tremendous pressure on polio survivors to conform if they wished to pass. Men were expected to find jobs and careers and to marry and support a family, regardless of their impairments. Women were expected to marry and to be able to raise a family, despite any lingering disability. Significant numbers of polio survivors passed in this way. They worked once their schooling was finished, and more than 85 percent of polio survivors eventually married.[56] Only Lorenzo Milam's provocatively titled *The Cripple Liberation Front Marching Band Blues* is both a polio memoir and a coming-out narrative. But even Milam married and fathered a child before coming out as a gay man.[57] By dating, marrying, and raising a family, and finding work to support that family, polio survivors conformed to the social expectations of the time. They may have done it differently and with more difficulty than their neighbors, but conforming to the social mores was one more way they could pass.

Ironically, polio survivors most easily passed when they wore a cast, either from breaking the leg or from one of the many surgeries. Onlookers typically assumed that the cast was temporary—the result of a fall, perhaps—and the wearer would soon be back to normal. Nudelman recalled going to a restaurant with a cast on after falling and breaking a leg. A man at the bar noticed the cast and commented, "Quite an accident, huh? How'ja do it, skiing?" Nudelman "flashed a grin and seized the moment." She replied, "Really took a big spill. Probably'll have to skip next ski season too." Skiing accidents happened to athletic types, and she appreciated the irony of the accident making her "appear less disabled" than she was.[58] One of the polio survivors Davis studied had a similar experience: Marvin Harris broke his leg while refusing to wear his brace. The young man was "not altogether unhappy about this, because when he was wearing the cast strangers often did not know that he was crippled." One day, a cab driver asked if he had broken his leg playing football, and Harris replied yes. After they exited the cab, Marvin told his mother, "Am I glad you didn't tell him I had polio! They just think I have a broken leg."[59] Richard Maus was teaching at a Minnesota high school when he broke his foot falling off a horse. He had worn many casts following surgery growing up, and he hated "being different, being disabled. This time, though, it was fun, not frustrating. For one thing, I knew my condition was only temporary." He also enjoyed showing off his crutch technique, learned following his many surgeries as a child and adolescent. This was better: "I finally had a glamorous reason to have a cast on my leg."[60] Breaking a leg was a normal activity, and for a while, at least, the temporary disability masked the permanent one. As Siebers has noted, "Temporary passing is empowering, producing brief moments of freedom from the prejudice and morbid curiosity often found to surround disability."[61] It is no wonder that Nudelman, Harris, and Maus took advantage of the opportunity to pass.

An interesting variant on passing is the way in which polio survivors and their families contrived to hide evidence of disability in photographs. The photographic memory was erased, which sometimes led even the polio survivor to doubt what happened. Mee "learned to pose for photographs in such a way that [his] crutches didn't show."[62] Serotte recalled a photograph taken at a cousin's wedding. She is seated next to the bride, but her braces are nowhere evident. Just before the photographer took the shot, her aunt arranged the wedding gown to cover Serotte's braced legs. In later years, something about the photograph bothered her, but not until her mother told her that the aunt had hidden the brace so Serotte would not have a "bad memory" of the time did she remember why: "It worked. My brace was so buried under the bridal gown that I even forgot I wore it. . . . Nothing at all to indicate a subterfuge. I thought for a long time that, because Lorraine's gown was so beautiful, they just wanted to show more of it than my taffeta skirt."[63] This fits a pattern noted by Marc Shell in which parents, for whatever reasons, encouraged not talking about polio in the hope of effacing the reality.[64] But there were consequences to this forgetting. As Serotte noted, "Thus began the mental and emotional, if not yet physical, eradication of polio in our family, and it lasted as long as I lived in their house. Polio as an idea evaporated; it just never happened."[65] But, of course, it had happened, and carefully posing family photos or not talking about the disease and its aftermath did not spare the individual with polio from the lifelong consequences of impairment and disability.

Passing for polio survivors did not generally mean that their disability was undetectable. Such invisibility was usually impossible, given withered limbs, twisted torsos, funny walks, braced legs, canes, crutches, and wheelchairs. Passing typically meant being able to do much of what you wanted; having family and friends who accepted you; being able to finish schooling, find a good job, marry and have a family. For polio survivors who passed, the disability did not disappear; rather, it diminished in importance relative to living a full life comparable to that led by "normals." In writing their memoirs, many polio survivors articulated this view of passing. Zola captured this notion when he wrote, "We are paid the greatest of compliments when someone tells us, 'You know, I never think of you as handicapped.'"[66]

Passing for polio survivors, however, carried a high price both physically and psychologically, as some of the individuals quoted above suggest. The physical costs included overuse of muscles affected by polio, unsteady walking and standing with the attendant danger of falling and injury, and ultimately hastening the onset of post-polio syndrome and its muscle weakness, fatigue, and pain. As Lipshultz put it, "*Passing*, unfortunately, came with a price. Who knew? Being 'normal' took an enormous amount of energy, both physical and emotional."[67] Gallagher recalled that during the decades he "passed," he ignored his body: "My paralyzed body was my obedient servant: it did what I forced it to do. I was numb to its aches and pains."[68] In those years, he transferred without assistance "onto strange toilets, even if the transfer was dangerous." He lifted himself "into hotel beds even if the effort left [him] breathless and [his] muscles cramping."[69] Like Gallagher, Finger, in her adolescent years, ignored pain to appear normal. When she applied for factory jobs, she left her crutches behind, and when she got a job packaging Bic pens eight hours a day, she stood the entire time rather than ask for a stool to sit on. She no longer remembers how her legs felt, but she knows they "must have ached and ached." But, she notes, "to have spoken of my aching legs would have been to break the compact I—along with so many others who had had polio—had made with the world—not to complain, to be a good sport, to soldier on, not to whine, to just keep going."[70] In other words, to pass, regardless of the pain.

Passing imposed psychological as well as physical burdens on polio survivors. Denying one's disability, and pushing ahead despite physical pain and the experience of stigmatization, pretending that everything was OK all took a psychological toll on those who sought to pass as normal. Lipshultz wrote that denial was hard work: "I am disabled. I just don't like to admit it. So, mentally of course, I am attempting to ward off those inner demons—the ones that are constantly reminding me of the source of my problems—and that takes a lot of effort, almost as much effort as it takes to walk." It took Lipshultz more than forty years before he accepted that he was disabled; he admits that "it was a high price to pay for passing, and, in retrospect maybe too high a price."[71] Mee revealed how conflicted he felt as he tried to pass for normal: "Sometimes I performed an intact outer self because it was what I wanted—to be normal and robust and optimistic. And sometimes I performed this self because it seemed the thing for a healthy person to do, and it was what others wanted of me. Some days I tried to find my own true path in life. I ran toward normality, and at the same time away from it, trying to pass for normal, and feeling it to be a lie."[72]

Others experienced a level of psychological distress that became pathological and incapacitating. In his autobiography, Gallagher acknowledged that "flat denial of hard reality can serve a useful purpose—it buys time for coming to terms with trauma." He also acknowledged that "this sort of thing can be effective, but it is exhausting and isolating." But denial never really worked for him psychologically. As he wrote, "I keened over my disability all the time, every day, all day; I just pretended to myself that I did not."[73] Finally, after several decades passing as a successful congressional aide and lobbyist, Gallagher fell into a deep depression that took years to emerge from. Beating back his depression occurred when he finally began to accept that he was significantly disabled.[74]

Like Gallagher, Anne Gross's mother, Carol Greenfeld Rosenstiel, experienced significant psychological distress related to passing. Gross has written a searing account of her mother's polio experience and her mother's efforts to pass. Her parents pushed Carol to succeed, to ignore the paralysis in her legs, and by some measures she did. She graduated from college; had a successful career as a professional musician and, later, as a therapist; and married a handsome young man and raised a family. Although she could walk awkwardly for short distances, Carol spent most of her time in a wheelchair. Her daughter writes that although her mother "lived under the illusion that she was integrated into society as if she were just like everybody else, she had paid a high price for it: she felt controlled by others and had internalized society's view of herself as being defective."[75] Anne Gross acknowledges that although her mother "seemed very well adjusted" to those who knew her, "her efforts to accommodate to the world of the non-disabled came at an enormous emotional cost."[76] She concludes that it was "the myth of 'normalcy'" that was her "mother's downfall, for it disavowed who she really was, leading to her intense feelings of anxiety, anger, isolation and pervasive unhappiness."[77] To be sure, not every polio survivor who passed experienced the deep psychological distress documented above, but many, if not all, experienced some level of emotional or psychological stress as a result of their efforts to pass as normal in spite of their impairments and the obstacles placed in their path by families, friends, and society at large.

The onset of post-polio syndrome some thirty to forty years after acute polio forced many polio survivors to reevaluate their efforts to pass. The new muscle weakness, pain, and fatigue often necessitated new assistive devices such as canes, braces, crutches, and scooters or wheelchairs that made disability more visible. In some cases, individuals were once again dependent on assistive devices they had not used since their original rehabilitation decades earlier. When post-polio struck, they found it much harder to fake it as they had for so many years. As he began to struggle with the effects of post-polio, Siebers reflected on his efforts to pass and admitted, "I have been fooling myself. It has all been an elaborate sight gag staged for my own ego. And I am beginning to pay the price for it."[78] Sheed had a similar experience: "when the so-called post-polio syndrome hit me in my mid-fifties, it weakened the whole physical apparatus just enough to call my bluff on all fronts at once—and no one could have been more surprised than I to realize quite how much I'd been faking it for all these years."[79] As post-polio increased Gallagher's disability, he admitted that "the fake facade became harder, ultimately impossible to maintain. And yet we were loath to let it go. So much of our pride, persona, self-image was invested in this heroic charade. It was the way we saw ourselves. It was our shield. With it we were invulnerable; without it, what are we?"[80] As all three men ultimately recognized, the time had come to cease pretending to be something they were not—namely, normal.

Reassessing their relationship to FDR was one consequence of abandoning the effort to pass as normal. Any polio survivor who attempted to pass did so in Roosevelt's shadow. He had been held up as their role model by doctors, therapists, family, and friends. If FDR had beaten polio and gone on to lead the country, there was no reason you, too, could not do great things, albeit on a somewhat less grand scale. From the 1930s on, many polio survivors did attempt to emulate FDR and pass as normal. But when post-polio syndrome struck, if not sooner, some questioned whether trying to be like Roosevelt had been either wise or possible. Zola identified part of the problem when he wrote that "few of us can control, manipulate, and overcome our environment the way FDR did."[81] Cass Irvin acknowledged that Roosevelt has been criticized as a "bad model" by some in the disability community because ordinary individuals with disabilities and lacking his resources cannot hope to pass as successfully as he did. Still, she admitted that she regards him as a "disability hero" because of what he achieved in spite of his disability. She acknowledges, however, that polio survivors who internalized his message—"that you cannot let them see how disabled you are not if you expect to succeed"—kept many polio survivors from joining disability "activist groups to change society."[82] Those who passed so successfully let society off the hook when it came to disability: society did not need to change; rather, the polio survivors made all the accommodations to pass as normal.[83]

While many polio survivors have had to renegotiate their relationship to FDR, Gallagher found it more challenging than most. In his *FDR's Splendid Deception,* he described what it took for Roosevelt to pass as normal, as a "cured cripple." For decades, Gallagher, like FDR, had performed normality: "throughout my life, I appeared cheerful but was unhappy. The appearance fooled family and friends and confused me badly. I was reluctant to give up the appearance for the fact, but it was necessary."[84] While writing about Roosevelt's physical and psychological struggles, Gallagher reassessed his own relationship to FDR as his role model. Sitting in "a cold and rainy parking lot," Gallagher "at last broke with the President of the United States. . . . I would be goddamned if I would follow him, stiff upper lip, good soldier to the last. I would shout out my hurt to the skies, curse the fates, both mourn and celebrate my loss. FDR was a great man, a magnificent leader of world scale, but he was no longer my role model. He was Super Crip; I opted for human."[85] Human, in this case, meant acknowledging the aches and pains of polio, the psychological trauma of significant disability, and the ultimate impossibility of passing as normal.

Passing, then, for polio survivors was a complicated performance. It was in part self-deception that one was still normal despite physical impairments and in part performance to convince others that one was not disabled, appearances to the contrary. Like all successful performances, it required both a skilled actor and a receptive audience. Roosevelt, of course, set a high standard. His performance as a "cured cripple"—despite the fact that millions had seen his braces, his awkward and dangerous walking, his being carried up stairs, and the ramps built for his convenience—was willingly accepted by most Americans in the 1930s and 1940s. They accepted his performance because they wanted and needed to believe that their president was normal.

The impairments of some polio survivors were so slight, perhaps a slight limp or an arm that did not work quite right, that they were able to pass largely without notice. Most, however, had a more visible disability, especially if they used any of the characteristic assistive devices, such as braces, canes, crutches, and wheelchairs. These more visibly handicapped individuals had to find ways to overcome physical and psychological barriers and to deflect attention away from what they could not do to what they could do. As we have seen, they employed a variety of techniques to make their way in the world of normality. They found ways to manage stigmatization in public and ways to convince family, friends, and potential teachers, employers, and lovers to look beyond their handicaps. But just as FDR's passing required a complicit nation, so, too, the passing of ordinary polio survivors required a complicit audience. Without the willingness of individuals in their network of friends, acquaintances, and colleagues to accept the performance of passing, most polio survivors could not have passed into the normal world.

Many polio survivors have noted the very real physical and psychological costs of passing. That raises a question: was it worth it? Each polio survivor will have his or her own answer, but for many the answer was yes, even if it was a qualified yes. They left rehabilitation and got on with their lives. They finished their education, found jobs, married, and had children—and, yes, sometimes divorced. They did what their friends and neighbors were doing in the late twentieth century, even if they did it more slowly and with greater difficulty. As we have seen, there were costs to the body and the psyche. But most, I suspect, would have made the same choice in similar circumstances. After all, what were their alternatives in a society and culture that made virtually no accommodations for individuals with disabilities? The choice in mid-twentieth-century America was between passing, or performing as normal, and being isolated in back rooms and institutions. Given those options, it is not surprising that those polio survivors who could sought to pass in the looming shadow of FDR, the passer-in-chief.

Notes

1. Wilfred Sheed, *In Love with Daylight: A Memoir of Recovery* (New York: Simon and Schuster, 1995), 45.

2. Ibid., 50.

3. For a full account of living with polio, see Daniel J. Wilson, *Living with Polio: The Epidemic and Its Survivors* (Chicago: University of Chicago Press, 2005).

4. Hugh Gregory Gallagher, *FDR's Splendid Deception*, rev. ed. (Arlington, Va.: Vandamere Press, 1994), 19.

5. Geoffrey C. Ward, *A First-Class Temperament: The Emergence of Franklin Roosevelt* (New York: Harper and Row, 1989), 616.

6. Gallagher, *Splendid Deception*, 65.

7. Ibid., 66.

8. Ibid., 63.

9. Ward, *First-Class Temperament*, 694.

10. Ibid., 694–697.

11. Ibid., 704.

12. Gallagher, *Splendid Deception*, 66.

13. Ibid., 71–75.

14. Ibid., 76–78.

15. Ibid., 91–93, 97–98.

16. Ibid., 91–92.

17. Ibid., 96.

18. Daniel J. Wilson, "A Crippling Fear: Experiencing Polio in the Era of FDR," *Bulletin of the History of Medicine* 72 (1998): 490.

19. Anne Finger, *Elegy for a Disease: A Personal and Cultural History of Polio* (New York: St. Martin's Press, 2006), 169.

20. Frederick Maynard and Sunny Roller discuss how polio survivors passed and minimized their disability in Frederick M. Maynard and Sunny Roller, "Recognizing Typical Coping Styles of Polio Survivors Can Improve Re-Rehabilitation: A Commentary," *American Journal of Physical Medicine and Rehabilitation* 70 (April 1991): 70–72.

21. Fred Davis, *Passage through Crisis: Polio Victims and Their Families* (1963), repr. ed. (New Brunswick, N.J.: Transaction Publishers, 1991), 139–141.

22. Ibid.

23. Tobin Siebers, "Disability as Masquerade," in Tobin Siebers, *Disability Theory* (Ann Arbor: University of Michigan Press, 2008), 117.

24. Lauro S. Halstead and Naomi Naierman, *Managing Post-Polio: A Guide to Living Well with Post-Polio Syndrome* (Washington, D.C.: NRH Press, 1998), 208.

25. Edmund J. Sass with George Gottfried and Anthony Sorem, *Polio's Legacy: An Oral History* (Lanham, Md.: University Press of America, 1996), 36.

26. Sheed, *In Love with Daylight*, 47.

27. Kathryn Rosemary Brigidt McGowan, "A Body History of Polio-Related Impairments in the United States: How Individuals' Experiences of their Polio-Related Impairments Responded to Socio-Cultural Shifts in Contemporary American Society" (Ph.D. diss., Case Western Reserve University, Cleveland, 2005), 533.

28. Ibid., 527.

29. Irving Kenneth Zola, *Missing Pieces: A Chronicle of Living with a Disability* (Philadelphia: Temple University Press, 1982), 203.

30. Ibid., 75.

31. Halstead and Naierman, *Managing Post-Polio*, 208.

32. McGowan, "Body History of Polio-Related Impairments," 538.

33. Finger, *Elegy for a Disease*, 101.

34. Brenda Serotte, *The Fortune Teller's Kiss* (Lincoln: University of Nebraska Press, 2006), 73.

35. Daniel J. Wilson, "And They Shall Walk: Ideal versus Reality in Polio Rehabilitation in the United States," *Asclepio* 61 (2009): 180.

36. McGowan, "Body History of Polio-Related Impairments," 506.

37. Ibid., 537.

38. Serotte, *The Fortune Teller's Kiss*, 170, 191.

39. Charles L. Mee, *A Nearly Normal Life: A Memoir* (Boston: Little, Brown and Company, 1999), 124.

40. Dorothea Nudelman and David Willingham, *Healing the Blues: Drug-Free Psychotherapy for Depression* (Pacific Grove, Calif.: Boxwood Press, 1994), 88.

41. Tobin Siebers, "My Withered Limb," *Michigan Quarterly Review* 37 (1998): 199, 204.

42. Sheed, *In Love with Daylight*, 50.

43. Sass, *Polio's Legacy*, 89.

44. Ibid., 82.

45. Nudelman and Willingham, *Healing the Blues*, 105.

46. Richard Daggett to Daniel Wilson, March 21, 2010.

47. Mee, *A Nearly Normal Life*, 104.

48. Zola, *Missing Pieces*, 208–209.

49. Finger, *Elegy for a Disease*, 50.

50. Martha Grimley Mason, *Life Prints: A Memoir of Healing and Discovery* (New York: Feminist Press, 2000), 98, 163.

51. Halstead and Naierman, *Managing Post-Polio*, 213.

52. Mee, *A Nearly Normal Life*, 168–169.

53. Mary P. Ryan, *Mysteries of Sex: Tracing Women and Men through American History* (Chapel Hill: University of North Carolina Press, 2006), 228, 230.

54. Michael Kimmel, *Manhood in America: A Cultural History* (New York: Free Press, 1996), 245.

55. Elaine Tyler May, *Homeward Bound: American Families in the Cold War Era* (New York: Basic Books, 1998), 185.

56. Wilson, *Living with Polio*, 203, 207.

57. Lorenzo W. Milam, *The Cripple Liberation Front Marching Band Blues* (San Diego: Mho and Mho Works, 1984), 123–125.

58. Nudelman and Willingham, *Healing the Blues*, 76.

59. Davis, *Passage through Crisis*, 139.

60. Richard Maus, *Lucky One: Making It Past Polio and Despair* (Northfield, Minn.: Anterior Publishing, 2006), 154–155.

61. Siebers, "Disability as Masquerade," 118.

62. Mee, *A Nearly Normal Life*, 170–171.

63. Serotte, *The Fortune Teller's Kiss*, 179–180.

64. Marc Shell, *Polio and Its Aftermath: The Paralysis of Culture* (Cambridge, Mass.: Harvard University Press, 2005), 52.

65. Serotte, *The Fortune Teller's Kiss*, 180.

66. Zola, *Missing Pieces*, 205.

67. Halstead and Naierman, *Managing Post-Polio*, 213–214.

68. Hugh Gregory Gallagher, *Black Bird Fly Away: Disabled in an Able-Bodied World* (Arlington, Va.: Vandamere Press, 1998), 108.

69. Ibid., 203.

70. Finger, *Elegy for a Disease*, 257–258.

71. Halstead and Naierman, *Managing Post-Polio*, 214.

72. Mee, *A Nearly Normal Life*, 166–167.

73. Gallagher, *Black Bird*, 4.

74. Ibid., 164–181.

75. Anne K. Gross, "The Polio Journals: Lessons from My Mother," typed manuscript in the author's possession, 5, 7.

76. Ibid., 112.

77. Ibid., 323.

78. Siebers, "My Withered Limb," 202.

79. Sheed, *In Love with Daylight*, 50.

80. Gallagher, *Black Bird*, 242.

81. Zola, *Missing Pieces*, 203–204.

82. Cass Irvin, *Home Bound: Growing Up with a Disability in America* (Philadelphia: Temple University Press, 2004), 94, 151.

83. Siebers makes a similar point in "Disability Masquerade," 117.

84. Gallagher, *Black Bird*, 177.

85. Ibid., 209.

3 The Multiple Layers of Disability Passing in Life, Literature, and Public Discourse

JEFFREY A. BRUNE

MOST OF THE TIME we think about passing on a concrete level—for example, an act by which someone conceals or overlooks the presence of disability in the body. However, passing also occurs on a more abstract level, as authors and audiences overlook the presence of disability in texts and in public discourse. It is this form of abstract passing that influences and suppresses discussions of disability. The "passing" of disability from texts and public discourses frequently frustrates disability scholars, summed up in Douglas Baynton's oft-quoted complaint that "disability is everywhere in history, once you begin looking for it, but conspicuously absent in the histories we write."[1]

While scholars often complain about the absence of disability in texts, no one has yet examined carefully the historical process by which disability becomes subverted in literature and public discourse. A good case for studying this process is the story of *Black Like Me,* John Howard Griffin's famous book from 1961 about passing as a black man and experiencing racist hate as he traveled through the Jim Crow South. Its creation and evolving legacy over the past six decades allow us to examine the process by which we erase the issue of disability from lives, literature, and public discourse.

The sixty-year story of disability passing related to Griffin and *Black Like Me* consists of three parts. In the author's life before *Black Like Me,* Griffin learned how to pass as a sighted person after a World War II injury blinded him for twelve years. During this time, he developed the skills for passing and became comfortable transgressing identity boundaries. Literature is then the second part of this story of disability passing. Although Griffin regained his vision before working on his famous book, his experience with disability exerted an important influence on *Black Like Me* that underlies much of the text. However, in the book he mentions his former disability only once and only briefly, allowing its influence to remain hidden between the lines. Response to the author and his work over the past fifty years has also failed to highlight the presence of disability, making public discourse the third part of the disability passing story. This became so complete that even some activists and scholars who felt inspired and applied the book to disability issues failed to realize disability's original influence on the text.

An examination of this history shows how individuals, authors, and audiences work to conceal the issue of disability from their bodies, literature, and public discourse. For those who have been interested in *Black Like Me* but have not considered carefully the issue of disability, a reconsideration of Griffin should open a new set of questions about one of the most neglected and important categories of historical analysis. For those who already care deeply about disability, this story should help us understand the process by which disability becomes buried beneath the surface of our texts and public discussions. The way people erase disability from bodies, literature, and public discourse are closely related and should be understood together.

Part I: Passing in Life

Disability became a major issue in Griffin's life in 1945, and with it, so did passing. He was serving in the South Pacific when a bomb blast from a Japanese attack injured him. From the moment he regained consciousness two days later, his vision began to fade. Within eighteen months, at age twenty-six, he could not see at all. As he lost his sight and became a disabled person, Griffin learned how to pass.

In his memoir of blindness, *Scattered Shadows,* Griffin describes the period after regaining consciousness and waking up in the army hospital. In the account, he pays little attention to the physical experience of going blind. Even in his recollection of the first days and weeks after regaining consciousness there are only a couple remarks about how his vision changed. His awareness of his injury only started to become apparent when he received mail for the first time and realized he could not read it.[2]

Griffin paid little attention to his physical experience of blindness because the social consequences of his disability were so much more profound. He quickly understood that the label of disability gave others the power to limit his freedom and opportunities. His first lesson in disability treatment came from the military: "To be hospitalized in the army was to be still in the army, to be a ward, to be under obedience, to be unfree. And after all the years of talking orders, we were avid for freedom."[3] Griffin was concerned mainly with getting out of the army, escaping the confines of hospital life, and seeing his family and friends again; the loss of vision thus was less significant than the freedom he desired. For him, the main effect of blindness was not physical; it was about how other people defined disability and used that definition to restrict him.

Because a disability label offered others the opportunity to limit his freedom and independence, Griffin resolved to make everyone think his vision was normal. Although he did not use the word himself, he was trying to pass as a sighted person, just as he would later try to pass as an African American: "I began to play the role against them. I perfected the role in all its details, with an obsessive patience and cunning—the role of a fully recovered man," he writes. "I feared they might never release me if my condition [of blindness] were discovered."[4] As he makes clear, fear motivated him to pass as sighted—fear that he would lose his freedom and independence.

Although there were many moments when his inability to see betrayed his condition, he pretended to read his letters and did other things to disguise his impairment. His doctors in the army hospital were not completely fooled and did not want to release him. However, his pleading and desire to return to his family convinced doctors to let him go, provided that he promised to see a specialist as soon as he arrived home. He won his freedom from the army and the hospital in part by passing as a nondisabled person.[5]

Griffin escaped the army hospital by hiding his disability, and passing became his modus operandi during the first couple years after his injury. After sailing back to the United States, he continued trying to hide his disability in official documents. His army discharge paperwork shows that he had the clerk indicate "none" in response to "wounds received in action." Another part of the form, although he received numerous decorations and citations, does not list a Purple Heart, which is normally awarded to any service member wounded or killed in action.[6] In his memoir of blindness, he describes his nervousness when he told the clerk that he had no injuries and feared that the man would question this assertion after looking at the medical record inside Griffin's file, but this did not happen.

His relief was short-lived, however, as he was soon ushered into another room for a physical examination that included an eye test. He was diagnosed with 20/200 vision and declared legally blind. He was shocked to hear he was legally blind, but more than that, he was worried that the diagnosis would delay his discharge. However, the war had just ended, and the vast number of returning soldiers overwhelmed the clerks.[7] He passed through without incident, but the story shows how much effort he had to put into passing and how much stress he had to endure. Evading the costs of being treated as a disabled man, he must have figured, was worth the price.

After he returned home, Griffin continued to pass as sighted in his dealings with the military and other government institutions. He decided not to file for the military disability pension he could have received for the same reasons he did not accept a Purple Heart: he wanted to escape the discrimination and low expectations that disabled people encountered. "I had rebelled against the attitude that placed a low ceiling and an empty future on the blind."[8] While he was correct that the label of disability would have lowered others' expectations for him, there is irony in his statement. A more active form of rebelling would have been to defy those expectations rather than try to pass as sighted and leave those assumptions unchallenged.

Part of the reason Griffin decided to pass was that he had internalized the stigma of disability and its association with pauperism. He was too embarrassed to identify as disabled and too ashamed to accept any public assistance for his disability, even when he and his family suffered financially because of the accommodations he required: "It was necessary for me to know that what little I earned by my work had not come from the taxpayers' pockets. It had been the same with the military provisions, because I refused to accept the medals I had been awarded or the disability pension to which I was legally entitled."[9] Notice that it was important *for him* to know he was not receiving benefits, even a high military honor, that he saw as tainted by the stigma of disability. This was also the time when notions of manhood seemed most incompatible with popular perceptions of disability, which was probably another reason Griffin rejected disability assistance. The problem had been building since the late nineteenth century, when independence and financial self-sufficiency became central to the American masculine ideal, and it only worsened in the postwar era. A new, more muscular male body became a symbol of national strength and the ideal to which many men aspired. Popular alarm about emasculation, reflected in films and elsewhere, placed more pressure on men to live up to masculine ideals that were increasingly antithetical to notions of disability.[10] Pride and the disability stigma he internalized were part of the reason he made such sacrifices to pass as nondisabled.[11]

There is irony, again, in the way that Griffin rejected government assistance to make himself feel more like a nondisabled, independent American man. The postwar popular belief in the independent middle-class man was more myth than reality. Nondisabled, white, middle-class men relied heavily on government subsidies and unpaid domestic labor, without which they could not maintain the façade of independence. They benefited from the educational and housing benefits of the GI Bill, military pensions, housing subsidies from tax deductions and the Federal Housing Authority, and other federal programs. Griffin did not benefit from any of those programs during this period. In addition, many white, middle-class men relied heavily on the unpaid domestic labor of their wives, which gave them the luxury of focusing their labor on money-earning employment. Many disability studies scholars also reject ableist notions of independence, pointing out the dependent or interdependent nature of all social relations. Griffin subscribed to ableist beliefs and thought that white American men supported themselves and their families independently; accepting government assistance would signal a failure in his battle against disability. However, the reality was that accepting government assistance would have brought Griffin into the mainstream of his era.[12] The main difference between him and nondisabled veterans was that Griffin's benefits carried more stigma.

Even though he rejected government help, Griffin, not surprisingly, still did not live independently. When he returned home after his discharge, at twenty-five, he moved in with his parents in the Fort Worth area. He had limited social contact with people he did not know but still did what he could to hide his visual impairment, even when he was with friends and family. He did not want to be the object of pity—

something he would later focus on in his writings. An eye specialist gave him a powerful magnifying glass to help him read, but in the house, "I kept the glass hidden to avoid the questions and concern it would evoke."[13] He did not want to remind his parents of his disability because they would feel bad and he would have to endure their pity. His deeply internalized desire to be "normal," independent, and free from pity drove his daily interactions as he worked to conceal the markers of his disability.

Griffin's ability to pass required effort on his part, but other people also played a role—an important theme that rarely appears in memoirs of passing. Scholars in queer studies have developed theories about the closet that help explain what makes passing so successful for disabled people. As Tobin Siebers explains, it can be easy for gay people to remain in the closet or pass as straight largely because many straight people *want* to overlook their difference and choose to ignore signs of a different identity. Siebers writes, "Passing is possible not only because people have sufficient genius to disguise their identity, but also because society has a general tendency to repress the embodiment of difference."[14] Griffin presents evidence of army doctors who knowingly allowed him to "pass" out of the hospital and clerks who allowed him to slip through his discharge even after he failed his eye exam simply because they were too overwhelmed with paperwork. His parents wanted to accommodate his wishes, and ignoring the signs of his blindness probably required a constant effort on their part. At the very least, they would have had to remain vigilant about not mentioning the topic that, at times, must have been an elephant in the room.

In 1946, while still trying to pass as sighted, Griffin decided to pursue his musical studies during what he knew would be his last months of partial vision. This came after he heeded the advice of his eye doctor, who told him that his declining vision would make it impossible to pursue a career in medicine. He enrolled in a conservatory in France, where he had gone to high school during the early part of World War II. In addition to providing him with a new potential career, the conservatory allowed him to live away from his parents, "independently," and be with people who did not know about his impairment. Despite the continued deterioration of his eyesight that would leave him completely blind within a year, he resolved to pass as sighted and not let any of his new acquaintances know about his condition. He felt relieved to make a fresh start. In the privacy of his room, he used his glasses and special magnifying glass to study, while in public he made every effort to pass as sighted.

During his period of trying to pass as sighted, Griffin had little training in how to function without sight and found it more difficult to pass as his vision faded completely. At the conservatory and while he was staying with friends in Paris, his lack of blind skills and his internalized shame made it hard to be around others. As he could not accept his own condition and could not tolerate the pity of others, he resolved to live a more isolated life. He requested and received permission to live at the Abbey of Solesmes, even though he had not yet converted to Catholicism. There he studied music and became an authority on Gregorian chant. Most important for him, his isolation meant he did not have to deal with the reactions of other people. "In such an atmosphere, awareness of my failing sight never became a drama of fear or morbidity," he writes. "If I had lost my sight elsewhere I would have been absorbed in fighting the opinions of those who judged it sad, fighting it with the exhausting aggressiveness that comes from weakness."[15] Alone, he could deal with the deterioration of his vision without worrying about how others viewed him and his unstable physical condition. His shame about being blind carried a heavy price and caused him to make great sacrifices to pass or to avoid other people when he was unable to pass.

Griffin lost the remainder of his sight in the spring of 1947. His life and studies became especially difficult, so he went back to his parents once he could not see at all. There he could get more training to learn how to function without sight, and his family could help create an environment to accommodate him. His parents sold their house and bought a farm twenty miles south of Fort Worth, in the town of Mansfield. He found the farm's isolation liberating, since it spared him from awkward social situations, and he focused on developing his skills for blindness. "Left alone on the farm during my first months of blindness, I was so immersed in discovery that I never stopped to dwell on my condition as tragic. I felt that I was simply living in a new and different way that fascinated me."[16] During this time he also realized he was not talented enough to make much money from music and began a career in animal husbandry. He won awards and wrote articles about his work, but animal husbandry was not a lucrative profession, and money was always tight for him and his family.

After a few months on the farm, Griffin sought out blind mentors so he could become more mobile and learn other skills, including Braille, to function more independently. This was at a time that most instructors were sighted and blind activists were just beginning to promote the idea of blind mentors.[17] In addition to teaching him new skills, his new mentors showed him a different way to be blind. They embraced a blind identity,[18] exhibited their blindness in public, and through their actions challenged the stigma of disability that Griffin had internalized.

Although Griffin did not try to pass during his remaining ten years of blindness, his embracing of a blind identity marked only a pause in the story of how he hid the presence of disability in his life. In January 1957, twelve years after his war injury, he unexpectedly regained his vision. It could have been a side effect of one of the drugs, strychnine, that he took for a different condition. The stimulant increases blood flow, which might have unknotted twisted blood vessels in his eyes. He found himself and his identity transformed and soon would try to dissociate himself from disability issues yet again.

The transition back to sighted was not easy; nor was it as euphoric as many people might expect. There was joy for Griffin, especially when he was able to see his wife and children for the first time, but an unexpected change of identity concerned him. Aside from being overwhelmed, both physically and psychologically, and receiving a great deal of publicity about "the blind veteran, suddenly cured,"[19] Griffin worried about how he would define himself. By this point, he identified as a blind man. To give up that identity was to lose a part of himself, and it frightened him. He wrote, "Dimly I thought of all those sightless people who had for so long been my brothers and sisters. Was I actually leaving their world, to which I had become so accustomed?"[20]

It appears as though he did, as there is little evidence that he stayed in touch with people in his blind community. However, the erasure of his disability experience would extend further than his social life and reach into his writing career.

Part II: Passing in Literature

After regaining his sight, Griffin ceased writing about blindness and disability. He failed to point out how disability influenced his later thinking and writing, allowing it to pass from his texts. But despite his reluctance to acknowledge disability's influence on him, it helped shape the book that made him famous and played an important role in America's civil rights history. As he made decisions about what to write—and what not to write—the issue of disability passing in his life entered a new phase: it became a textual rather than a physical performance.

Griffin's first literary act of disability passing was to cease work on his memoir of blindness. *Scattered Shadows* was a book he had been planning for years, but when he regained his sight, he abandoned this project. It was only forty years later, after Griffin's death, that his friend Robert Bonazzi edited and published the memoir. To do so, Bonazzi took the early chapters of the book, which Griffin had completed while he was still blind, and combined them with passages from Griffin's journal that chronicled the later years of his disability. There are problems with the later parts of the book, since Griffin was not able to edit his journal entries and because he did not reflect on the experience and its lasting influence on him, as one would expect a memoir to do. Had Griffin completed *Scattered Shadows* himself, it would have revealed much to audiences—and to himself—about disability's continuing influence in his life and on his work, including his involvement in civil rights and the writing of *Black Like Me*. When he decided to cease writing about how disability affected him, Griffin dissociated himself from disability issues. This happened just when he was about to become a famous public figure.

Only two years after regaining his sight, Griffin shifted all of his attention to racism. In 1959, he darkened his skin, crossed the racial line, and tried to write about the experience of African Americans in the Jim Crow South.[21] He never addressed directly the links between his disability experience and *Black Like Me,* but the influences are many, extending from the act of passing to the themes and style of the work itself.

It is not difficult to see how passing as a sighted man would have been useful when Griffin later tried to alter his identity and pass as a black man. Blind people have written memoirs that describe their experience passing as sighted and the knowledge they gained about how to pass. The memoirist and scholar Georgina Kleege explains that many blind people change their expressions, appearance, and habits to deflect people's attention and conceal the markers of their disability. Blind people who pass as sighted "compose their faces in expressions of preoccupation, she writes. "They walk fast, purposefully; they do not ask directions. Forced to read something, they pat their pockets for reading glasses they do not own. When they make mistakes, they feign absentmindedness, slapping their foreheads and blinking." Passing as sighted is not a casual act or one that depends on simple imitation; it requires deliberation. The sociologist Tanya Titchkosky explains that blind passing relies not on mimicry but on knowledge. "Passing means knowing," she writes. "It means knowing the minutest details of how everyday existence is oriented to the expectation that sight is an ever present feature of that existence; it means knowing the customs, habits, and signs of seeing people. Passing means knowing how to do things with eyes, and knowing what to do that looks sighted when one is unsure of what to do because one cannot see."[22]

Methods that Griffin mentions for learning to pass include pretending to read, not wearing his dark glasses, and not carrying his cane or using his magnifying glass when others could see him. Even after he developed his politicized blind identity, Griffin continued learning skills from blindness training that would have made him better at passing. For example, in 1949 he went to New Orleans to develop his skills with the well-known blind mentor Sadie Jacobs. Jacobs focused on teaching students empowerment as well as skills for everyday living. Even though she did not want her students to pass as sighted, she taught them to conceal many of the physical markers and mannerisms associated with blindness. She helped Griffin eliminate the "blind look," which he said some people "brutally but accurately termed 'the dumb look.'" She told him that when he conversed with people, he held his head too high, kept his neck too stiff, and did not look people in the eye—all habits that made him look different and awkward to sighted people. He took to heart his teacher's advice that "you will have succeeded only when you can make people forget that you are blind."[23]

Throughout his training, Griffin continued developing his knowledge of how to change the physical markers that determined how people perceived and identified him. Griffin became an expert in people's body language customs, and he learned it through deliberate study rather than practicing it merely from habit. He gained a detailed understanding of how people looked at each other, how they tilted their heads, how they smiled, what they wore, how they walked through a room, what they did with their hands while walking, how they blinked, how they greeted each other, how they used voice inflection, how they avoided encounters with others, and many other mannerisms. Griffin never wrote about how this knowledge helped him when he decided to pass as a black man, but it is not difficult to imagine how he would have drawn from that knowledge and experience to shift his identity once again. Passing as sighted may have affected the way Griffin passed as black, or even got the idea of passing in the first place.

While his experience with blindness likely affected the way he carried out the six-week racial experiment, there is stronger evidence showing how his disability experience affected the book's most powerful literary elements. His studies of people's habits, expression, and visual communication appear to have influenced his prose, which is fixated on visual imagery and the way people use their vision. *Black Like Me* is, on its surface, about how people look at each other. Parts of the book even reflect specific passages from Griffin's earlier journal entries and draw on the same visual themes and literary devices that he used to write about blindness and disability. His experience with blindness seems to have played a key role in shaping his prose, yet *Black Like Me* passes as a book that has nothing to do with disability.

Some of *Black Like Me*'s most powerful and memorable passages describe Griffin's encounters with the "hate stare" coming from racist whites. Describing what it was like to be the object of that stare, he writes:

> Once again a "hate stare" drew my attention like a magnet. It came from a middle-aged, heavyset, well-dressed white man. He sat a few yards away, fixing his eyes on me. Nothing can describe the withering horror of this. You feel lost, sick at heart before such unmasked hatred, not so much because it threatens you as because it shows humans in such an inhuman light. You see a kind of insanity, something so obscene the very obscenity of it (rather than its threat) terrifies you. It was so new I could not take my eyes from the man's face. I felt like saying: "What in God's name are you doing to yourself?"[24]

What Griffin fails to mention, or allows to pass, in this oft-quoted passage is that prior to his racial experiment he had thought deeply about staring and how people use their eyes to communicate. Five years earlier he wrote in his journal, "In themselves, handicaps are nowise tragic, but through the eyes of others, through their voices and their actions, we are made constantly aware that it is, and the sea of these 'white missionaries' is so overwhelmingly great that they make converts of us—some of us falling rapidly into their concept of our conditions, and some of us, less fortunate, struggling against this lie of tragedy."[25]

When he became blind, Griffin understood quickly how his visual appearance had changed and how that affected the way people *looked* at him. Note his sensitivity to visual gaze, as he argues that tragedy is created "through the eyes of others." He appreciated the visual dimension of constructing disability and imbuing it with meaning, and his was not a unique experience for a disabled person. As Rosemarie Garland-Thomson argues, the "image of the disabled body as a visual assault, a shocking spectacle to the normate eye, captures a defining aspect of disabled experience. . . . The disabled body is the object of the stare. . . . As every person with a visible disability knows intimately, managing, deflecting, resisting, or renouncing that stare is part of the daily business of life."[26]

Although the stare he encountered as a disabled man was different from the one he received when posing as a black man, Griffin's claim that the stare from the racist white man "was so new" is only partly true. He already had written about the power of staring and what it meant to be the object of a stare. Before his famous racial experiment, he already had thought about how people use their gaze, or stare, to communicate and to oppress. In addition to being the object of stares as a disabled man, as a blind person he developed a detailed knowledge of how people use their eyes to communicate. This earlier knowledge of staring and visual communication is probably why he was able to write about the hate stare so accurately, powerfully, and clearly. That he made no mention of his previous experience with staring and visual communication is one of the many ways that he allowed disability to pass from his text.

Another of *Black Like Me*'s most powerful passages deals directly with vision and physical appearance. It bears an even more striking resemblance to one of his earlier journal entries about blindness and vision. As he puts the final touches on his African American guise, he looks into the mirror. "The transformation was total and shocking," he writes. "I had expected to see myself disguised, but this was something else. . . . All traces of the John Griffin I had been were wiped from existence. Even the senses underwent a change so profound it filled me with distress. . . . The completeness of this transformation appalled me. It was unlike anything I had imagined."[27] At other times in the story, he goes back to the mirror to set up discussions about identity and physical appearance.

Griffin writes about the encounter with the mirror as if it were a new and unexpected experience. However, long before, during his time of blindness, he wrote about what it would be like to look in the mirror and see a shocking, unfamiliar image. In one journal entry from 1954, he writes, "I wonder how I should feel if I could suddenly see my face in a mirror after these long years of blindness. What did I look like? I remember no face of mine in any mirror, but I do remember my face in photographs. Would I be shocked at the change? . . . Would I look anything like I think I look?"[28] That journal entry, with its focus on the mirror, visual imagery, and shock, is remarkably similar to his memorable passage from *Black Like Me.* It contradicts his claim that seeing an unfamiliar face in the mirror was an experience he had never contemplated. During his time of blindness, he gained a keen and deliberate sense of visual imagery and developed some of the visual touchstones—such as the mirror—that would give his famous book much of its literary power. Yet in that passage from *Black Like Me,* he fails to mention that blindness had already made him think about seeing a shocking image in the mirror, allowing the issue of disability to pass from his text yet again.

Another connection between disability and *Black Like Me* is that Griffin became concerned with racism and prejudice during his years of blindness. Some blind activists dislike the association between blindness and antiracism, which often assumes, incorrectly, that without the ability to see there can be no distinction of race. Positive stereotypes of blind people as pure and inspiring can be as harmful as they are false. Nonetheless, during his time of blindness Griffin wrote about how sightlessness was leading him to reassess his racial views. Raised in Texas in the 1920s, Griffin admitted that he accepted racial prejudice as he grew up. However, during the 1950s he became preoccupied with issues of racism, which he attributed to a confluence of factors, including his religious conversion, academic studies, and experience with blindness. In a passage that would make some blind advocates cringe, Griffin wrote in his journal, "For the blind man, the whole issue of racism on the basis of inferiority according to color or race is solved axiomatically. He can only see the heart and intelligence of a man, and nothing in these things indicates in the slightest whether a man is white or black, but only whether he is good or bad, wise or foolish."[29]

Griffin was not the only World War II veteran who linked his blindness from a war injury to his later fight against racism, and his narrative is somewhat typical. In his study of the Blinded Veterans Association (BVA), the historian David Gerber interviewed white veterans involved in this progressive organization who told similar stories about how blindness had led them to their egalitarian, antiracist politics. Whatever the reasons, many white veterans in the postwar era made a connection between the experience of blindness and antiracist activism. Yet in *Black Like Me*, Griffin never mentions the disability experience that he earlier credited for leading him toward his antiracist work. Once again, he allowed the issue to pass from the text.[30]

Despite the influences of disability and blindness on his life and the introspective nature of the book, Griffin mentions his former blindness only once in *Black Like Me* and, excuse the pun, only in passing. It happens when he goes to New Orleans to begin his experiment and remembers going there ten years before. "Strange experience," he writes. "When I was blind I came here and learned cane-walking in the French Quarter. Now, the most intense excitement filled me as I saw the places I visited while blind. I walked miles, trying to locate everything by sight that I once knew only by smell and sound."[31] With only this brief mention, Griffin makes no attempt to explain how his experiences with disability affected him, his experiment, and his book.

Aside from ignoring the significance of his blindness, those three sentences repress the issue of disability further because they make more sense when reading his "blindness" metaphorically rather than literally. In Western culture—and not just in modern times—"blindness" is usually used as a metaphor. Normally it is pejorative and refers to spiritual or cognitive incapacity: blind faith, the blind leading the blind, turning a blind eye, blind love, blind luck, blind devotion, and so on.[32] The narrative of *Black Like Me* provides a context for understanding those three sentences only if you read them metaphorically. "When I was blind" fits within the book's story of how Griffin had ignored, or been "blind" to, racial oppression earlier in his life. With his newfound awareness of injustice, he could suddenly "see" things clearly: "now, the most intense excitement filled me as I saw the places I visited while blind." However, if you read "blindness" literally, those sentences have no meaningful context within the book's pages. When a description of impairment fits neatly into popular metaphors, it helps issues of disability escape notice and pass from texts. It is no wonder that many people who have read the book tell me they do not remember Griffin had been blind.

Throughout most of the book, the absence of disability—at least on the surface of the text—is striking, but perhaps nowhere is it more glaring than in the preface. There Griffin compares the oppression of African Americans with that of other minority groups: "I could have been a Jew in Germany, a Mexican in a number of states, or a member of any 'inferior' group." Why he did not relate his own experience and mention disabled people—a group who suffered from prejudice and discrimination and was a target of the Nazi Holocaust and American eugenics campaigns—is puzzling, especially given his past disability activism.[33] After he ceased trying to pass as sighted and embraced a blind identity, he became involved with the National Federation of the Blind (NFB), one of the leading disability civil rights organizations in the postwar era. He contributed to its developing set of politics that emphasized blind empowerment and societal accommodation.[34] He wrote pamphlets for the NFB, including a handbook for how the sighted should treat blind people, and gave lectures on behalf of the organization.

That someone with this résumé would later cover up issues of disability in his writing shows the strong tendency even for modern progressive writers to bury the issue and allow it to pass out of texts. In Griffin's case, it is hard to say why, but perhaps it is because after his body underwent changes, he felt uncomfortable with the issue. Maybe he felt self-conscious, as if he betrayed the community when he regained his sight. (It would be ironic if, in 1959, he felt too much like an outsider to write about disability, since at that time he was a white man writing about what it was like to be "black like me.") Or perhaps he thought the issue would not resonate with audiences and would distract them, thereby lessening the book's impact. Griffin's motives for casting aside his disability politics are not clear, but the costs of disability passing in this seminal work are. In his fight against racism, Griffin squandered the opportunity to subvert another form of oppression and highlight the intersections and parallels between race and disability. Imagine if, at the moment Griffin successfully persuaded many whites to think about racial oppression, he had also gotten them to think about disability rights. Disability passing, whether in life or literature, has its costs.

Part III: Passing in Public Discourse

Given that Griffin hid disability in his writing, it is not surprising that most of the public discourse about the book over the past fifty years has also failed to highlight the issue.[35] Among the early responses to the work there was one notable exception. Louis Lomax, the African American author and journalist, connected *Black Like Me* to the author's disability experience: "*Black Like Me* comes from the heart of a man who learned the meaning of suffering from a temporary bout with blindness. And it was while John Howard Griffin was at the altar of darkness that he first knew the pain of being different."[36] Lomax wrote his response after he had a conversation with Griffin, and it is not clear whether he would have seen the relationship between the book and disability without that meeting. It is still, at the very least, interesting that an African American writer interested in civil rights would be the one to point out the parallel otherness in the categories of disability and race. Nonetheless, Lomax seemed to have been a lone voice; disability was rarely mentioned in relation to *Black Like Me* during the first four decades that followed the book's publication.

The absence of disability in conversations about *Black Like Me* is unfortunate and troubling but not shocking. General and academic audiences alike tend to ignore the significant social aspects of disability, and Griffin's own attempts to bury the issue made this easy to accomplish. However, what is most intriguing is that this story of disability passing even involves disability activists and scholars. The most distinguished of those who played a role was Irving Zola, one of the most important disability scholars and activists of the twentieth century. Physically disabled as a result of polio and a car accident, Zola was one of the founders of the Society for Disability Studies and played a key role in the emergence of disability as a scholarly field, which he believed should be closely linked to activism.

With the publication of Zola's seminal work, *Missing Pieces*, in 1982, the disability passing of *Black Like Me* reached a new level. Although physically disabled, Zola did not use a wheelchair in the 1970s but decided to do so as a sociological experiment when he joined a community of wheelchair users in the Dutch village of Het Dorp. The town was designed for severely disabled adults, and there Zola, in a wheelchair for the first time in years, explored issues of disability and identity. On the inside of the book's dust jacket, he singles out Griffin for tribute: "*Missing Pieces* is an unraveling of a social problem in the manner of *Black Like Me*. Like its author, I, too, am a trained social observer, but for me 'passing' was not an issue. For I already have the stigmata of the disabled—the braces, the limp, the cane—though I have spent much of my life denying their existence."

That brief statement, displayed prominently in the front matter of the book, is rich in irony. Zola cites *Black Like Me* as the inspiration for his disability magnum opus without mentioning the role that disability

played in Griffin's life and work. Doing so would have made Zola's connection to Griffin more meaningful and added to his arguments about
the importance of disability and identity. Instead, by positioning himself as the link between disability and *Black Like Me,* Zola further
obscures the more direct connections between the two. Unfortunately,
there is no way to know why this happened. Although it is hard to
believe that one of the field's keenest scholars would have missed seeing
the importance of disability in a work he held dear, it is even harder to
believe that he would have failed to raise the issue if he had been aware
of it. Disability had become so opaque that even one of the leaders in
the field allowed it to pass yet again from Griffin's life and work.

However, Zola's use of Griffin may also speak to the irrepressibility
of disability. While efforts to suppress the issue appeared successful,
disability remained embedded in Griffin's work. All that was required to
bring the latent issue to light was a reading by disabled people, even if
they remained unaware they were connecting with the underpinnings
of the book.

Zola was not the only disability activist and scholar involved in this
story. Another was Victoria Lewis, an activist and artist in disability
theater who read *Black Like Me* when she was in high school in the early
1960s. Reading *Black Like Me* as a disabled youth with post-polio syndrome put Lewis on a path that eventually led to disability rights. "Not
to reduce the journey to a formula," she writes, "but first came an understanding of racial justice, and a decade or two later, the fight for wom-
en's rights, then disability rights. Underlying these several conversions
was the founding understanding of the social construction of identity
and my first encounter with that was the reading of Griffin's book."[37]

Lewis does not remember ever knowing that Griffin had been disabled, and although learning about this surprised her, it also made
sense. Even though it took years before she consciously applied the
book to disability activism, it resonated with her because she could
relate it to her experience as a visibly disabled person. Interestingly,
and tellingly, she even mentions Zola as she explains why *Black Like
Me* captivated her in high school: "I already had a glimmering of being
what Irving Zola called a 'shrewd sociologist' as a disabled person, of
negotiating people's perceptions of me, or at least those I knew were a
result of them seeing me as a little crippled girl. So perhaps Griffin's
narrative echoed my own experience of dealing with the world."[38] Lewis
also offers a thought that connects to Lomax's review of *Black Like Me*

of 1961, which looks at the parallels between race and disability: "I have often wondered if my disability figured into my receptivity to the civil rights movement, if the marginalization I experienced (as polite as it was) made me feel a kinship with other marginalized figures." Even though it took Lewis years to apply *Black Like Me* consciously to disability, she recalls her experience with disability as the reason that Griffin's work rang true and put her on a path toward activism. That path eventually led Lewis to disability rights, which brings the story full circle. That she—and probably Zola, as well—connected with *Black Like Me* while remaining unaware of disability's original influence on the text shows both the irrepressibility of disability in modern America and the success of efforts to pass over the issue. This paradox is key for understanding disability's role in modern life and discourse.

This story of disability passing in public discourse has slowly begun to take a new turn over the past decade, although how significant it will become remains to be seen. In 1997, Griffin's good friend Robert Bonazzi, who also married Griffin's widow, published an authorized biography, *Man in the Mirror: John Howard Griffin and the Story of Black Like Me*. Much of that book focuses on how blindness and disability affected Griffin and his work. Perhaps most important, after finishing the biography Bonazzi edited and published Griffin's incomplete memoir of blindness, *Scattered Shadows,* which does even more to highlight the influence of disability in Griffin's life.

The results of Bonazzi's "rediscovery" of disability in Griffin's life are mixed. They have gotten some notice from scholars and journalists interested in Griffin. Kleege called scholars' attention to *Scattered Shadows* in an extended review, and the articles that occasionally surface on the Internet and in magazines usually reference Bonazzi's work and are now more likely to mention Griffin's disability, even if only briefly.[39] Yet scholars, at least outside the field of disability studies, are paying less attention to Griffin, presumably because there is now widespread consensus that it is problematic to use his text to understand the African American experience.

Whatever happens with academic, journalistic, and activist discussions of Griffin, *Black Like Me* continues to be popular with general audiences. Academics, activists, and journalists now play only a minor role in the reception of *Black Like Me*. Fifty years after its publication, sales are still strong; on Amazon.com, it is still the twentieth-best-selling book in African American studies, outselling even Harriet

Jacobs's *Incidents in the Life of a Slave Girl.* In the category of biographies and memoirs about authors, it ranks twenty-fourth and is one of the few books on that list not published within the past ten years.[40] On Amazon.com, *Black Like Me* continues to elicit new, positive, lengthy reviews from lay readers, most of which would trouble academics and activists because they use the book to try to understand the African American experience in the Jim Crow South. Almost none of the customer reviews mention disability or blindness. So while there have been some changes among scholarly and activist audiences, there do not seem to be any drastic changes in the way that lay white audiences read the book, at least based on Internet reviews.

Yet I still hope that Griffin's work, after fifty years, can have a new life with two outcomes. First, I hope people can start to read *Black Like Me* with disability issues in mind. I hope that people will start to read it alongside *Scattered Shadows* and use it to probe issues of disability. As Kleege points out, many people introduced Griffin as "the former Negro" when he gave lectures in the 1960s and 1970s, and Griffin adopted the moniker himself for a time, yet almost no one refers to him as a former blind man.[41] The latter moniker is more accurate and useful than the former and will prompt people to think more deeply about the importance of disability in American society.

Second, I hope people, and especially disability scholars, can use this layered story to consider how we pass over issues of disability in ways that go beyond physical performance. It is useful to consider the relationship between physical and discursive passing, which often go hand in hand. Understanding the process by which disability becomes buried will help us to exhume the issue from other stories and bring it more of the attention that it needs. While this sixty-year story shows the success of efforts to hide disability, it also shows how irrepressible disability issues are in modern America. This paradox is one of the reasons that disability studies has so much potential as a field of scholarly inquiry.

Notes

1. Douglas C. Baynton, "Disability and the Justification of Inequality in American History," in *The New Disability History: American Perspectives,* ed. Paul K. Longmore and Lauri Umansky (New York: New York University Press, 2001), 52.

2. John Howard Griffin, *Scattered Shadows: A Memoir of Blindness and Vision* (Maryknoll, N.Y.: Orbis Books, 2004), 33.

3. Ibid., 35.

4. Ibid., 33–34.

5. Ibid., 34.

6. "Enlisted Record and Report of Separation: Honorable Discharge," October 27, 1945, 1:13, John Howard Griffin Papers, Rare Book and Manuscript Library, Columbia University Library.

7. Griffin, *Scattered Shadows*, 35–36.

8. Ibid., 123.

9. Ibid.

10. In a forthcoming work, I focus on the intersecting issues of disability and masculinity in Griffin's life, which provides an instructive example for understanding identity in postwar America. For the relevant history of masculinity, see Michael S. Kimmel, *Manhood in America: A Cultural History*, 2nd ed. (New York: Oxford University Press, 2006); E. Anthony Rotundo, *American Manhood: Transformations in Masculinity from the Revolution to the Modern Era* (New York: Basic Books, 1993); Christina S. Jarvis, *The Male Body at War: American Masculinity during World War II* (DeKalb: Northern Illinois University Press, 2004); Tom Pendergast, *Creating the Modern Man: American Magazines and Consumer Culture, 1900–1950* (Columbia: University of Missouri Press, 2000); Jessica Weiss, *To Have and to Hold: Marriage, the Baby Boom, and Social Change* (Chicago: University of Chicago Press, 2000); David A. Gerber, "Blind and Enlightened: The Contested Origins of the Egalitarian Politics of the Blinded Veterans Association," in *The New Disability History: American Perspectives*, ed. Paul K. Longmore and Lauri Umansky (New York: New York University Press, 2001).

11. For work on the internalization of disability stigma, see Fiona Kumari Campbell, *Contours of Ableism: The Production of Disability and Ableness* (New York: Palgrave Macmillan, 2009), 16–29. Campbell builds on the work of Oliver Cromwell Cox, whose work eventually helped inspire critical race theory. Although Cox discussed the internalization of disability stigma in tandem with the internalization of racism, critical race theorists failed to follow his lead and decided to "pass" over the issue of disability: Oliver C. Cox, *Caste, Class, and Race: A Study in Social Dynamics* (Garden City, N.Y.: Doubleday, 1948), 383.

12. Kenneth T. Jackson, *Crabgrass Frontier: The Suburbanization of the United States* (New York: Oxford University Press, 1985); Eva Feder Kittay, *Love's Labor: Essays on Women, Equality, and Dependency* (New York: Routledge, 1999); Allison Carey, "Beyond the Medical Model: A Reconsideration of 'Feeblemindedness,' Citizenship, and Eugenic Restrictions," *Disability and Society* 18, no. 4 (2003): 411–430; Roxana Galusca, "From Fictive Ability to National Identity: Disability, Medical Inspection, and Public Health Regulations on Ellis Island," *Cultural Critique* 72 (Spring 2009): 137–163; Margaret Price, *Mad at School: Rhetorics of Mental Disability and Academic Life* (Ann Arbor: University of Michigan Press, 2011), chap. 6; Susan Wendell, *The Rejected Body: Feminist Philosophical Reflections on Disability* (New York: Routledge, 1996); Susan Wendell,

"Unhealthy Disabled: Treating Chronic Illnesses as Disabilities," *Hypatia* 16, no. 4 (Fall 2001): 17–33.

13. Griffin, *Scattered Shadows*, 39.

14. Tobin Siebers, "Disability as Masquerade," *Literature and Medicine* 23, no. 1 (Spring 2004): 1–22.

15. Griffin, *Scattered Shadows*, 95.

16. Ibid., 117.

17. For the history of blindness training, see Frances A. Koestler, *The Unseen Minority: A Social History of Blindness in America* (New York: D. McKay, 1976).

18. I am not trying to make an argument in favor of a singular, overarching blind (or Blind) identity. Rather I am talking about *a* blind identity, or *his* blind identity, looking at how Griffin and some people within his blind social network defined and politicized their disability identity.

19. Stories about blind people who regain their vision have been popular for millennia, going back at least as far as the Bible. This literary tradition helps explain the public fascination with Griffin's story of regaining his eyesight: see Moshe Barasch, *Blindness: The History of a Mental Image in Western Thought* (New York: Routledge, 2001), 47–56; Elisabeth G. Gitter, "The Blind Daughter in Charles Dickens's Cricket on the Hearth," *Studies in English Literature 1500–1900* 39, no. 4 (Autumn 1999): 675–689.

20. Griffin, *Scattered Shadows*, 219.

21. Griffin got the idea for this experiment when he was a writer for *Sepia*, an African American magazine. *Sepia* ran the story in serial format before Griffin published it as a book in 1961.

22. Georgina Kleege, *Sight Unseen* (New Haven, Conn.: Yale University Press, 1999), 18; Tanya Titchkosky, *Disability, Self, and Society* (Toronto: University of Toronto Press, 2003), 70. For other memoirs of blind people who tell of their earlier experiences passing, see Stephen Kuusisto, *Planet of the Blind* (New York: Delta Trade Paperbacks, 1999); Stephen Kuusisto, *Eavesdropping: A Memoir of Blindness and Listening* (New York: W. W. Norton, 2006); Ryan Knighton, *Cockeyed: A Memoir* (New York: Public Affairs, 2006); Russell Targ, "Do You See What I See: Memoirs of a Blind Biker," n.d., available online at http://irvalibrary.com/papers/DoYouSeeWhatISee.pdf; Rod Michalko, *The Difference That Disability Makes* (Philadelphia: Temple University Press, 2002); Rod Michalko, *The Mystery of the Eye and the Shadow of Blindness* (Toronto: University of Toronto Press, 1998).

23. Griffin, *Scattered Shadows*, 129.

24. John Howard Griffin, *Black Like Me* (1961), repr. ed. (New York: Signet, 1996), 51.

25. John Howard Griffin, "Journal Vol. III," n.d., 454, 33:825, John Howard Griffin Papers, Rare Book and Manuscript Library, Columbia University Library; emphasis added. Although it may seem ironic that he referred disdainfully to "white missionaries" before becoming involved in black civil rights, he never

attempted to save, teach, or reform African Americans in a missionary way. Instead, his civil rights goal was to raise awareness of racial injustice, just as he had wanted nondisabled people to become more aware of how they treated and looked at people with disabilities. *Black Like Me* is voyeuristic and raises questions about the author's authenticity, but disability taught Griffin to avoid a missionary approach when dealing with the problems of other groups.

26. Rosemarie Garland-Thomson, *Extraordinary Bodies: Figuring Physical Disability in American Culture and Literature* (New York: Columbia University Press, 1997), 26. See also Garland-Thomson's *Staring: How We Look* (Oxford: Oxford University Press, 2009).

27. Griffin, *Black Like Me*, 10–11.

28. Griffin, "Journal Vol. III," 454.

29. Quoted in Robert Bonazzi, *Man in the Mirror: John Howard Griffin and the Story of Black Like Me* (Maryknoll, N.Y.: Orbis Books, 1997), 23.

30. Gerber, "Blind and Enlightened," 313–334.

31. Griffin, *Black Like Me*, 5.

32. Kleege, *Sight Unseen*, 21.

33. While there are problems with analogizing between different categories of oppression, given the era in which he lived and how Griffin compared different groups, it would have been appropriate for him to include disability in this preface. For problems with analogizing between disability and race, gender, class, and sexuality, see Jeffrey A. Brune, "Minority," in *Keywords in Disability Studies*, ed. Rachel Adams, Benjamin Reiss, and David Serlin (New York: New York University Press, forthcoming); Susan M. Schweik, *The Ugly Laws: Disability in Public* (New York: New York University Press, 2009), 142–143.

34. For a history of the NFB, see Koestler, *The Unseen Minority*.

35. For an overview of the critical response to *Black Like Me*, see Bonazzi, *Man in the Mirror*, 169–192.

36. Louis Lomax, "It's Like This," *Saturday Review*, December 1961.

37. Victoria Ann Lewis, e-mail message to author, July 2, 2010.

38. Ibid.

39. Georgina Kleege, "The Strange Life and Times of John Howard Griffin," *Raritan* 26, no. 4 (Spring 2007): 96–112. For examples of recent nonacademic articles about Griffin and *Black Like Me*, see "John Howard Griffin," *African American Registry*, May 31, 2008, available online at http://www.aaregistry.com/african_american_history/955/A_revolutionary_writer_John_H_Griffin; Michael Miner, "Black Like Him," April 22, 2010, available online at http://www.chicago reader.com/gyrobase/black-like-me-50th-anniversary-john-howard-griffin/Content?oid=1691012&showFullText=true; Bruce Watson, "Black Like Me, 50 Years Later," *Smithsonian Magazine*, October 2011, available online at http://www.smithsonianmag.com/arts-culture/Black-Like-Me-50-Years-Later.html.

40. On August 27, 2010. Precise rankings change regularly, but sales of *Black Like Me* stay fairly steady.

41. Kleege, "The Strange Life and Times of John Howard Griffin," 96.

4 The Menstrual Masquerade

DAVID LINTON

T HE SOCIAL menstrual ecology is a most peculiar environment, full of contradictions, ambiguities, and layers of cultural construction. More than half the population of the globe is presumed to be a future menstruator, a periodic menstruator, or a former menstruator, yet at the same time, all of the members of the menstrual class are expected, even required at the risk of shame, embarrassment, and ostracism, to deny their membership.

The importance of passing as a non-menstruator—we might call it "menstrual denial"—is taught in the home and school, strenuously reinforced by social custom, and promoted through the marketing of a variety of products that are guaranteed to help one pass as having a uterus that *does not* occasionally shed its lining. The menstrual marketplace, traditionally dominated by pad and tampon manufacturers, now sees the arrival of a new generation of drugs that promise to eliminate— or, at least, sharply curtail—the menstrual cycle, thereby altering the landscape. However, the expectation that one is to hide the physical evidence of one's cycle remains as strong as ever. This essay explores the nuances and history of the menstrual masquerade.

Despite the advances in terms of women's greater freedom and general sexual frankness, the power of the menstrual taboo and the continuing need to keep menses closeted is still strong. It was made vivid when President Barack Obama nominated Sonia Sotomayor to a seat on the U.S. Supreme Court, as the following story illustrates: G. Gordon Liddy was one of the Watergate burglars in 1972. He was convicted of conspiracy, burglary, and illegal wiretapping for which he served four and a half years in prison. He is now the host of a right-wing radio talk show with a program that is syndicated in 160 markets and is on both Sirius Satellite Radio and XM Satellite Radio. In late May 2009, Liddy was discussing Sotomayor's nomination and said, "Let's hope that the key conferences aren't when she's menstruating . . . or just before she's going to menstruate. That would really be bad." What Liddy apparently believes is that Judge Sotomayor should be denied employment because she has a disabling condition known as "being a woman."

Over the centuries, a constellation of myths, lore, and prejudices developed across many cultures, times, and locations that gave women ample motivation to hide their periods. The "punishments" for being a menstruator were sometimes severe.[1] The rewards for passing as a non-menstruator were considerable: greater acceptance and social integration. Even though it was recognized that at any moment a woman might become a menstruator and thereby be deemed socially or psychologically unfit, as long as the woman could keep to herself the knowledge of when her period was at hand, she had a better chance of shaping her social status independently. However, the negative side of the situation is that since the exact days of the period are unknown, the fact that a woman might be menstruating can be used against her even when she is not or has entered menopause, as the Sotomayor story demonstrates.

This circumstance prevails today as men can be still be heard to say, whenever they want to dismiss a woman's comments or behavior, "Must be that time of the month." To make matters worse, women cannot combat the criticism by saying that it is not so, because it would mean agreeing that if it were that time of the month, then the dismissal would be warranted. Furthermore, the only way to prove the negative would be to expose one's non-menstruating genitals—an unthinkable tactic. (An exception to and reversal of this ploy is depicted in the movie *Showgirls,* when a woman refuses sex with a man because she is menstruating and invites him to touch her and get blood on his fingers to prove that she is telling the truth. He does so, but then he says he does not care, but she still maintains the taboo against menstrual sex.[2])

One of the primary reasons that menstruation has been stigmatized is because it has been long associated with illness and the desire of healthy individuals to avoid the unhealthy in fear of contamination. This is hardly surprising, as in the case of men in particular, their own experience of bleeding was when a man was sick or injured. As a result, women have good reason to hide evidence of menses, despite the fact that, ironically, a regular menstrual cycle is a sign of *good health* for them. However, the notion that menstruation is an illness has become so pervasive and the necessity of hiding one's period has become so thoroughly internalized that advertising for menstrual products can easily exploit the fears and, in doing so, reinforce them.

Disability studies scholars have repeatedly pointed out that disability is commonly seen, in Paul Longmore's words, "as a defect located in individuals that requires corrective treatments."[3] This is the source of the tendency to use a medical model when framing social responses to disabling conditions. Simi Linton has observed that the idea is similar to the argument that women's roles and status are biologically determined.[4]

I believe it is generally conceded that in American consumer culture, the structure and content of product advertising acts to both reflect and reinforce prevailing social values. Therefore, an examination of advertising for menstrual products can demonstrate how ads have used notions of disability to perpetuate feelings of inadequacy that must be "treated" and hidden via purchase and use of particular products. The effect has been to view the period as some sort of malady or disease that, thankfully, can be cured. However, at the same time, the disabling condition must be kept secret (especially from men), much as individuals with various disabilities historically have been institutionalized or otherwise denied public presence to spare the nondisabled from their discomforting appearance.

The most thorough theoretical analysis to date of the politics of passing as a non-menstruator was written by Sharra L. Vostral, who refers to "the technological politics of passing . . . [that] allow women to present themselves as non-menstruators."[5] Vostral focuses on the history of "menstrual technologies" (disposable pads and tampons) over more than a century (1870–1980); however, the end date of her study precludes consideration of the impact of menstrual cessation drugs that can eliminate the period completely rather than simply hiding the days during which it is occurring. Nonetheless, Vostral's contention is appropriate to any discussion of the social practices involving hiding, disguising, or denying menstrual realities: "Menstrual hygiene technologies are hidden artifacts that have enabled women to pass to overcome prejudice leveled against a bleeding body."[6]

Despite the high level of efficacy of menstrual products, whether referring to pads, tampons, cups, or pharmaceutical products, there is a significant difference between menstrual passing and other forms of the phenomenon, such as gendered, racial, or disability passing. In the case of the latter forms, an individual might spend an entire lifetime embedded in the chosen masquerade, at least to a portion of one's social circle. For instance, the literary critic Anatole Broyard, a man of mixed race,[7] succeeded in spending his entire professional and personal life passing as "white," and similar successes are convincingly depicted in the novels *Passing* by Nella Larsen and *The Human Stain* by Philip Roth, to name just two of many compelling examples. No such long-term reprieve exists when it comes to menstruation. The temporal rules are completely different. While a "black" individual might pass perpetually as "white," if skin tones are ambiguous enough, and a person might swap genders convincingly (as seen in the films *Boys Don't Cry* and *Albert Nobbs*), at least in public presentation women, even if they do not menstruate at all due to a biological anomaly or medical condition or age, are always assumed to menstruate or to have menstruated at *some time*. The question comes down to the difference between "when" and "whether." Social circumstances and traditions require women to behave as though they never menstruate, although it is presumed that in fact they actually do; it is just not known on which day of the month they are doing so.

While the historian Roland Marchand has documented how advertising practices in the 1920s invited consumers to seek the trappings of "sophisticated" and "upper-class" identities so as to meet consumer-capitalist expectations,[8] the specific admonitions to completely hide a crucial aspect of one's basic biology have not been thoroughly explored. Therefore, consider a representative set of magazine ads from the 1920s, an especially fruitful decade for the study of both disability and the lives of women, including their menstrual lives. This was a time of rapid social change on many levels, not the least of which were changes in menstrual management technologies. Perhaps the most important change ever in this area was the invention of the cheap, disposable sanitary napkin, a product given the name Kotex, which stood for "cotton texture," although the pads were made of wood pulp. Ironically, according to the manufacturer's description of the product, Kotex was created originally not for use by women but as a field dressing to help men deal with their periodic bleeding: the bleeding caused by battlefield wounds.

The prototype for the very first Kotex ad in 1920 shows a woman in a nurse's outfit standing between two seated men, both of whom show signs of having been wounded.[9] One has his leg in a cast, and the other's arm is in a sling. The woman faces the man in the sling, and they gaze affectionately at each other while she holds in front of her, just below her waist, a sanitary bandage. Today, virtually everyone has some idea what Kotex is, but when it was introduced, the ad made no overt mention of what to do with the product. The headline reads, "To Save Men's Lives Science Discovered Kotex," suggesting that it is something good for men, and the copy reinforces this notion.

There are some hints at the product's purpose, but they are as subtle as the picture itself. The intimate gaze between the soldier and the nurse as she holds the Kotex in front of the part of her body where the pad will be used conveys a touchingly sweet bond between them as they share the knowledge that this simple device can help each of them. Although Kotex was invented, as the ad states, "to save men's lives," now that the war is over, women can use it to make their own lives more "comfortable" and "safe." The echoing use of the words "save" and "safe" subtly suggests a sort of rough similarity between the two kinds of bleeding, menstrual and military, a balancing that dramatizes women's periodic bleeding and puts it on a par with that which a man experiences when wounded in battle. The illustration emphasizes the relationship by centering the pad between the army nurse and the army soldier.

This is a remarkable ad for several reasons. In the decades to come, there was very little presence of men in ads for menstrual products, and not for at least eighty more years were we to see a woman actually handling a menstrual product in the presence of any men other than those in the role of a health-care professional. A set of examples from Kotex campaigns during the 1920s further demonstrates the ways that passing as a non-menstruator became the norm.

One of the most common inducements to hiding menstruation has been the belief that menstrual fluid exudes an offensive odor that is a cause of social rejection. The phrase most commonly used to describe this condition was women's "oldest hygienic problem," as in an ad from 1925.[10] Furthermore, the ad plays on the notion that menstruation is a "handicap" that must be kept out of sight. However, at least in this case, there is a reward for passing as a non-menstruator, as one can wear the "sheerest frocks"—that is, be fully fashionable—thanks to the product.

The importance of hiding one's "handicap" was a central theme in most Kotex ads through the 1920s, an indication of social values concerning both menstruation and disability. Frequent use of the term "hygienic handicap," coupled with repeated claims that the product "deodorizes" the period, worked to induce a bodily insecurity that not only sold the product but encouraged frequent changing of pads, thereby further increasing sales.

One of the most blatant calls for menstrual secrecy motivated by fear of social rejection is found in a Kotex ad from 1929 whose large headline promised "Concealment Assured" above a picture of two smiling young women about to drive off in a sporty convertible.[11] Their freedom and lack of care, implied by the convertible and their fashionable outfits and hairstyles, are made possible because "this new sanitary pad assure[s] complete concealment." Not only does Kotex promise that the pad is visually "non-detectable, even under your lightest, filmiest clothes" because "there is no awkward bulk," but there is also nothing to fear from one's bad odor during summer months, because "Kotex deodorizes, too—so much more important when weather is warm."

The most intriguing and subtle ad in the series was published in *Pictorial Review* and elsewhere in 1929. It shows two slender young women lounging on the deck of an ocean liner dressed for the evening's shipboard festivities, an image of high sophistication in the 1920s. The way we know that they are aboard a liner is the presence of a round life preserver attached to the railing beside them. The name of the ship, as was the common practice, is printed in large letters on the device. They are aboard *The Nepenthe*.[12]

This is an extraordinary detail, perhaps chosen by an English major turned copywriter who remembered fondly Edgar Allan Poe's well known and often taught "The Raven." Poe's poem, the tale of a grief-stricken man unable to overcome the loss of his dead lover, pleads with the stolid, unflinching raven for "surcease of sorrow," some balm or drug to slake his misery, such as the mythic potion alluded to in Homer's *Odyssey* and Edmund Spenser's *The Faerie Queen,* as well as in works by Milton, Shelley, Chapman, and Pope: the mysterious elixir, *nepenthe,* the drug that banishes sorrow by making the user forget his woes, the antidepressant of the ancients. The narrator implores the raven,

> "Wretch," I cried, "thy God hath lent thee—by these angels he
>   hath sent thee
> Respite—respite and nepenthe from thy memories of Lenore!
> Quaff, oh quaff this kind nepenthe and forget this lost Lenore!"
>   Quoth the Raven, "Nevermore."

The young women in the ad have set sail on the good ship *Kotex Nepenthe,* the miracle conveyance that will carry them away from conscious need to worry or grieve over the burden of their menstruating bodies. This is the most extreme form of menstrual passing: passing against one's self. It is as if one of the women is saying, "I didn't even know I was wearing it."

What does it mean to board the *Kotex Nepenthe*? What port is being left behind? Where have the women set sail for? The ad copy provides three answers. First, as the headline and the first sentence of the text assert, one can advance one's class, "Why 9 out of 10 smart women instinctively prefer this new sanitary protection," states the headline, and the copy adds, "It is easy to see why the use of Kotex has become a habit among women who set the standard of good taste." Furthermore, as one "smart matron" puts it, "Now I wouldn't go back to the old way. This is so much more civilized—how did we ever get along without it?" By implication, women who continue to use old rags are of a primitive nature. And note the use of the phrase "Kotex has become a habit," an apt coinage for a drug-use metaphor.

Second, as the photo illustration and the copy confirm, a Kotex user can feel young and glamorous: "For such women have young ideas, young minds."

Third, and most significant, Kotex can help one hide the olfactory and visible signs of one's very gender: the scent of menses and the sight of a pad beneath one's dress: "ROUNDED, TAPERED CORNERS—make for inconspicuous protection," and "DEODORIZES . . . safely, thoroughly, by a patented process."

The ad embodies, both metaphorically and literally, the major theme that runs through the ninety-year history of advertising for disposable menstrual products: secrecy—that is, that one can pass through the decades of one's menstrual life as one who does not menstruate.

Some Historical Perspectives

Although the patterns of menstrual secrecy or denial and the importance of passing became fully developed through the twentieth century and correspond with the maturation of consumer capitalism, there have been instances when the menstrual taboos have been reversed and actually played to a woman's advantage.

Probably the oldest recorded incident of a woman exploiting her menstrual stigma to gain ascendency over a man is found in the biblical book of Genesis, the story of how Rachel defeated her hated father, Laban, and saved her life, as well. Rachel had stolen her father's household gods, a collection of teraphim, and run away with Jacob, her husband. When Laban caught up with the fleeing couple and their entourage, he was set on vengeance. The icons were hidden in the blankets under a camel saddle that Rachel sat on in her tent. Laban had searched every other tent, container and saddle bag, coming to Rachel last. They faced each other across the space, decades of pent-up anger hovering over them. Rachel's hatred for her domineering, abusive father inspired her to employ the severe strictures laid out in chapter 15 of the book of Leviticus: "When a woman has a discharge of blood which is her regular discharge from her body, she shall be in her impurity for seven days, and whoever touches her shall be unclean until the evening." Without budging from her seat, she said to Laban, "Let not my lord be angry that I cannot rise before you, for the way of women is upon me."

Imagine the tension in that moment. Laban had no way to know whether Rachel really was menstruating. If she was, and the teraphim were under her, his gods were defiled, and if he touched her blanket, he also would be unclean. On the surface, it might seem that she was dutifully protecting him from menstrual contamination by warning him of the danger her condition placed him in. But if she was feigning menses, he could get his gods back and punish his defiant, wayward daughter. He chose not to take the risk, stormed out of the tent, and allowed Jacob with his wives, servants, and followers to go their way. Thus, a key turning point in the history of Judeo-Christian culture pivots on an incident of one woman's decision to unmask herself— or seem to. We will never know which. The richly layered ambiguity in the story of Rachel's confrontation with Laban captures a set of practices still firmly in place. Women are supposed to keep their periods private matters. However, when they do choose to "go public" with mention of their periods, whether it actually is occurring or not, men are expected to accept the claim and behave in accord with whatever the prevailing menstrual protocols require.

Actually, although forms of the menstrual taboo are ancient, the practice of fully hiding the fact that one is menstruating is relatively recent. Advances in menstrual management technologies (pads, tampons, cups, pills) have driven the period under cover. The statement of Rachel to her father was not, on the face of it, transgressive.

In preindustrial societies, women did not (indeed, could not) worry about passing as non-menstruators. The onset of a girl's menarche and each ensuing period were readily apparent to her immediate circle of acquaintances. Even in cultural contexts that required women to remove themselves to a menstrual hut or tent or other quarantined space, it was known why they were gone, and they often had responsibilities to perform before they left, such as preparing enough food to feed the family during their menstrual confinement.

In circumstances in which one cannot pass due to close quarters, poor sanitation, and so on—village life, in other words—one absents oneself (having internalized the operant value systems) into a social quarantine such as a menstrual hut or tent, during which everyone knows but is spared the exposure and possible contamination. Historically, there has been a widely held belief that there's something contagious about menstrual blood.[13] Socially, the menstrual hut resembles a convalescent, rehabilitation facility, with its required bed rest and quarantine, as occurs during an epidemic. And following the required isolation, one emerges as a *survivor*—at least, until the next affliction predictably sets in. Men sometimes take on the role of menstrual victim, as well, with their own rituals of avoiding women who are menstruating. Among the most recent manifestations of this phenomenon is the fact that there are software applications on computer systems that allow men to register the dates of the menstrual cycles of women in their lives so they can avoid contact with them—or, at least, enact defenses appropriate to the perceived threat. Each month, one receives an email reminder of the impending period. One of the more creative of these sites is PMSBuddy.com. The most offensive is TrackYourBitch.com.

At some point, a profound change took place in the menstrual ecology of post-tribal societies. It is unclear why the change occurred, and its meaning and impact on the very nature of gender construction is not yet fully understood although Chris Knight, Leonard Shlain, Penelope Shuttle and Peter Redgrove, among others, have postulated explanations.[14] The change involved moving from a cultural practice of openly acknowledging the presence of menstruation but requiring that women have no contact with men during the period to a requirement that women hide the fact that they are menstruating while still engaging in their customary activities. In those settings that required women to remove themselves to the menstrual hut, or in ultra-traditional societies such as Hasidic sects, a woman's menstrual cycle is commonly recognized as when a girl is no longer allowed to sit with her father in the temple after her first period or a woman goes to the *mikva* following every period. Living in close quarters with simple sanitary arrangements, it is impossible to hide evidence of menstrual bleeding, so to deal with the taboos spelled out in ancient texts, such as those in Leviticus, detailed protocols were established and fully internalized by men and women. Although, as Margaret Mead pointed out in 1949, occasions did arise when a young girl might try to pass as a non-menstruator at the onset of her first periods to delay the inevitable arranged marriage, the menstrual cycle was no secret.[15]

We can only surmise when and why women began to abandon (or defy) the menstrual rules of order by hiding the discernible evidence. Surely, material advances in the availability of absorbent fabric, combined with social and psychological factors such as a desire to participate more fully in some activities and a wish to avoid the disdain or even repugnance that men sometimes expressed toward them, were among the influences.

As with most other social practices, the longer a custom is in place, the less likely it is to be questioned. It usually takes a social upheaval of some sort to require a reexamination and modification of established practices. Just such an upheaval occurred in 1941 with the onset of World War II. The extensive draft of men into military service required that factory jobs and other non-domestic employment be open to women. The urgency of defense-plant productivity required reliable workers and, therefore, recognition of women's menstrual-cycle needs. That, in turn, led to wider availability of product dispensers and more frank advertising practices, even including the claim that having a period need not interfere with engaging in sex with one's mate when he was home on leave. At the same time, the rapidly growing acceptance of the more convenient and discreet tampons that were widely marketed starting in 1936 made it even easier for women to keep their periods a secret. According to Vostral, "By 1940 Tampax, Inc. placed ads in over 47 different magazines with a total circulation of over 45 million people."[16]

When the war ended in 1945, the extensive social, economic, and employment gains women had made during the war were quickly reversed, including the more open recognition and acceptance of the menstrual cycle. Ads once again stressed the importance of odor control and discretion and the importance of hiding any sign of the period and the paraphernalia associated with it. The most blatant—and, by contemporary standards, most offensive—was a series of ads for Zonite, a douching product, that appeared in magazines such as *Screen Stories* and *Modern Romance* in 1950 and 1951.[17] The Zonite ads repeatedly used a line that was calculated to convince women that their genitals exuded a foul odor that they themselves were unaware of, a smell that drove their husbands away, ruined their social lives, and deprived them of sex: "There's a womanly offense—greater than body odor or bad breath . . . an odor she may not detect herself but is so apparent to other people."

Within a few years of the end of the war, many of the social and economic gains made by women during the war were lost, including the gains having to do with denying and hiding the menstrual realities.

Menstrual Anti-passing: Reversing the Flow

One of the unique aspects of the social taboos surrounding menstruation is that sometimes, even when she is not menstruating, a woman may claim to be doing so. In the realm of disability, Tobin Siebers uses the term "masquerade" to describe this phenomenon: "exaggerating or performing difference, when that difference is a stigma, marks one as a target, but it also exposes and resists the prejudices of society."[18] There is a sort of jiu-jitsu quality to this gambit: by redirecting the force of the negative social energy against its customary source (commonly men), women have been able to gain power, at least momentarily. Colloquially, this is sometimes called "playing the menstrual card," and its workings are described in some detail the essay "Not Tonight, Dear."[19]

There is even a form of menstrual activism embodied in the work of some feminists, most famously in an oft-cited essay by Gloria Steinem "If Men Could Menstruate,"[20] and that of female comics such as Margaret Cho, Sarah Silverman, and Whoopi Goldberg, who openly discuss the period in such a way as to defy the concealment culture's demands. The contradictions and absurdities of the situation were aptly mocked by Karen Houppert when she posed the following comparison:

> People with runny noses do not hide their tissues from colleagues and family members. They do not die of embarrass-

ment when they sneeze in public. Young girls do not cringe if a
boy spies them buying a box of Kleenex. . . . No one celebrates
congestion. . . . But those who suffer publicly—ahchoo!—are
casually blessed. It is, in essence, no big deal.[21]

Houppert does not propose going to the opposite extreme of
endorsing menstrual coming-out parties, but she does encourage efforts
to demystify and normalize the period. Currently, women are far from
having achieved that end, though there are some signs of change. For
instance, it is becoming common for television programs, especially
situation comedies, to include references to menstruation, and although
they are often played for laughs and even ridicule, the taboos and menstrual anxieties are just as often held up for examination and exposure.
To cite just a few, *The Cosby Show, 7th Heaven, Roseanne, Beverly Hills
90210, Degrassi, The Larry David Show,* and *Everwood* have done episodes depicting first periods in sympathetic ways that reject the shame
and embarrassment tropes that traditionally have dominated the value
system and that necessitated menstrual denial.

Or consider the fact that a major female sports figure, the tennis
star Serena Williams, has appeared in a running series of magazine ads
for Tampax Pearl tampons that present her as being able to continue to
win her matches, regardless of the fact that she has her period. Williams
is the first celebrity of such status who has "come out" so publicly as a
menstruator.

The menstrual unmasking described here is far from universal in
capitalist-consumer cultures, let alone more traditional non-Western
settings. Yet if present trends continue, we may be entering a new era
of menstrual enlightenment.

Notes

1. Janice Delaney, Mary Jane Lupton, and Emily Toth, *The Curse: A Cultural History of Menstruation* (Chicago: University of Illinois Press, 1988).

2. Paul Verhoeven, dir., *Showgirls,* 128 min., 1995.

3. Paul Longmore, *Why I Burned My Book and Other Essays on Disability*
(Philadelphia: Temple University Press, 2003), 4.

4. Simi Linton, *Claiming Disability: Knowledge and Identity* (New York: New
York University Press, 1988).

5. Sharra L. Vostral, *Under Wraps: A History of Menstrual Hygiene Technology* (Lanham, Md.: Lexington Books, 2008), 3.

6. Ibid., 10.

7. Bliss Broyard, *One Drop: My Father's Hidden Life—A Story of Race and Family Secrets* (New York: Little, Brown, 2007).

8. Roland Marchand, *Advertising the American Dream: Making the Way for Modernity, 1920–1940* (Berkeley: University of California Press, 1985).

9. An image of this ad, "To Save Men's Lives," is available online at http://www.mum.org/urkotex.htm (accessed November 10, 2012).

10. An image of this ad, "Woman's Happiness," is available online at http://library.duke.edu/digitalcollections/adaccess.BH0009/pg.1 (accessed November 10, 2012).

11. An image of this ad, "Concealment Assured," is available online at http://library.duke.edu/digitalcollections/adaccess.BH0022/pg.1 (accessed November 10, 2012).

12. An image of this ad, "Why 9 Out of 10 Smart Women," is available online at http://library.duke.edu/digitalcollections/adaccess.BH0260/pg.1 (accessed November 10, 2012).

13. Delaney et al., *The Curse.*

14. Chris Knight, *Blood Relations* (New Haven, Conn.: Yale University Press, 1991); Leonard Shlain, *Sex, Time and Power: How Women's Sexuality Shaped Human Evolution* (New York: Viking, 2003); Penelope Shuttle and Peter Redgrove, *The Wise Wound: Menstruation and Everywoman* (New York: Marion Boyars, 1978).

15. Margaret Mead, *Male and Female* (New York: William Morrow, 1949).

16. Vostral, *Under Wraps,* 74.

17. An image of this ad, "How Can He Explain to His Sensitive Young Wife?" is available online at http://library.duke.edu/digitalcollections/adaccess_BH0214/ (accessed November 10, 2012).

18. Tobin Siebers, "Disability as Masquerade," *Literature and Medicine* 23 (Spring 2004): 19.

19. "'Not Tonight, Dear': Taboos of Sex," in Delaney et al., *The Curse.*

20. Gloria Steinem, "If Men Could Menstruate," *Ms. Magazine,* October 1978.

21. Karen Houppert, *The Curse: Confronting the Last Unmentionable Taboo: Menstruation* (New York: Farrar, Straus and Giroux, 1999), 4.

5 ## "I Made Up My Mind to Act Both Deaf and Dumb"

Displays of Disability and Slave Resistance in the Antebellum American South

DEA H. BOSTER

I N **1839**, Jacob D. Green, a domestic slave and errand boy on a large plantation in Maryland, made his first attempt to run away from his master. The resourceful Green had begun to use deception and tricks at a young age to torment his white masters and get revenge on fellow slaves who humiliated or wronged him, but, in Green's words, "I firmly believed to run away from my master would be to sin against the Holy Ghost." However, after his wife of six years—a former concubine of their master—and the couple's children were sold away without warning, Green immediately began to plan his escape, earning money by selling stolen chickens and lying to obtain a horse from his master's father-in-law.[1] On his way to Delaware, Green fell asleep in a barn, where seven white men discovered him after he fell out of the hayloft. The men demanded to know who Green was and why he was there, but Green refused to reply, even after the men brought him before a magistrate. His silence indicated to the men that Green might be mute, an assumption that Green decided to use to his advantage: "When I remembered I had not given evidence of speech, I determined to act as if I was dumb; and when the magistrate called to me, I also thought deafness was often united with dumbness, and I made up my mind to act both deaf and dumb, and when he called, 'Boy, come here,' I took no notice, and did not appear to hear . . . and so effectually that he discharged me, convinced I was a valueless deaf and dumb nigger."[2]

Although Green was later arrested and returned to his master in Maryland, his successful ruse of being deaf and dumb—and, by association, "valueless"—is a telling example of the power that slaves had to perform disability in antebellum Southern society. Green's feigned muteness was arguably not "visible" the way a limp or deformed limb would be, but it was highly conspicuous; his refusal to answer his white captors' questions was, in the antebellum South, a serious offense that could have resulted in an arrest, a whipping, or both. By making his feigned impairment so prominent in the encounter, Green challenged his white oppressors to render his "disabled" body invisible again and succeeded when they turned him loose instead of whipping him, charging him with trespass, or publicizing his capture.

For many slaves, there were significant advantages to being considered "disabled," and displays of feigned, exaggerated, or self-inflicted disability in their bodies was an important way for slaves to negotiate control over the bodies and resist the authority of their masters.[3] The success of "passing" as disabled lay in the ability of slaves to perform the most obvious signs of disability, making those signs impossible to ignore and tapping into pervasive concerns about "disorderly bodies." Almost paradoxically, performing disability—a condition normally associated with dependence and powerlessness—and forcing white authority figures to contend with their conditions could allow slaves to achieve a degree of independence and control in many different situations.[4] Slaves "passing" as disabled to resist their bondage did so by relying on complex intersections between race, gender, social class and the physical body in the antebellum American South.[5]

Historians since the 1970s have debated the prevalence of such performances, mainly in the context of slave malingering. In their statistical study *Time on the Cross*, Robert Fogel and Stanley Engerman claimed that feigned illness was rare among slaves on the plantations they analyzed, and white observers did not always assume that ill slaves were malingerers; instead, they argued, planters "were generally more concerned about losing slaves or impairing their health through the neglect of real illness."[6] However, many other historians—including Herbert Gutman, Kenneth Stampp, Peter Wood, Eugene Genovese, Todd Savitt, and Sharla Fett—have argued against this view, claiming that malingering was a pervasive and effective tool of day-to-day resistance and was a prominent concern for slaveholders and the doctors they employed to care for their slaves.[7] These authors discuss the discourse of slave malingering in the antebellum South—many white observers assumed that feigned illness and impairment was widespread among African American bondspeople, and there were numerous admissions of the practice in the narratives of former slaves—but pay little attention to the underlying mechanisms of malingering. As Heidi M. Hackford points out, feigned illness requires a conformity to a shared set of ideas about health and bodies; feigned disability provided, in a sense, a "contested space" for masters and slaves to negotiate authority over enslaved bodies. Evidence from trickster tales indicates that techniques of feigning illness or disability were common knowledge among slaves but were also considered risky and were a matter of debate among slaves, as well.[8]

However, while Hackford argues that slave malingering was largely a domestic concern,[9] many slaves who feigned disability often did so publicly. Indeed, many different sites in antebellum slave society—including plantations and work sites, jails, and auction blocks—provided opportunities for slaves to stage visible performances to "pass" as disabled. A more useful model for discussing malingering slaves, therefore, is the concept of masquerade. In "Disability as Masquerade," Tobin Siebers describes exaggerations of disability as "structurally akin to passing," but a kind of passing that makes a physical difference impossible to ignore. Individuals may "perform" disability to adjust or control how observers react to them in certain situations. The masquerade of disability is therefore a response to the "logic of compulsory able-bodiedness," which dictates that "the more visible the disability, the greater the chance that the disabled person will be repressed from public view and forgotten."[10] Siebers theorizes the concept of the masquerade politically as "a resource for changing the meaning of disability,"[11] but for African American slaves, adopting "masquerades" of disability could change the meanings of their bondage. In antebellum slave society, where enslaved bodies were routinely objectified in practice and discourse, individuals who donned masquerades of disability—as "unsoundness," defect, or impairment—made their bodies more conspicuous for their disorderliness than for their enslavement. Thus, slaves compelled uncomfortable observers to pity, ignore, or conceal them, since the visibility of the disability paradoxically could serve to make the disabled person invisible. Slaves performing disability, whether it was genuine or feigned, could capitalize on a variety of reactions, including sympathy, fear, and disgust, to negotiate the terms of their bondage.

Most important, however, they relied on cultural habits, prevalent in white and black communities alike, of hiding and ignoring the disabled. Ultimately, slaves' performances of disability and "passing" as disabled—as well as the ambivalence some slaves expressed about being identified as disabled after they achieved freedom—upheld prevalent negative assumptions about disability in antebellum society.

F ROM A SLAVE'S PERSPECTIVE, there were certainly a number of benefits to being considered ill or disabled, although there were significant differences between feigning an acute illness and a chronic impairment. Several scholars have indicated that the primary motive for slave malingering was to avoid labor; a short-term illness could provide a temporary respite from work, but a long-term ailment or disability—including vague presentations such as paralysis, rheumatism, or loss of limb function—could allow a slave to obtain lighter work assignments permanently or even be retired.[12] A diagnosis of disability could also allow a slave to avoid punishment for crimes and, more frequently, to halt undesired sales. Evidence of a disability—even an obviously counterfeit one—could lower their prospective values and even terminate dealings with prospective buyers, a phenomenon well-known to many slaves.[13] John Boggs, a field hand from Maryland, describes being sold for one thousand dollars to a cotton planter in Georgia, "but he wouldn't take me because I had been disfigured by poison-oak, and the loss of a finger; so my master had to put in two other young fellows instead of me. I would have been in a cotton-field forty years ago if it hadn't been for that."[14] Boggs's condition was a genuine "unsoundness" that prevented him from being sold to an undesirable location and master. He identified his disability as good fortune in that circumstance, an opinion that many other slaves at market shared. Some slaves also may have exaggerated their age to be excused from hard labor, as well as to garner respect within the plantation community.[15] In his 1843 discussion of factors influencing the collection of slaves' vital statistics, the statistician Samuel Forry noted the phenomenon of slaves' lying about their real age "from the circumstance that it flatters [their] self-love, enhances [their] dignity, and excuses [them] from labor. . . . [D]ignity and ease depend on [their] years."[16]

Some scholars claim that feigned disability was more common among female slaves, whose "soundness" was often linked with their reproductive health. Reproductive problems were easier to simulate, and although such ailments were difficult to authenticate, white slaveholders eager to protect the fecundity of their female chattel were more likely to heed their bondswomen's complaints.[17] Occasionally, enslaved women pretended to be pregnant to obtain more food rations as well as a decreased workload, but such a deception was difficult to maintain. More frequently, female slaves simulated or exaggerated chronic disorders such as menstrual pain and amenorrhea to mitigate their work.[18] Some bondswomen also feigned sterility or miscarriage to avoid being used as plantation "breeders" or to quietly terminate pregnancies from forced sexual relations. In an article published in 1860 in the *Nashville Journal of Medicine and Surgery,* John H. Morgan, a physician in Murfreesboro, Tennessee, argued that many black women were "willing and even anxious to avail themselves of an opportunity to effect an abortion or to derange menstruation," secretly using herbal abortifacients and other substances to create a ruse of sterility or miscarriage.[19] There is evidence that such malingering could be successful. For instance, on April 2, 1857, James Abney, a slaveholder in South Carolina, purchased three slaves—one woman and two children—at a discounted rate because "they were diseased, and were sold as unsound." The nature of the woman's supposed defect seems to have been her barrenness, but after emancipation, she bore three children, which prompted the administration of the seller's estate to sue for compensation in 1868.[20] Such examples indicate the complicated intersection of race, gender, and ability in slaveholders' assessments of their chattel's "soundness," as well as the multitude of benefits that slave men and women could reap from performing disability in the antebellum South.

Despite the numerous advantages to being considered disabled or "unsound," slave folklore included warnings about being discovered while feigning or exaggerating disease or debility. As the historian Sharla Fett has observed, trickster tales that circulated in slave communities describe opportunities for "strategic illness," as well as punishment of slaves who were caught fooling their masters.[21] In one tale, a retired man named Uncle Daniel moved into the "old quarters" of his plantation, with an enslaved boy assigned to attend his needs. However, Uncle Daniel was mean to the boy and snuck out at night to steal milk and sweet potatoes, so the boy told the master that Daniel was embellishing his infirmity. Soon after, the master told several men to carry Uncle Daniel to a haystack to get some sun, then set the haystack on fire: "that old man see that fire and jumped over top the stack and got up and outrun everybody. So they took him and put him back in the fields."[22] Thus, many slaves understood the benefits as well as the pitfalls of malingering and had to judge their situations carefully before attempting to feign disability.

Suspicions of invented illness, or "possuming," in slaves were particularly strong among Southern masters, traders, and medical professionals. The prominent Southern physician Samuel A. Cartwright even argued that malingering was an inherent trait among African Americans.[23] Evidence from plantation records and medical discourse suggests that, while some slaveholders certainly were concerned about their slaves' well-being, masters often doubted the authenticity of health complaints and physical weakness among their bondspeople. Slaveholders faced the prospect of wasted capital and productivity by allowing feigned illnesses to go unnoticed or unpunished, and white doctors risked losing their lucrative practices if they were deceived by black patients. Thus, many members of white slaveholding society often assumed that ailing slaves feigned their conditions and conducted rigorous investigations to ensure that slaves' health problems were genuine before seeking or administering treatment. Moses McLoud, a medical student in South Carolina, even recommended that slaves' "complaints demand at the hands of the Physician a more careful investigation than those of whites" because deception was supposedly so widespread and could have serious implications for labor systems and the treatment of slaves.[24] It is difficult to verify many cases of suspected malingering, especially since its occurrence could have serious social consequences for members of the slaveholding class. However, it is clear that feigned disability was a common occurrence among Southern slaves, as well as a prominent concern for their masters.

A LTHOUGH WHITE authority figures often suspected slaves with apparent disabilities of malingering, there are numerous accounts of slaves able to use displays of genuine or feigned disability to negotiate their circumstances, including labor conditions and sales. Narratives of former slaves, correspondence about slaveholding and plantation records, and observations in antislavery publications indicate that bondspeople could "pass" as disabled by making signs of disability highly conspicuous and impossible to ignore. Employing Siebers's concept of the logic of compulsory able-bodiedness, it is possible to sur-mise that the masquerade of disability forced observers to react to seemingly "disabled" slaves by pitying or repressing them in efforts to make their disorderly bodies less visible. Thus, an injured laborer would be excused from work and sent to the privacy of his home; a disabled runaway would be kept out of public spaces such as jails and court-rooms; or an "unsound" property would be removed from an auction block without being sold. Such performances relied on a widespread cultural habit of obscuring disabled individuals and could be used to serve the interests of the slaves, whether their conditions were genuine or not.

There is strong evidence that slaves attempted to exaggerate dis-abling conditions to avoid working, if not always successfully. In 1844, the Louisiana planter Bennet H. Barrow suspected a man named Demps of exaggerating a vision problem to get out of working; on June 12, Barrow complained in his journal that "Demps has been doing nothing since Last November[;] Dr King tending him for Loss of his Eye sight, gave him up—to appearance seemed as well as ever gave him 25 cuts yesterday morning & ordered him to work Blind or not. to show the scoundrel." After that punishment, Demps absconded, causing Barrow to vow that he would "make him see sights as Long as I live."[25] This jour-nal entry indicates that Demps was able to use his blindness—which he made prominent enough to earn the attention of a physician—to absent himself from work for more than six months, much to the frustration of his master. Demps's conspicuous blindness failed to provide him with a longer absence from work, however, and Barrow eventually turned the tables on him by ordering him to work in full view of others, despite his blindness and the disfiguring injury of "25 cuts." Demps responded by physically removing himself from the plantation, which confirmed his malingering in Barrow's mind. Thus, Demps relied on assumptions about blindness to compel his master and overseer to "obscure" his disability by absenting him from work; when that ulti-mately did not work, Demps absented himself by running away.

Other slaves had more success in using exaggerations of disability to negotiate the terms of their labor. The West Indies slave Mary Prince experienced debilitating rheumatism and other injuries from physical abuse and required assistance to perform her duties as a laundress. Often, her condition so frustrated her masters that they would send her away to find another owner, although they always changed their minds about selling her. Prince's disability was a very conspicuous one; she notes that she had to use a stick to walk and was often laid up because of her rheumatism, "But whether sick or well, I had my work to do."[26] In her narrative, she presents her ailments as a form of resistance. Prince notes that her impairments inhibited her from washing her mistress' clothes "to satisfaction," but not other forms of labor that were directly profitable to her: "When my master and mistress went from home, as they sometimes did, and left me to take care of the house and premises, I had a good deal of time to myself, and made the most of it. I took in washing, and sold coffee and yams and other provisions to the captains of ships. I did not sit still idling during the absence of my owners; for I wanted, by all honest means, to earn money to buy my freedom."[27]

Although Prince's condition did not completely excuse her from her assigned duties, she was certainly aware that she could use her condition to adjust her work routines. Indeed, as Barbara Baumgartner argues, "It seems plausible that Prince rhetorically manipulates her bodily affliction as a means of explaining and defending her inability (i.e. refusal) to work."[28]

In another example, James L. Smith, who had been disabled by a broken leg in his adolescence and was assigned to scaring crows in a cornfield every day of the week, recalled an attempt to use malingering to "break up, or put an end to [his] Sunday employment." At first, Smith considered feigning a stomachache but was worried that Mr. and Mrs. Mitchell, his masters, would administer "something that would physic me to death."[29] Thus, he devised to pretend to re-fracture his disabled leg. Mr. Mitchell threatened Smith with the lash if he did not get back to his duties, injured or not, but Smith, "groaning and crying with every step," did not make it back to the field before Mitchell relented. After eating some breakfast, Smith went to his bedroom to lie on the floor: "[I] pretended that I was in so much pain that I could not raise myself." Mrs. Mitchell found him there, and after bathing his seemingly injured leg with a camphor liniment and binding him up, she "rebuked her husband by telling him he had no business to send me out in the field . . . for I was not able to be there." Smith remained in his room for two weeks, until he received news that the crows had moved on from the cornfield. "After hearing this joyful news I began to grow better very fast," he recalled. "When Saturday came I could walk quite a distance to see my mother, who lived some ten miles off."[30] Although they could not be certain of their masters' reactions and risked severe punishment,

Prince and Smith were able to capitalize on existing impairments to negotiate the terms of their bondage, exaggerating their disabilities with very conspicuous, visible performances to mitigate forced labor but proudly described their ability to perform physical tasks of their choosing, such as Prince's laundry for profit and Smith's ten-mile walk to visit his mother.

Some slaves, like Jacob D. Green in the opening example of this chapter, used displays of disability as a means of escape. Henry Box Brown aggravated an injury to make a disability more visible and impairing, forcing his overseer to excuse him from work and thus making the slave himself "invisible" and giving him time to plan his flight unnoticed. Prior to his escape from Virginia in a railroad cargo box, Brown attempted to obtain a break from work "in consequence of a disabled finger." When his overseer refused "on the ground that [Brown's] hand was not lame enough," Brown made his injury worse with oil of vitriol, which ate through his flesh down to the bone. As Brown described the situation to the abolitionist Charles Stearns of Boston, "The overseer then was obliged to allow me to absent myself from business, for it was impossible for me to work in that situation." However, he "did not waste his precious furlough in idle mourning over his fate" but "armed [him]self with determined energy, for action," to plan his escape.[31] It is significant that Brown's narrative does not describe the pain and suffering of his wound, which he admits was more extreme than he had intended, but instead focuses on his disabling injury as a means to an end. In this respect, his injured finger—a highly conspicuous sign of disability for his overseer—became a means of transcendence, allowing him to overcome the burden of his duties and plan his eventual flight from bondage in the relative obscurity that disability provided to him.

The strategy of feigning disability outright is apparent in the memoir of Israel Campbell, who had enjoyed relative independence as a craftsman in Kentucky but was arrested on suspicion of a planned escape after he shoed his horse and purchased a new bridle. Campbell attempted to get out of jail by feigning a fit, which he felt he could accomplish because he had witnessed fits in other people. In his published narrative, Campbell described his plan:

> Seeing that there was not much prospect of their making any effort to find out whether I was guilty or not, I put my wits to

work to try and escape. The plan I adopted was to have a fit, and make great noise and get very sick. This plan I began to carry out the following night. About twelve o'clock I commenced hollowing, groaning and shaking my legs, and made a desperate noise, which so frightened the white [inmate], that he called the other man and roused the jailer and told him to bring a light, that Israel had a fit.[32]

Campbell's striking performance fooled the jailer and white prisoners, all of whom were afraid that he was dying and responded to his masquerade with sympathy and horror. Campbell's master, however, was not convinced and had a physician confirm Campbell's deceit by examining his pulse and tongue.[33] One may conclude that the master and physician were simply more knowledgeable about the diagnosis of epileptic fits than an ignorant jailer and inmates, but the fact that Campbell even warranted the attention of his master and a doctor indicates that his performance was powerful and difficult to ignore. This episode indicates a deep power struggle between Campbell, a slave who attempted to use a performance of disability to negotiate his freedom from jail, and his owner, who potentially had much to lose if Campbell's feigned fit went unnoticed and enabled the slave to escape.

More frequently, the auction block—where African American bodies were made highly visible—was an important stage for displays of disability.[34] Auctioneers and masters were often frustrated by slaves who performed conspicuous signs of "unsoundness"—including paralysis, insanity, mental incapacity, and epileptic fits—in front of prospective buyers. As the Alabama trader A. J. McElveen noted in an letter to his partner J. B. Oakes in 1856, "James is cutting up. . . . I could Sell him like hot cakes if he would talk Right. . . . [T]he Boy is trying to make himself *unsound*."[35] Slaves who made a real or counterfeit disability conspicuous on the auction block were in a powerful position to negotiate the terms of their sale. For instance, J. Winston Coleman Jr.'s monograph *Slavery Times in Kentucky* describes an auction in Winchester, Kentucky, at which a slaveholder named Mr. Anderson offered his slave, George, with a standard guarantee that the man was "sound of mind and body and a slave for life." However, during the "lively" bidding process, "George suddenly assumed a strange appearance—his head was thrown back, his eyes rolled wildly, his body and limbs began to twitch and jerk in an unheard of manner." Exclaiming that he was suffering from "fits," George fell off the block and was immediately removed for a doctor's examination. Apparently, the physician was unable to determine whether the slave's fit had been genuine and recommended that he remain in the jailer's care overnight; however, "next morning, when the jailer brought in breakfast, he found the bed empty. George was gone, and nothing was heard of him again until word came, several weeks later, that he was safe in Canada."[36]

In this example, George used his prominent visibility on the raised auction block, in a crowded room of observers, to stage a violent epileptic fit for all to see. This performance of disability not only called his soundness as property into question (as well as his master's honor, by negating the guarantee of health he had given minutes before), it also provided George with a means of escape. The trader and doctor removed his "disabled" body from the public site of the auction to a more private, concealed setting where he was left unattended overnight, so he seized the opportunity to flee. In this instance, George capitalized on the extreme visibility on the auction block to present his body as disabled and disorderly and thereby challenged observers to repress or conceal him by removing him from the block.

One intriguing example of a potentially feigned disability that enabled a slave to avoid both a sale and punishment is the case of a fifteen-year-old woman named Virginia who was sentenced to hang for arson in Richmond on March 15, 1843. Virginia allegedly had committed the crime in the home of her hired-out master, William Rushmer, and had been kept at the city jail for more than one month prior to her trial. After pronouncing her sentence, the aldermen of Richmond and other witnesses estimated Virginia's value as a convicted slave at $300 and remanded her to the jail until her execution date.[37] Her owner, Archibald Govan, appealed to Governor James McDowell for clemency, and on March 22, the governor granted Virginia full pardon on the condition that she leave the commonwealth permanently at the expense of her owners, who hoped to sell her farther South. However, on the day that Govan brought Virginia to the "private jail" of the prominent Richmond slave trader Bacon Tait, "She was seized with Epeleptick fits." The episodes continued frequently for more than two months before both the trader and a physician concluded that she could not be sold in her condition,[38] indicating that her fits were a more effective barrier to a sale than her conviction for arson. Thus, despite the governor's directive, Virginia returned to the Govans and her own family and remained there as late as June17, when her owner Lucy Govan remarked in a letter to her father that Virginia's "health ha[d] greatly improved, [and] she looks as fat and well as I have ever seen her."[39]

Virginia's highly visible "unsoundness" seemed to have been an isolated phenomenon. Writing to his father-in-law, Archibald Govan mentioned that the day he moved Virginia to Bacon Tait's slave jail was "not the first time" she experienced fits,[40] but there is nothing else in the records to indicate that Virginia had a history of epilepsy or that her frequent convulsions continued after she returned to the Govan household. This absence is especially conspicuous in the court records of Virginia's arson trial; given the disease's associations with insanity, a history of epileptic fits presumably would have been important information for the court to consider in determining Virginia's guilt. The main reason that Bacon Tait offered for removing Virginia from his slave jail was his assertion that the "malady with which the girl is afflicted has hitherto baffled all effort to effect a sale" and "the girl cannot be sold even at nominal price as long as she may labour under her present malady."[41] This claim indicates that Virginia's value as a convicted felon plummeted from an estimated $300—not much lower than that of other young, female slaves in Richmond's markets at the time[42]—to virtually nothing in less than three months as a result of her convulsions. The short-lived intensity of Virginia's epilepsy raises the possibility that she used performances of fits as a strategy to avoid a sale and incarceration. Whether or not Virginia intentionally feigned her condition, it is clear that the daily fits she displayed were impossible for the trader, the physician, or any prospective buyers to ignore. They responded to her condition by removing her from public space altogether, thereby rendering her uncontrolled body "invisible" and allowing Virginia to return to her family.

In many respects, Virginia's experience closely resembles that of Denmark Vesey, the leader of a failed slave rebellion in South Carolina in 1822. As a young man known as Télémaque, he had served as a cabin "pet" aboard Captain Joseph Vesey's ship but was sold to a Haitian sugar plantation in 1781. Captain Vesey departed for St. Thomas, but he returned to Haiti approximately one month later to learn that Télémaque had experienced frequent epileptic fits in his absence. According to one account, "The boy was examined by the city physician, who required Capt[ain] Vesey to take him back; and Denmark served him faithfully, with no trouble from epilepsy, for twenty years."[43] Antebellum antislavery accounts of Denmark Vesey's life highlight this episode—especially the fact that his fits were an isolated occurrence and never returned after Vesey left Haiti—as an early indication of Vesey's cunning and desire to resist his bondage rather than evidence of any genuine disability. As the abolitionist Archibald Grimké observed, "It is by no means clear . . . whether those epileptic fits were real or whether they were in truth feigned, and therefore the initial *ruse de guerre* of that bright young intelligence in its long battle with slavery."[44] Grimké is reluctant to claim outright that Vesey feigned his epileptic fits but clearly indicates that simulating illness or disability to avoid or reverse a sales agreement was a successful practice for antebellum slaves. Both Virginia and Vesey experienced (or, at least, appeared to experience) a seriously disabling condition, and their fits were apparently prominent enough to warrant the attention of doctors, slaveholders, and traders. Also, in both cases, the diagnoses that marked them as disabled, "unsound," and worthless at market prompted white authorities to send them away from public spaces and back to their original owners, which was a more favorable circumstance.

Denmark Vesey's example also indicates that the appearance of disability, whether genuine or feigned, in a slave could affect sales even after they were finalized. The fact that buyers could sue for breach of warranty if slaves they had purchased turned out to be "unsound," usually due to a hidden defect, provided another motive for slave malingering. Such "hidden defects" in redhibitory cases included any number of conditions, including peritonitis, scrofula, venereal diseases, and leg ailments, as well as epileptic fits and insanity.[45] As Judith K. Schafer and Ariela J. Gross have noted, it is likely that many slaves were aware that disease or disability could legally negate sales, and may feigned or exaggerated hidden defects to reverse an undesirable sale.[46] By performing disability after a sale was finalized, slaves turned apparent hidden defects into public spectacles, openly calling into question the honor and integrity of the slaveholders who sold them and inspiring the majority of litigation in the antebellum South.

In some cases, slaves intentionally disabled themselves as a form of sabotage. The historians Kenneth Stampp and Leslie Howard Owens have cited several examples of self-mutilation, including that of a woman in Kentucky who repeatedly stuck her hand into a beehive to aggravate a disabling "swelling in her arms" and that of a male "prime hand" who chopped off several of his toes to prevent a sale away from his wife and family. In Arkansas, one slave discovered that he could "throw his left shoulder out of place" and thereby avoid "an hour's work," and a man named Yellow Jacob, after receiving a kick from a mule, deliberately kept his bruises from healing to avoid going back to work.[47] In *This Species of Property,* Owens argues that these mutilations were examples of slaves, frustrated by their oppression, striking out against their own bodies as a form of aggression.[48] This conclusion, however, overlooks the possibility that slaves could benefit from creating disability in themselves, particularly if they did so publicly or if their self-inflicted defects were highly visible. In antislavery publications and the narratives of former slaves, there are several accounts of slaves' attempting to negate sales agreements by sabotaging their own bodies.[49] The abolitionist James Redpath described an encounter with a young woman offered for auction in a Richmond market whose "right hand was entirely useless—'dead,' as she aptly called it":

> One finger had been cut off by a doctor, and the auctioneer stated that she herself chopped off the other finger—her forefinger—because it hurt her, and she thought that to cut it off would cure it. This remark raised a laugh among the crowd. . . .
>
> "Didn't you cut your finger off," asked a man, "'kase you was mad?"
>
> She looked at him quietly, but with a glance of contempt, and said:
>
> "No, you see it was sort o' sore, and I thought it would be better to cut it off than be plagued with it."
>
> Several persons around me expressed the opinion that she had done it willfully, "to spite her master or mistress, or to keep her from being sold down South."
>
> I do not doubt it.[50]

Similarly, *Domestic Manners of the Americans,* Frances Trollope's popular travel memoir and account of life in the United States, contains an example of a man in Virginia who was to be sold farther South. According to Trollope, "Within an hour after it was made known to him, he sharpened the hatchet with which he had been felling timber, and with his right hand severed his left from the wrist,"[51] presumably to decrease his value as a field laborer. The fugitive slave Milton Clarke, writing with his brother Lewis in 1846, described a carpenter in Lexington named Ennis, whose master, General Leslie Coombs, negotiated to sell him "down the river" to work on a cotton plantation. Clarke notes, "Ennis was determined not to go. He took a broadaxe and cut one hand off; then contrived to lift the axe, with his arm pressing it to his body, and let it fall upon the other, cutting off the ends of the fingers." Ennis was sold anyway, albeit "for a nominal price," to a Louisiana planter.[52]

In all of these examples, slaves about to be sold intentionally disabled their bodies with very visible, disfiguring injuries. While it is likely that they chose to chop off fingers, hands, and toes because it was expedient—slaves had easy access to sharp tools and could quickly complete the task without interference—it is also remarkable that such injuries were impossible to ignore at auction. Hands and feet were important elements of a prospective buyer's inspection, and slave traders could not afford to conceal such defects as missing digits or extremities. Furthermore, it is significant that these slaves sabotaged their bodies publicly, by committing the act in front of others or admitting to their actions after the fact. Marking their bodies as disabled allowed slaves to claim an element of control over themselves, but it also tempted observers to read other kinds of "unsoundness" into their bodies. For example, the woman who claimed to cut off her own finger because it was "sore" invited prospective buyers to question her mental state; those who laughed at her claim and asked her if she was "mad" read her deliberate injury as a sign of possible stupidity or insanity. Thus, slaves who employed displays of "unsoundness" in sales situations relied on conspicuous signs of disability, as well as complex, intersecting assumptions about race, social status, and physical bodies, to manipulate observers' reactions. In doing so, slaves passing as disabled could gain a measure of control over their own bodies.

I T IS CLEAR that many slaves admitted to using performances of disability in bondage as a resistance strategy. However, evidence from the narratives of former slaves published before and after the Civil War indicates a strong current of discomfort with the association of free individuals with disability, whether or not those disabling conditions were genuine. Just as abolitionists used images of disability and fetters to describe the oppression and despair of bondage, they used images of physical strength and ability to represent freedom for African Americans.

This metaphorical pairing had tremendous power in American anti-slavery culture, which prized independence—physical as well as social and political—and celebrated free labor. The tension between images of disabled slaves and able-bodied freedpeople influenced narrative descriptions of performances of slave disability.

Former-slave narrators and white abolitionist editors who use disabled bodies as texts to recite the horrors of the institution often uphold the image of disabled bodies as objects of pity, lust, or revulsion. At the same time, slave narrators often attempted to remove themselves from the crippling effects of slavery to prove their abilities as free individuals to themselves and their audience. The centrality of successful escapes in fugitive narratives both literally and metaphorically distanced narrators from the disabling characteristics of bondage and from the disabled bodies of slaves themselves. Fugitives therefore do not describe themselves as objects of pity, because they were "able" to escape the South and join free society. In their published narratives, they present themselves as free, able individuals. In this respect, fugitive narratives ultimately reified the "normalizing" effects of freedom and the able-bodiedness it represented.

In some cases, former slaves who had used disability performances as a resistance strategy seem to separate themselves from their feigned disabled identities to demonstrate their honesty to free society. In this sense, their imposture as disabled is only a necessary tool under bondage but unneeded and not a part of their free personae. This is apparent in the escape narrative of Lavinia Bell, printed in the *Montreal Gazette* on January 31, 1861. Bell had worked as a field hand in Texas, where she was subjected to a number of cruel punishments for "rascality" and repeated escape attempts and became severely crippled and disfigured. An editor's note following the newspaper article notes that "in the fore-going account we have omitted many particulars communicated to us by the woman, the many ruses she practiced, counterfeiting madness, inability to walk, &c., in order to throw off suspicion."[53] Thus, the editors admit that Bell feigned disabilities but indicate that such "rascality" in bondage was secondary to the physical suffering she endured. They therefore invite readers to sympathize with Bell's "real" physical condition that resulted from her servitude rather than judge her for her malingering ploys.[54] Furthermore, the editors provided a physician's statement to verify Bell's condition and clearly stated that Bell did not seek any financial support for herself, despite her inability to work. This account was intended to arouse the pity of readers but also suggests a desire to distance Bell as a freedwoman from her image as a helpless, burdensome, and dishonest slave.

ONE FAMOUS EXAMPLE of a slave's disability performance, as well as ambivalence about adopting a disability identity, was the flight of William and Ellen Craft, a young enslaved couple from Macon, Georgia. In December 1848, they devised a daring and unusual plan to escape their bondage. Disguising Ellen as a young male planter traveling with her male servant William, the pair relied exclusively on public transportation for a four-day journey to Philadelphia.[55] To transform Ellen into "Mr. Johnson," the Crafts applied a number of feigned physical impairments to her disguise. They used handkerchiefs and poultices to cover her smooth face and feminine jaw line and green spectacles to shield her eyes. Since she was illiterate, they put her right arm in a sling so she would have an excuse not to write, and feigned deafness would excuse her from talking to fellow white passengers. Ellen sewed herself a pair of trousers and a shirt, and William, a craftsman, used his money to pay for their journey. Before dawn on the morning of their escape, William cut his wife's hair short, and she donned her slings and bandages over her fine men's clothing. The Crafts traveled through Savannah, Charleston, Wilmington, Washington, D.C., and Baltimore—staying in fine hotels and booking passage on first-class rail carriages and steamers—before they reached Philadelphia on Christmas Day.[56]

Many historians and literary scholars have analyzed William Craft's narrative, emphasizing the cultural disruptions inherent in the couple's escape. However, Ellen's "passing" as a white, male slaveholder—her transgression of race, gender, and class boundaries—has received far more critical attention than her masquerade of disability.[57] Ellen Samuels's 2006 article "'A Complication of Complaints': Untangling Disability, Race, and Gender in William and Ellen Craft's *Running a Thousand Miles for Freedom*" is the only critical publication to date that explores the meanings of disability in the Crafts' narrative, and explores "the intimate and constitutive relationship of race, gender, class, and disability" that Ellen's disguise represents.[58] Samuels argues convincingly that Ellen Craft was only able to "pass" as a white, male slaveholder because she artfully used the pretense of disability.

William Craft's narrative of their escape contains many descriptions of how other passengers reacted to Mr. Johnson's impairments along their journey. In most cases, according to Craft, the genteel Mr. Johnson was received with sympathy and treated very gently. At several times along the journey, William and Ellen faced deterrents and possible discovery, but pity for the disabled Mr. Johnson—who acquired new impairments whenever it seemed necessary—prevented them from being caught.[59] For instance, shortly after fleeing their plantation, Ellen Craft encountered a man she knew named Mr. Cray, a friend of her master's, and believed that he would be able to identify her as a slave. When Mr. Cray attempted to draw Mr. Johnson into conversation, Ellen "resolved to feign deafness as the only means of self-defence":

> After a little while, Mr. Cray said to my master, "It is a very fine morning, sir." The latter took no notice, but kept looking out of the window. Mr. Cray soon repeated this remark, in a little louder tone, but my master remained as before. This indifference attracted the attention of the passengers near, one of whom laughed out. This, I suppose, annoyed the old gentleman; so he said, "I will make him hear;" and in a loud tone of voice repeated, "It is a very fine morning, sir." My master turned his head, and with a polite bow said, "Yes," and commenced looking out of the window again. One of the gentlemen remarked that it was a very great deprivation to be deaf. "Yes," replied Mr. Cray, "and I shall not trouble that fellow any more." This enabled my master to breathe a little easier, and to feel that Mr. Cray was not his pursuer after all.[60]

In this instance, Ellen Craft feigned deafness to arouse the sympathy of her fellow passengers, particularly Mr. Cray, the man most likely to identify her as a slave. Her guise elicited a number of responses in this instance, including Mr. Cray's annoyance and the amusement of other passengers. Ultimately, however, pity for Mr. Johnson's hearing impairment, "a very great deprivation," enabled Ellen to adopt the invisibility of a disabled person to continue this leg of her journey without discovery or capture.

Sympathy for the "poor invalid" Mr. Johnson also aided the Crafts at other critical moments in their escape. For instance, as they prepared to board a train from Baltimore to Philadelphia, a railroad officer attempted to detain them because Mr. Johnson could not prove that William was his slave. As the "eagle-eyed officer" explained to the Crafts, the railroad did not want to assume liability for a slave who escaped to a free state. Of course, Ellen had no certification that William belonged to her, but their "deliberation" with the officer attracted a lot of attention from other passengers, who "thought my master was a slaveholder and invalid gentleman, and therefore it was wrong to detain him." As the train prepared to leave, the railroad officer finally decided "as he is not well, it is a pity to stop him here" and allowed William and Ellen to board the train.[61]

The story of the Crafts' daring escape was popular in abolitionist circles, but although their narrative and interviews proudly describe their adopted disguises, they also convey the couple's ambivalence about portraying Ellen Craft as a disabled male planter. On the one hand, William's account goes into great detail about Ellen's "invalid" disguise and expresses how impressive it was that she could adopt many signs of impairment so convincingly. On the other hand, there are also clear descriptions of how Ellen did not identify with her character of Mr. Johnson. Early in the narrative, William Craft notes that they chose to disguise Ellen as the "invalid master" only because it would have been impossible for them to travel together as a man and woman, even if Ellen could pass as a white slaveholding mistress. In William's words, "My wife had no ambition whatever to assume the disguise, and would not have done so had it been possible to have obtained our liberty by more simple means."[62] Throughout their four-day journey, Ellen was terrified and uncomfortable, relying on William's assistance and voice in many different situations. Upon arriving in Philadelphia, the couple took a cab from the train station to a boardinghouse run by an abolitionist, whom one of the guards on the train from Baltimore had recommended to William. Apparently, Ellen had been emotionally overcome after they reached Philadelphia and was "in reality so weak and faint that she could scarcely stand alone" when they reached the house but had recovered and changed out of her costume even before they met the landlord.[63] These descriptions of Ellen's physical state and appearance after they reached Philadelphia distance her both from the invalid Mr. Johnson and from the image of a dependent, weak female slave. Instead, Ellen was almost magically transformed into the completely able-bodied freedperson that abolitionist rhetoric had been espousing for decades. Postbellum reviews of William's narrative also emphasize this metamorphosis. Writing in 1876, for instance, Thomas Wallace Knox provides an account the Crafts' journey in *Underground; or, Life Below the Surface,* describing the different signs of disability that Ellen donned in a section Knox titled "The Deformed Transformed." As Knox points out, adding various impairments to Ellen's disguise provided the solution to most of the problems with the Crafts' plan and ultimately "relieve[d] Ellen from the attentions which she was desirous of avoiding."[64] However, "As soon they arrived [in Philadelphia] the rheumatism departed, also the deafness, also the lameness in the arm, also the toothache. The young planter was transformed into a woman, and assumed the proper dress."[65] Samuels has observed that the retellings of William and Ellen Craft's daring escape in abolitionist "melodramas" by William Wells Brown and Lydia Maria Child also downplay the disability disguise that Ellen adopted, which was "probably motivated by [a] dislike for portraying . . . slave heroes as weak or damaged."[66] Thus, Ellen's transgressive disguise disappeared as soon as she obtained her freedom, and most fictional and nonfictional accounts of the Crafts' escape—including William's narrative—emphasize her immediate return to able-bodied femininity, downplaying her feigned identity as a disabled slaveholder.

The ambivalence of portraying Ellen as "disabled" is also evident in an engraving of Ellen disguised as Mr. Johnson. The image was printed for sale to audiences on the abolitionist lecture circuit, and was included as the frontispiece of the Crafts' narrative when it was published in 1860. Ellen is portrayed with cropped hair and is dressed in a gentleman's finery, with a silk tie and stovepipe hat to give the illusion of greater height. She wears a tartan sash across her chest, and tassels hang by her right shoulder. She sits in three-quarter profile but with her face turned completely forward, making eye contact with her viewers through clear spectacles while a hint of a smile plays on her lips. While the engraving certainly provides a detailed image of Ellen as the "master," most elements of Ellen as "invalid" have been removed. She has no bandages or poultices on her head, her right arm is not bound, she holds no cane, and her green spectacles have been replaced with clear lenses. The only element of her disguised impairments in the image is a white linen sling around her neck, but the sling is tucked back against the left side of her body. As Samuels has suggested, the confusing image of Ellen Craft in "quasi-disguise" reduces all functional signs of disability to near-invisibility. Thus, while the image emphasizes Ellen's racial

Ellen Craft (ca. 1851)

and gender subversions, it completely removes itself from any implications that Ellen—even as Mr. Johnson—was disabled.[67] As prominent former-slave speakers, William and Ellen Craft—like other fugitives who spoke in abolitionist lectures and published their narratives—had to demonstrate their ability to participate in free society as able-bodied individuals. Thus, the engraved image of Ellen as Mr. Johnson seems to normalize Ellen as an able-bodied freedwoman, even in her disguise.

For slaves like Jacob D. Green and the Crafts, there were recognizable benefits to "donning" disability like a cloak, concealing their true identities and motives from slaveholders and would-be captors. The guise of a disability, made highly visible and performed in public, provided them with a means to negotiate the terms of their servitude and change their situation. Slaves who used displays of genuine or feigned disability relied on prevalent clues of and assumptions about impairment to take advantage of the invisibility of disabled individuals in larger society. However, in using disability to transgress their enslaved roles, Green and the Crafts ultimately did not question the meanings of disability itself. Indeed, after they obtained their freedom, they sought to distance themselves from the image of disability they put on. Even the title of William Craft's narrative serves this function; as African American slaves, the Crafts were "running" for their freedom, but as a white planter, Ellen was in fact barely limping. In this regard, the narrative is not just a simple account of the trials of two "passing" fugitive slaves, but an implicit claim that those slaves were able to run for freedom, and participate in free society as able-bodied individuals.

THE VOLUME OF EVIDENCE that slaves could, and did, use displays of disability indicates that there were significant advantages for slaves to be considered "disabled," and slaves' ability to deceive their masters was an important tool in their resistance arsenal. As Ira Berlin has noted, "Even when their power was reduced to a mere trifle, slaves still had enough to threaten their owners—a last card, which, as their owners well understood, could be played at any time."[68] Performances of disability were an undeniably powerful tool of subversion for antebellum slaves who relied on common emotional reactions to disabled individuals, as well as the cultural impetus to conceal or obscure those individuals. In this regard, slaves could use feigned, exaggerated, or self-inflicted disability to challenge the terms of their bondage, but such displays largely did not challenge prevalent ideas about disability. As the example of William and Ellen Craft indicates, slaves who used feigned disability to achieve their goals often did not want the association with disability to carry over to their identity as freedpeople. Echoing popular metaphors of freedom as ability, some former slaves' narratives make explicit claims of honest able-bodiedness in freedom, reifying prevalent notions of disability as weakness and dependence.

Notes

1. J. D. Green, *Narrative of the Life of J. D. Green, a Runaway Slave, from Kentucky, Containing an Account of His Three Escapes, in 1839, 1846, and 1848* (Huddersfield: Henry Fielding, 1864), 22–23. Portions of this essay are excerpted from Dea H. Boster, "An 'Epeleptick' Bondswoman: Fits, Slavery, and Power in

the Antebellum South," *Bulletin of the History of Medicine* 83 (Summer 2009): 271–301.

2. Green, *Narrative of the Life of J. D. Green*, 26.

3. See Laird W. Bergad, *The Comparative Histories of Slavery in Brazil, Cuba, and the United States* (New York: Cambridge University Press, 2007), 166; Norrece T. Jones Jr., *Born a Child of Freedom, yet a Slave: Mechanisms of Control and Strategies of Resistance in Antebellum South Carolina* (Hanover, N.H.: University Press of New England, 1990), 137; Peter H. Wood, *Black Majority: Negroes in Colonial South Carolina from 1670 through the Stono Rebellion* (New York: W. W. Norton, 1974), 285–286.

4. See Saidiya Hartman, *Scenes of Subjection: Terror, Slavery, and Self-Making in Nineteenth-Century America* (New York; Oxford: Oxford University Press, 1997), 22; Heidi M. Hackford, "Malingering: Representations of Feigned Disease in American History, 1800–1920" (Ph.D. Dissertation, American University, 2004), 99; Tobin Siebers, "Disability as Masquerade," *Literature and Medicine* 23 (Spring 2004): 3.

5. See Susan M. Schweik, *The Ugly Laws: Disability in Public* (New York: New York University Press, 2009), 184–204.

6. Robert William Fogel and Stanley L. Engerman, *Time on the Cross: The Economics of American Negro Slavery* (Boston: Little, Brown, 1974), 119, 126. See also Gregory Brian Durling, "Female Labor, Malingering, and the Abuse of Equipment under Slavery: Evidence from the Marydale Plantation," *Southern Studies* 5 (Spring–Summer 1994): 37–38, 40, 42, 45.

7. See Herbert G. Gutman, *Slavery and the Numbers Game: A Critique of Time on the Cross* (Urbana: University of Illinois Press, 2003), xii, 85–87; Kenneth M. Stampp, *The Peculiar Institution: Slavery in the Ante-Bellum South* (New York: Alfred A. Knopf, 1956), 103–105; Wood, *Black Majority*, 285–286; Eugene D. Genovese, *Roll, Jordan, Roll: The World the Slaves Made* (New York: Vintage, 1974), 620; Todd L. Savitt, *Medicine and Slavery: The Diseases and Health Care of Blacks in Antebellum Virginia* (Urbana: University of Illinois Press, 1978), 114–116, 162–165; Sharla M. Fett, *Working Cures: Healing, Health, and Power on Southern Slave Plantations* (Chapel Hill: University of North Carolina Press, 2002), 177. See also Boster, "An 'Epeleptick' Bondswoman," 289.

8. Hackford, "Malingering," 5, 10, 43, 45, 47, 49, 61, 86.

9. Ibid., 44–45, 56.

10. Siebers, "Disability as Masquerade," 2–4, 6, 10, 19.

11. Ibid., 12.

12. Edwin Adams Davis, ed., *Plantation Life in the Florida Parishes of Louisiana 1836–1846, as Reflected in the Diary of Bennet H. Barrow* (New York: Columbia University Press, 1943), 43–44; Raymond A. Bauer and Alice H. Bauer, "Day to Day Resistance to Slavery," *Journal of Negro History* 27 (October 1942): 406–407; Leslie J. Pollard, *Complaint to the Lord: Historical Perspectives on the African American Elderly* (Selinsgrove: Susquehanna University Press, 1996), 41.

13. Bauer and Bauer, "Day to Day Resistance," 406–407. For an example of a slave whose obvious malingering compromised her sale, see Tyre Glen to Isaac Jarratt, Huntsville (March 24, 1832), Jarratt-Puryear Papers, Correspondence and Papers, 1807–1849, box 1, folder 1830–1833, Rare Book, Manuscript, and Special Collections Library, Duke University, Durham, N.C.

14. Samuel G. Howe, interview with John Boggs, cited in *Slave Testimony: Two Centuries of Letters, Speeches, Interviews, and Autobiographies,* ed. John W. Blassingame (Baton Rouge: Louisiana State University Press, 1977), 422.

15. Although Deborah Gray White has argued that feeble enslaved men experienced decreased status on plantations because of their loss of strength and able-bodiedness, elderly slaves were often revered by masters and fellow slaves alike: Deborah Gray White, *Ar'n't I a Woman? Female Slaves in the Plantation South,* rev. ed. (New York: W. W. Norton, 1999), 114–115, 130. See also Margaret Washington Creel, *"A Peculiar People": Slave Religion and Community-Culture among the Gullahs* (New York: New York University Press, 1988), 58; Genovese, *Roll, Jordan, Roll,* 521; Jones, *Born a Child of Freedom,* 54; Mrs. George A. Hickox (née Mary Catherine Brisbane), "This Paper Was Read at the Monday Club Held at Washington, Connecticut, about the Year 1898," vertical file 30-21-1 (African Americans; General), South Carolina Historical Society, Charleston, 4–5; Emily Burke, *Pleasure and Pain: Reminiscences of Georgia in the 1840's* (Savannah: Beehive Press, 1991), 33.

16. Samuel Forry, "Vital Statistics Furnished by the Sixth Census of the United States, Bearing upon the Question of the Unity of the Human Race," *New York Journal of Medicine, and the Collateral Sciences* 1 (September 1843): 155.

17. Brenda E. Stevenson, *Life in Black and White: Family and Community in the Slave South* (New York: Oxford University Press, 1996), 192–193; Jenny Bourne Wahl, *The Bondsman's Burden: An Economic Analysis of the Common Law of Southern Slavery* (Cambridge: Cambridge University Press, 1998), 37–38; White, *Ar'n't I a Woman,* 79–83; Fett, *Working Cures,* 191.

18. Bauer and Bauer, "Day to Day Resistance," 406–407; Stampp, *Peculiar Institution,* 103–104; Savitt, *Medicine and Slavery,* 115–116; Fett, *Working Cures,* 179; Hackford, "Malingering," 73.

19. John H. Morgan, "An Essay on the Causes of the Production of Abortion among our Negro Population," *Nashville Journal of Medicine and Surgery* 19 (1860): 117–119 (quote on 117).

20. *James B. Floyd, Adm'r v. James M. Abney and Others,* 1 S.C. 114, 1869 S.C. LEXIS 12 (1869), cited in Helen Tunnicliff Catterall, ed., *Judicial Cases Concerning American Slavery and the Negro,,* vol. 2 (Washington, D.C.: Carnegie Institution of Washington, 1929), 475); White, *Ar'n't I a Woman,* 85.

21. Fett, *Working Cures,* 181. See also Hackford, "Malingering," 43, 47, 49, 61, 86.

22. Daryl Cumber Dance, *Shuckin' and Jivin': Folklore from Contemporary Black Americans* (Bloomington: Indiana University Press, 1978), 186–187.

23. James O. Breeden, ed., *Advice among Masters: The Ideal in Slave Management in the Old South* (Westport, Conn.: Greenwood Press, 1980), 193; M. D. McLoud, "Hints on the Medical Treatment of Negroes" (M.D. thesis, Medical College of the State of South Carolina, 1850), Waring Historical Library, Medical University of South Carolina, Charleston, 2; Stanley Feldstein, *Once a Slave: The Slave's View of Slavery* (New York: William Morrow, 1971), 182–183; Steven M. Stowe, *Doctoring the South: Southern Physicians and Everyday Medicine in the Mid-Nineteenth Century* (Chapel Hill: University of North Carolina Press, 2004), 162–174, 216; Hackford, "Malingering," 54. Assumptions that slave malingering was widespread were not limited to the South. For instance, in *The Opal*, a newsletter published by patients at the New York State Insane Asylum in the 1850s, a fictional conversation written between "two southern gentlemen and a negro" indicates that a thieving slave who claimed to be "crazy" might receive a lighter punishment. As the slave Bob told his owner in the story, "It is so fashionable to be crazy, master, it saves many a fellow from the State's Prison and Gallows": "A Dialogue between Two Southern Gentlemen and a Negro, Part 1," *The Opal*, May 1852, available online at http://www.disabilitymuseum.org/lib/docs/1258 .htm (accessed December 15, 2008).

24. McLoud, "Hints on Medical Treatment," 1. See also Stowe, *Doctoring the South*, 139–140; Hackford, "Malingering," 25, 65–68, 79–80.

25. Davis, *Plantation Life*, 329.

26. Mary Prince, *The History of Mary Prince, a West Indian Slave*, 3rd ed. (Edinburgh: Waugh and Innes, 1831), 14, 18.

27. Ibid., 15–16.

28. Barbara Baumgartner, "The Body as Evidence: Resistance, Collaboration, and Appropriation in 'The History of Mary Prince,'" *Callaloo* 24 (Winter 2001): 258.

29. James L. Smith, *Autobiography of James L. Smith, Including, also, Reminiscences of Slave Life, Recollections of the War, Education of Freedmen, Causes of the Exodus, Etc.* (Norwich, Conn.: Press of the Bulletin Company, 1881), 21.

30. Ibid., 23–24. Smith also describes walking long distances to attend prayer meetings on Saturday evenings (ibid., 26), indicating his ability to overcome his disability to claim independence and do something important to him.

31. Charles Stearns, *Narrative of Henry Box Brown, Who Escaped from Slavery Enclosed in a Box 3 Feet Long and 2 Wide* (Boston: Brown and Stearns, 1849), 58.

32. Israel Campbell, *An Autobiography, Bond and Free; or, Yearnings for Freedom, from My Green Brier House. Being the Story of My Life in Bondage, and My Life in Freedom* (Philadelphia: C. E. P. Brinckloe, 1861), 134–135.

33. Ibid., 136; Boster, "An 'Epeleptick' Bondswoman," 291–292.

34. Walter Johnson, *Soul by Soul: Life Inside the Antebellum Slave Market* (Cambridge, Mass.: Harvard University Press, 1999), 162–188; Bauer and Bauer, "Day to Day Resistance," 412. See also John Parker Autobiography, Rankin-Parker Papers, Rare Book, Manuscript, and Special Collections Library, Duke

University, Durham, N.C., 3, cited in Steven Deyle, *Carry Me Back: The Domestic Slave Trade in American Life* (New York: Oxford University Press, 2005), 265.

35. A. J. McElveen to Z. B. Oakes, Hayneville, Ala., October 21, 1856, cited in *Broke by the War: Letters of a Slave Trader,* ed. Edmund L. Drago (Columbia: University of South Carolina Press, 1991), 134.

36. J. Winston Coleman, *Slavery Times in Kentucky* (Chapel Hill: University of North Carolina Press, 1940), 129–130. See also Bauer and Bauer, "Day to Day Resistance," 412–413.

37. Hustings Court of Richmond, Minutes Book 15 (1842–1844), Library of Virginia, Richmond, 261, 278; Deposition of Mrs. Ruschmer (*sic*), Office of the Governor, Record Group 3, James McDowell (1843–1846), Letters Received, Box 373, Archives and Manuscripts Room, Library of Virginia, Richmond. See also Philip J. Schwarz, *Slave Laws in Virginia* (Athens: University of Georgia Press, 1996), 7; Boster, "An 'Epeleptick' Bondswoman," 271–272, 279, 295.

38. Lucy Ann (Waller) Govan to William Macon Waller (March 21, 1843), William Macon Waller Papers (1843–1850), and Archibald Govan to William Macon Waller ([June 18?] 1843), William Macon Waller Papers (1843–1850), Virginia Historical Society, Richmond; Bacon Tait to Governor James McDowell (June 1, 1843), and G. G. Minor to Governor James McDowell (June 1, 1843), Office of the Governor, Record Group 3, James McDowell (1843–1846), Letters Received, Box 373, Archives and Manuscripts Room, Library of Virginia, Richmond. See also James Campbell, "'The Victim of Prejudice and Hasty Consideration': The Slave Trial System in Richmond, Virginia, 1830–61," *Slavery and Abolition* 26 (April 2005): 79–81.

39. Lucy Ann Govan to William Macon Waller (June 17, 1843), William Macon Waller Papers (1843–1850), Virginia Historical Society, Richmond.

40. Archibald Govan to William Macon Waller ([June 18?] 1843).

41. Bacon Tait to Governor James McDowell (June 1, 1843).

42. The historian Michael Tadman estimates that, in 1846, the average price for bondswomen age ten to fifteen was between $275 and $350 in Richmond: Michael Tadman, *Speculators and Slaves: Masters, Traders, and Slaves in the Old South* (Madison: University of Wisconsin Press, 1989), 289. Furthermore, on a trip to Mississippi to sell slaves in 1847, Virginia's original master, William Macon Waller, observed that "high prices" for female plantation slaves were between $375 and $400: William Macon Waller to Henry Loving, 4 December 1847, William Macon Waller Papers (1843–1850), Virginia Historical Society, Richmond. Comparing these numbers with the estimate made at Virginia's trial, it seems that the Richmond aldermen did not take epilepsy into account as a permanent defect, indicating that her condition was unknown prior to her arrival at Tait's slave jail. This may be another clue that Virginia feigned epilepsy after the trial was over.

43. Thomas Wentworth Higginson, *Travelers and Outlaws: Episodes in American History* (Boston: Lee and Sheppard, 1889), reprinted in *Denmark Vesey* (Los Angeles: Vanguard Society of America, 1962), 4–5, Labadie Collec-

tion, University of Michigan, Ann Arbor. See also James Hamilton, *Negro Plot: An Account of the Late Intended Insurrection among a Portion of the Blacks of the City of Charleston, South Carolina* (Boston: Joseph W. Ingraham, 1822), 17; Orville J. Victor, *The History of American Conspiracies: A Record of Treason, Insurrection, Rebellion, &c. in the United States of America, from 1760 to 1860* (New York: J. D. Torrey, 1863), 375–376.

44. Archibald Henry Grimké, *Right on the Scaffold, or the Martyrs of 1822* (Washington, D.C.: American Negro Academy, 1901), 5. See also David Brion Davis, *Inhuman Bondage: The Rise and Fall of Slavery in the New World* (New York: Oxford University Press, 2006), 223; Boster, "An 'Epeleptick' Bondswoman," 299.

45. Ariela J. Gross, "Pandora's Box: Slave Character on Trial in the Antebellum Deep South," *Yale Journal of Law and the Humanities* 7 (1995): 309; Wahl, *Bondsman's Burden*, 42, 200, n. 55.

46. Judith K. Schafer, "'Guaranteed against the Vices and Maladies Prescribed by Law': Consumer Protection, the Law of Slave Sales, and the Supreme Court in Antebellum Louisiana," *American Journal of Legal History* 31 (October 1987): 310–311; Ariela J. Gross, *Double Character: Slavery and Mastery in the Antebellum Southern Courtroom* (Princeton, N.J.: Princeton University Press, 2000), 54, 66.

47. Leslie Howard Owens, *This Species of Property: Slave Life and Culture in the Old South* (New York: Oxford University Press, 1976), 93–94; Stampp, *Peculiar Institution*, 128.

48. Owens, *This Species of Property*, 94.

49. See Jones, *Born a Child of Freedom*, 61.

50. James Redpath, *The Roving Editor; or, Talks with Slaves in the Southern States* (1859), repr. ed. (New York: Negro Universities Press, 1968), 252–253. See also Bauer and Bauer, "Day to Day Resistance," 413.

51. Frances Trollope, *Domestic Manners of the Americans, Volume 2*, 4th ed. (London: Whittaker, Treacher, 1832), 51. See also Owens, *This Species of Property*, 93.

52. Lewis Garrard Clarke and Milton Clarke, *Narratives of the Sufferings of Lewis and Milton Clarke, Sons of a Soldier of the Revolution, During a Captivity of More than Twenty Years Among the Slaveholders of Kentucky, One of the So-Called Christian States of North America* (Boston: Bela Marsh, 1846), 125. See also Bauer and Bauer, "Day to Day Resistance," 414. Like the Virginia man Trollope described, Ennis likely attacked his hands to disable himself from the kind of field labor expected of a slave in the deep South, but he was sold anyway. One may speculate that his malingering ploy failed because Coombs wanted to punish Ennis for deliberately injuring himself, or because the master wanted to recoup some of the financial loss that Ennis generated.

53. Interview of Lavinia Bell, originally published in the *Montreal Gazette*, January 31, 1861, in Blassingame, ed., *Slave Testimony*, 345.

54. Ibid., 342.

55. In his account in 1849 of the escape of William Box Brown, the abolitionist Charles Stearns compared Brown's escape to the Crafts', noting that William and Ellen's use of public transportation was extremely risky. Unlike Brown, however, "They had the benefit of their eyes and ears," even as Ellen feigned deafness and helplessness: Stearns, *Narrative of Henry Box Brown,* vii.

56. William Craft, *Running a Thousand Miles for Freedom; or, the Escape of William and Ellen Craft from Slavery* (London: William Tweedie, 1860), 34–35, 51–52.

57. See Lindon Barrett, "Hand-Writing: Legibility and the White Body in *Running a Thousand Miles for Freedom,*" *American Literature* 69 (June 1997): 319, 322, 330–332; Sterling Lecatur Bland, *Voices of the Fugitives: Runaway Slave Stories and Their Fictions of Self-Creation* (Westport, Conn.: Greenwood Press, 2000), 8, 22, 141, 156; Michael A. Chaney, *Fugitive Vision: Slave Image and Black Identity in Antebellum Narrative* (Bloomington: Indiana University Press, 2007), 80–82, 97; Jennifer Fleischner, *Mastering Slavery: Memory, Family, and Identity in Women's Slave Narratives* (New York: New York University Press, 1996), 35; Susan Gubar, *Racechanges: White Skin, Black Face in American Culture* (New York: Oxford University Press, 2000), 13; Charles J. Heglar, *Rethinking the Slave Narrative: Slave Marriage and the Narratives of Henry Bibb and William and Ellen Craft* (Westport, Conn.: Greenwood Press, 2001), 81–86; Barbara McCaskill, "'Yours Very Truly': Ellen Craft—The Fugitive as Text and Artifact," *African American Review* 28 (Winter 1994): 510–511; Ellen M. Weinauer, "'A Most Respectable Looking Gentleman': Passing, Possession, and Transgression in *Running a Thousand Miles for Freedom,*" in *Passing and the Fictions of Identity,* ed. Elaine K. Ginsberg (Durham, N.C.: Duke University Press, 1996), 38–39, 44–45.

58. Ellen Samuels, "'A Complication of Complaints': Untangling Disability, Race, and Gender in William and Ellen Craft's *Running a Thousand Miles for Freedom,*" *MELUS* 31 (Fall 2006): 16.

59. Interview of William and Ellen Craft, originally published in *Chambers' Edinburgh Journal* 15, series 2 (March 15, 1861), in Blassingame, *Slave Testimony,* 270–271. See also Samuels, "A Complication of Complaints," 17.

60. Craft, *Running a Thousand Miles,* 44.

61. Ibid., 71–73; interview of William and Ellen Craft, in Blassingame, *Slave Testimony,* 272–273.

62. Craft, *Running a Thousand Miles,* 35–36.

63. Ibid., 79, 81.

64. Thomas Wallace Knox, *Underground; or, Life Below the Surface* (Hartford, Conn.: J. B. Burr, 1876), 433.

65. Ibid., 434.

66. Samuels, "A Complication of Complaints," 28–29.

67. Ibid., 20–22.

68. Ira Berlin, *Generations of Captivity: A History of African-American Slaves* (Cambridge, Mass.: Harvard University Press, 2003), 3.

6 Passing as Sane, or How to Get People to Sit Next to You on the Bus

PETA COX

FOR THE PAST FIVE YEARS, I have been taking public transport in Sydney, Australia. I ride on buses, trains, and the occasional ferry.[1] My experiences have prompted me to develop the following rules for appearing sane on public transport:

1. Do not talk to yourself. This includes not mumbling obscenities under your breath about the late arrival of the train or bus or about the incompetence of the driver. It does not include pretending to talk on a mobile phone that then rings. For this you will be deemed a jerk, not mad.[2]

2. Avoid eye movements that are too fast or too slow. Do not stare at a person, although staring at the ground or toward the middle distance is fine. Try not to show your agitation by looking repeatedly around the vehicle. If you are concerned about someone or something coming into the vehicle, look up from your book or focus point every ten seconds, fix your eyes in the middle distance, and scan, using your peripheral vision.

3. Do not wring your hands or self-soothe. Keep your hands still, though not rigid. Playing a game on your mobile, with the sound off to indicate an awareness of other passengers, is a good middle-ground activity.

4. If you must avoid touching poles, seats, and other surfaces that could transmit germs, make this avoidance appear casual.

Where possible, remain seated until the vehicle has stopped so you do not need to grab anything for balance. If you *have* to stand in a vehicle, do not cover your hands with the sleeve of your jacket; rather, lean against a wall or balance pole with a part of your body already covered by clothing.

5. Do not attempt to converse with others. Asking questions that require one-word answers is OK ("Do you know what this stop is?" "Can you tell me the time?"), as are rhetorical questions ("Bloody hot day today, eh?").

6. Observe the dress code. Try to look unremarkable—avoid wearing five different shades of pink or a wizard outfit. A clean appearance always helps.[3]

As these examples highlight, passing as sane occurs when a person who is experiencing psychological distress or non-normative emotional states or cognition manages to avoid displaying these states in the presence of others. "Passing" therefore occurs when others do not perceive the person as distressed.[4] Passing is particularly important for people diagnosed with a mental illness, because the costs of not passing can be quite high—including, in some instances, nonconsensual treatment and involuntary hospitalization.[5]

This chapter uses feminist accounts of performativity to examine the complex relationships among acts of passing, experiences of embodiment, and identification as a person with a mental illness. Theories of performativity destabilize the distinction between "being" and "acting" and, in so doing, help us understand the experience of passing as sane as a complex undertaking that can either increase or decrease an individual's distress.

Passing as sane often depends on a person's embodiment, specifically how an individual's body is held, placed, and experienced by that individual, as well as how others interpret this embodiment. Popular understandings of embodiment routinely position it either as a meaningless but unavoidable result of having a body or as an expression of personality. Scholars who use the concept of performativity dispute these understandings of embodiment and assert that certain repeated actions become culturally significant because they *give the sense,* both to the individual and to observers, that the individual is a particular type of person.

Although some feminist accounts position passing as a legitimate aspect of subjectivity, passing is more routinely considered a negative pursuit, the unfortunate result of personal shame and social stigma. For example, Tobin Siebers positions passing as a negative action in which, at times, people are "locked in the closet." While this is true in some circumstances, it is equally true that some people find it comforting to be able to lock the door and protect themselves from the outside world.[6] Thus, a deeper understanding of passing as sane leads us to understand such strategic actions in less absolute moral terms and acknowledge that the actions are legitimate choices regarding when and where attributes or identities are on display.

To understand what it means to pass as sane, a definition of sanity is required. The definition is culturally represented as the normalized and nearly invisible opposite of mental illness.[7] Yet while mental illness may be entrenched in the cultural imaginary, defining it remains extremely difficult. The emotional and cognitive states and behaviors that are understood as "sick" vary significantly over time and place.[8] Such changes reflect the morals and norms of a particular period and location. For instance, the removal of homosexuality from the *Diagnostic and Statistical Manual of Mental Disorders* (DSM) was, in large part, a response to activism by gay and lesbian people as part of the gay pride movement in the 1970s.[9] Throughout most of the twentieth century, the moral and social norms regarding sexual orientation supported understanding homosexuality as a sickness. Similarly, over the past two millennia, understandings of extreme sadness have included various explanations, such as an imbalance in the humors, a vice, a sin, a type of pathological mourning, and a chemical imbalance in the brain.[10] Each explanation made sense and was consistent with explanatory and moral frameworks of the period when it was used.

These examples demonstrate how cultural norms both create and restrict definitions of mental illness. However, this insight does not negate the lived experience of distress; it simply acknowledges that this lived experience is influenced by the available explanatory discourses.[11] Emily Martin's definition of manic depression demonstrates this social constructionist perspective:

Will I be claiming that manic depression is not "real"? Not at all. I will claim that the reality of manic depression lies in more than whatever biological traits may accompany it. The "reality" of manic depression lies in the cultural contexts that give particular meanings to its oscillations and multiplicities. Will I be claiming that people living under the description of manic depression do not need treatment? Not at all. I will claim that whatever suffering attends the condition should be treated by any means possible. But I will also say that manic depression is culturally inflected: its "irrational" heights and depths are entwined in the present-day cultural imagination.[12]

Performativity theorists extend social constructionism and argue that our sense of self is a construct created through repeated and ritualized action. Judith Butler argues that rather than *being* a gender, we continuously *enact* a gender, and through this we construct a sense of a gendered core that is both continuous and immovable. For Butler there is no self, no "doer behind the deed"; instead, the stylized repetition of gendered acts gives the impression that there is such a core. Butler notes that there are limits to the types of selves that can be constructed through performativity, as it is a "compulsory repetition of prior and subjectivating norms, ones which cannot be thrown off at will, but which work, animate, and constrain the gendered subject."[13]

Similar to the deliberate act of passing, in which a person seeks a particular type of reaction from others, gender performativity occurs through relation: "One does not 'do' one's gender alone. One is always 'doing' with or for another, even if that other is only imaginary."[14] However, most theorists agree that there is a categorical distinction between choosing to act in a particular way and repeated enactments of social norms that create a particular sense of self. Butler makes this distinction plain when she states:

> In no sense can it be concluded that the part of gender that is performed is the truth of gender; performance as bounded "act" is distinguished from performativity insofar as the latter consists in a reiteration of norms which precede, constrain, and exceed the performer and in that sense cannot be taken as the fabrication of the performer's "will" or "choice." . . . The reduction of performativity to performance would be a mistake.[15]

This differentiation means that many gender studies scholars consider arguments that merge gender performance and gender performativity

suspect or inaccurate. However, as discussed later, separating performance and performativity is less useful when dealing with passing as
sane, since the experiences of managing emotional distress often disrupt
a distinction between deliberate and ritualized presentations of self.

Another key aspect of performativity theory is that there is no original gender or gendered relationship that is "copied" by non-normative
others (e.g., butch lesbians, drag queens, femme gay men). Rather, all
genders are enactments.[16] Thus, the concept of performativity implies
that all behavior is a type of performance or enactment.

Thinking of mental illness as performative means that every person, regardless of the perceived "reality" of that individual's mental state,
passes as sane or insane. In other words, every action is a construction
of self that gives the perception of an internal sane or insane self.

While theories of performativity are useful as a starting point in
examining passing as sane, there are fundamental differences between
gender and mental illness that limit the applicability of this theory. The
link between deliberate performance and successful enactment of self-
hood for gendered presentation differs from that for mental health. In
the case of masculinity, men who feel they are *acting* masculine often
report that they feel they are failing at *being* masculine; thus, deliberately "walking like a man" may feel like a less successful enactment of
masculinity than if such actions were to "come naturally."[17] By contrast,
the *acting* of mental health, even when a person experiences that acting
as a false presentation, is an aspect of *being* "mentally healthy." Western
culture understands the "ability to continue acting 'normal'" as part of
the definition, and the experience, of good mental health.

To demonstrate the relationship between acting "normal," passing
as sane, and *experiencing* oneself as sane, imagine two people diagnosed
with depression. Both report feeling the same level of sadness and
despair. Yet one goes to work and the other takes the day off. Is it still
reasonable to say that these two individuals are equally unwell? Similarly, imagine the person who hears voices but does not yell back at
them in the street, or the person who has a panic attack but does not
run down the road yelling that the world is ending. Is this performance,
this enactment for self and audience of a lack of distress, not actually
the same as *having* less distress? Thus, in both the commonsense and the
medical understanding of these experiences, how one reacts to physical
and emotional manifestations of distress (i.e., symptoms) may be understood as a symptom in and of itself.

Similarly, both laypeople and professionals interpret an individual's long-term reactions to symptoms as indicators of how "mentally ill" that person is. Such assessments are not based on what a person thinks or feels. Rather, these assessments focus on what one does, and does not do, with one's body. For example, some ways of coping with emotional distress are deemed indicators of mental illness (excessive use of alcohol, self-harm, engagement in crime, forced vomiting, and suicidal ideation and behavior are, respectively, part of the DSM-IV-TR criteria for alcohol dependence, borderline personality disorder, conduct disorder, bulimia, and depression).[18] A person who engages in particular embodied practices may be classified as mentally ill or may be deemed *more severely* mentally ill. In comparison, a person who takes medication, goes to a psychiatrist, stays at a hospital, does exercise, and practices meditation is typically considered *less* mentally ill.[19] It is thus not solely a person's symptoms or internal state but, rather, that individual's embodied responses to the symptoms that determine how "mentally ill" the person is deemed to be.

Mainstream interventions for affective disorders such as desensitization also focus on reactions to symptoms, with the goal of allowing the individual to pass as non-symptomatic. Some psychologists use desensitization to treat anxiety and phobias. Desensitization involves graded exposure: controlled engagement with the phobic object or situation, increasing in intensity over time.[20] For example, L. J. Gilroy and colleagues' system for graded exposure to a spider involves individuals' relating to a live spider enclosed in a container placed on a table. Step one is to enter the room; step four is to touch the container in which the spider is enclosed; and the final step involves holding the spider with both hands.[21] At each stage, the person feels afraid but proceeds with the required action. In other words, the person acts "normal" (performs "normally").

Mainstream therapies such as desensitization and cognitive-behavioral therapy are often coupled with skills training. While the aim of such training is to enable people to function better in their day-to-day lives, the training also teaches individuals how to pass as sane. Skills learned might include breathing techniques and ways to remain calm and continue to function in distressing situations. In these instances, the practitioner assesses as less impaired the client who can *act* in ways that *appear* normal—the client who does not, for example, obviously hyperventilate or run out of a confined place. In other words, practitioners routinely assess impairment as reduced when the client can pass as sane. However, clients are likely to think of themselves as "cured" of their anxiety only when they are not experiencing symptoms. Thus, for many practitioners and their clients, "cure" occurs when the deliberate *performance* of being OK can routinely be used as a mechanism to stop distressing emotional or embodied states. Unlike gender performativity, in which embodiment, subjectivity, ritual, and performance are typically considered part of a singular lived experience, the performativity of mental health may involve more stratification. Specifically, the deliberate *performance* of being OK may at times be either enmeshed within or very distinct from the subjective embodiment of being OK or asymptomatic. Or to put this in colloquial self-help terms, both mindfulness and desensitization are therapies based on "fake it 'til you make it."[22]

This use of performance to preempt performativity also occurs in more everyday situations. For some people, being told by friends or family members, "You are not going to get upset," will stop them from becoming more distressed. In these instances, the first few minutes of trying not to be upset may involve some form of quivering-lip, teary-eyed pretending. However, when this type of intervention is successful, a few minutes later the lips stop quivering, the eyes dry, and the pretense is no longer needed, because the person really *is* OK. In other words, the emotional spiral is abated by an approximation of the embodiment of OK-ness. What has been a solely physical shift (stopping crying) becomes a psychological one (a lack of distress). Thus, the performance has become performativity.

The ability to fake it 'til you make it, or pass as sane, relies heavily on knowing what behaviors signify mental health in a particular community. Expectations of sane behavior vary across communities and identities; most people's expectation of the "sane" behavior of a middle-aged white woman differs from their expectation of the "sane" behavior of a teenage African American male.[23] In fact, the ability to pass as sane does not depend on a singular set of criteria for sanity. Rather, passing as sane requires that a person refrain from breaking the social norms regarding other aspects of that individual's identity; one's sanity falls into question if one does not act appropriately for one's gender, race, class, sexuality, religion, and so on.[24] In the Australian context, the identity-dependent nature of passing as sane is apparent when we examine published accounts of the different coping behaviors of men and women with depression. Whereas women describe managing their symptoms by taking bubble baths, reading quietly, cooking, receiving affirmation from a lover, and looking after their children, men report that they manage their symptoms by drinking with "mates" or by themselves, joking, distancing themselves from family and friends, and damaging property.[25] In these instances, adherence to gender norms (women doing womanly things and men doing manly things) is a key aspect of being understood as sane. Had these people deviated from conservative gender norms—if the men had enjoyed bubble baths or the women had damaged property—it is likely that they would have been perceived as more mentally ill than they would have been had they remained appropriately gendered. Passing as sane depends on a wide range of social markers, such as race, gender, class, and sexuality.

WHILE PASSING may be therapeutically useful as a mechanism for encouraging individuals to fake it 'til they make it, for many people passing as sane remains a deliberate and strategic performance that is morally devalued because it is considered a signifier of shame. As the social scientist Kenneth Paterson notes, the person who feels that it is necessary to "wear a mask" to continue relationships with friends and family may also feel that this behavior requires universal rejection of the person's "true" self.[26]

This understanding of passing appears to be centered on a belief that the need to pass is, in itself, an indication that a person is experiencing a mental illness. For instance, on an Australian Internet forum about experiences of depression, an anonymous participant writes: "For what feels like forever I have been pretending that I'm ok. I go through everyday with a fake smile just biding my time until I can go home and curl up in a ball and sleep."[27] In this instance, the "fakeness" of the coping is presented by the author as evidence of being unwell. Ironically, a person may interpret the very actions that promote the appearance of sanity as evidence of *in*sanity, so passing behaviors may augment rather than diminish distress. In these circumstances—when it remains a continuous, and self-conscious, "acting"—passing as sane is likely to be experienced as a destructive or negative behavior.

For people diagnosed with a mental illness, masquerading as insane may have a variety of benefits. Siebers uses the term "masquerade" to describe the act of exhibiting an impairment or implying that one has a different form of disability. He argues, "The masquerade represents an alternative method of managing social stigma through disguise, one relying not on the imitation of a dominant social role but on the assumption of an identity marked as stigmatized, marginal, or inferior."[28] In line with Siebers's understanding of "masquerade," passing as insane or intentionally exhibiting insane behavior may grant access to services that passing as sane would not. As a participant in Paterson's study of Australians living with depression notes, "I wouldn't have bothered applying [for federal aid] if I wasn't just continuing weeping from the eyes, and just completely dysfunctional. . . . I wouldn't have been able to get the appointment. What's the point? They're not going to believe me."[29] This example depicts a participant who felt compelled to exhibit mental illness, or masquerade as insane, when applying for mental-health–related support from the government.

For some, passing as insane provides a valuable sense of community and enjoyment, as is the case with the members of a bipolar support group that the anthropologist Emily Martin observed:

> The next moment, a man who had come to meetings week after week, but who always sat quietly, saying nothing, with a gloomy expression and dejected appearance said, "I don't usually say anything at all, I have been silent here for weeks and weeks, but tonight I realize I can't hold it all in. I have to let it out." Then, he launched into a string of shockingly barbed and funny jokes. Startled, everyone looked around the table hesitantly. Smiles bloomed as a rapid "eye flash"—eye contact that moved rapidly around the group—signalled the start of a hilarious session of joke telling that took up the entire rest of the two-hour meeting.[30]

Martin describes the support group as engaging in what Siebers defines as masquerade. Specifically, the group members exaggerate their manic symptoms deliberately as part of their social interaction.[31] This example counters the characterization of passing as always the shameful or undesired behavior described earlier in the chapter, as the group members appear to enjoy their exaggerated interactions. Moreover, passing as (in)sane has a surprisingly strong link to pleasure; passing as sane often helps to reduce distress, while passing as insane, at least in some instances, can be both amusing and joyful.

Both passing as sane and passing as insane are cultural and reflexive practices. Passing as sane (or insane) is a constant enactment of self that depends on knowing social norms of sanity and a range of other social identities, such as gender, sexuality, class, and race. Passing as sane plays on the edge between acting and being, which is also the edge between performance and performativity. At times, people diagnosed with a mental illness can use the tension between acting and being as a way to manage their symptoms or to maintain social engagement despite their distress. However, at other times, such passing may exacerbate distress. At its most extreme, passing as (in)sane may collapse the division between acting and being, so that what was once a deliberate act becomes a ritualized construction of self. In this way, the experiences of those with mental illness suggest a merging between performance and performativity that offers us new insight into passing and other issues of identity presentation.

Notes

1. Although I am based in Australia, my research and observations are relevant to the American context because modern beliefs about insanity in Western countries such as Australia and the United States have a close link to the American Psychiatric Association's *Diagnostic and Statistical Manual of Mental Disorders* and the mainstream use of psychopharmacology, which is heavily promoted within the United States. See Catherine Coleborne and Dolly MacKinnon, *Madness in Australia: Histories, Heritage and Asylum* (Brisbane, Australia: University of Queensland Press, 2003); Peter Conrad and Joseph Schneider, *Deviance and Medicalization: From Badness to Sickness* (St. Louis, Mo.: Mosby, 1980); Peter Kramer, *Listening to Prozac* (New York: Penguin, 1993); Adam Phillips, *Going Sane* (New York: Penguin, 2005).

2. See also Margaret Price, *Mad at School: Rhetorics of Mental Disability and Academic Life* (Ann Arbor: University of Michigan Press, 2011).

3. This set of "rules" is specific to mental illness. No other illnesses and conditions will have their own sets of behaviors that, in public places, are understood to be indicative of "sickness." For an extended discussion of disability in public, see Susan Marie Schweik, *The Ugly Laws: Disability in Public* (New York: New York University Press, 2009).

4. I use the terms "sane" and "insane" because they are meaningful social and moral categories in modern Western culture. This does not suggest that I support the negative stereotypes often associated with these terms.

5. For a social constructionist definition of mental illness, see Juliet Foster, *Journeys through Mental Illness: Client Experiences and Understandings of Mental Distress* (Basingstoke, U.K.: Palgrave Macmillan, 2007); David Healy, *Mania: A*

Short History of Bipolar Disorder (Baltimore: Johns Hopkins University Press, 2008); David Pilgrim and Richard Bentall, "The Medicalisation of Misery: A Critical Realist Analysis of the Concept of Depression," *Journal of Mental Health* 8 (1999): 261–274.

6. Tobin Siebers, "Disability as Masquerade," *Literature and Medicine* 23 (Spring 2004): 19.

7. Phillips, *Going Sane*.

8. Robert Daly, "Before Depression: The Medieval Vice of Acedia," *Psychiatry* 70, no. 1 (2007): 30; Emily Martin, *Bipolar Expeditions: Mania and Depression in American Culture* (Princeton, N.J.: Princeton University Press, 2007); Healy, *Mania*.

9. Ronald Bayer, *Homosexuality and American Psychiatry: The Politics of Diagnosis* (New York: Basic Books, 1981); Robert Spitzer, "The Diagnostic Status of Homosexuality in DSM-III: A Reformulation of the Issues," *American Journal of Psychiatry* 138 (1981): 210–215; Ronald Bayer and Robert Spitzer, "Edited Correspondence on the Status of Homosexuality in DSM-III," *Journal of the History of the Behavioral Sciences* 18, no. 1 (1982): 32–52; Gerald Davison, "Politics, Ethics, and Therapy for Homosexuality," *American Behavioral Scientist* 25, no. 4 (1982): 423–434; Richard Friedman and Jennifer Downey, "Psychoanalysis and the Model of Homosexuality as Psychopathology: A Historical Overview," *American Journal of Psychoanalysis* 58, no. 3 (1998): 249–270; Gary Greenberg, "Right Answers, Wrong Reasons: Revisiting the Deletion of Homosexuality from the DSM," *Review of General Psychology* 1, no. 3 (1997): 256–270; Charles Silverstein, "The Implications of Removing Homosexuality from the DSM as a Mental Disorder," *Archives of Sexual Behavior* 38, no. 2 (2009): 161–163.

10. Daly, "Before Depression," 30; Martin, *Bipolar Expeditions,* 16–28; Healy, *Mania,* 1–51.

11. Marino Perez-Alvarez, Louis Sass, and José Garcia-Montes, "More Aristotle, Less DSM: The Ontology of Mental Disorders in Constructivist Perspective," *Philosophy, Psychiatry, and Psychology* 15, no. 3 (2009): 212.

12. Martin, *Bipolar Expeditions,* 29.

13. Judith Butler, "Critically Queer," *GLQ: A Journal of Lesbian and Gay Studies* 1, no. 1 (1993): 22; Edwina Barvosa-Carter, "Strange Tempest: Agency, Poststructuralism, and the Shape of Feminist Politics to Come," in *Butler Matters: Judith Butler's Impact on Feminist and Queer Studies,* ed. Margaret Sönser Breen and Warren J. Blumefeld (London: Ashgate Publishing, 2005), 176; Judith Butler, *Gender Trouble* (New York: Routledge, 1990); Butler, "Critically Queer," 22.

14. Judith Butler, *Undoing Gender* (New York: Routledge, 2004), 1.

15. Butler, "Critically Queer," 24; italics in the original.

16. Butler, *Undoing Gender,* 209.

17. R. W. Connell, *Gender* (Cambridge: Polity Press, 2002).

18. American Psychiatric Association, *Diagnostic and Statistical Manual of Mental Disorders: DSM-IV-TR,* 4th ed. (Washington, D.C.: American Psychiatric Association, 2000).

19. Ironically, in these examples, it is behavior indicating that a person believes he or she has a mental illness that positions that person as *less* severely mentally ill, because such behavior positions the individual as being rational and responsible (i.e., the person is taking responsibility for his or her own health and minimizing any self-inflicted harm and/or harm to others)—characteristics that in Western culture are not associated with severe mental illness.

20. M. Gelder, I. Marks, and H. Wolff, "Desensitization and Psychotherapy in the Treatment of Phobic States: A Controlled Inquiry," *British Journal of Psychiatry* 113 (1967): 53–73; Jeffrey Bedell, Robert Archer, and Michael Rosmann, "Relaxation Therapy, Desensitization, and the Treatment of Anxiety-Based Disorders," *Journal of Clinical Psychology* 35, no. 4 (2006): 840–843.

21. Lisa J. Gilroy, Kenneth C. Kirkby, Brett A. Daniels, Ross G. Menzies, and Iain M. Montgomery, "Controlled Comparison of Computer-Aided Vicarious Exposure versus Live Exposure in the Treatment of Spider Phobia," *Behavior Therapy* 31, no. 4 (2000): 733–744.

22. See, e.g., Katie Evans, *Understanding Depression and Addiction Pamphlet* (Center City, Minn.: Hazelden Publishing, 2003).

23. See Peter Sedgwick, *Psycho Politics: Laing, Foucault, Goffman, Szasz, and the Future of Mass Psychiatry* (New York: Harper and Row, 1982), 45.

24. See Barvosa-Carter, "Strange Tempest," 179.

25. Tessa Wigney, Kerrie Eyers, and Gordon Parker, *Journeys with the Black Dog: Inspirational Stories of Bringing Depression to Heel* (Sydney: Allen and Unwin Academic, 2008), 47, 247; Penelope Rowe and Jessica Rowe, *The Best of Times, the Worst of Times: Our Family's Journey with Bipolar* (Sydney: Allen and Unwin, 2005), 38, 46; Craig Hamilton, *Broken Open* (Sydney: Bantam, 2004), 56, 123.

26. Kenneth Paterson, "Living with Depression: Resisting Labels and Constructing Pathways to Empowerment" (Ph.D. diss., University of Queensland, Brisbane, Australia, 2009), 82.

27. "Blue Board," Centre for Mental Health Research, Australian National University, available online at http://www.blueboard.anu.edu.au (accessed June 1, 2011).

28. Siebers, "Disability as Masquerade," 5.

29. Paterson, "Living with Depression," 102.

30. Martin, *Bipolar Expeditions,* 75.

31. Ibid., 75–76.

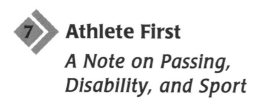

7 ⟩⟩ Athlete First
A Note on Passing, Disability, and Sport

MICHAEL A. REMBIS

F OR SOME DISABLED PEOPLE, being viewed as an athlete first is the ultimate compliment, and the ultimate goal. Deborah, for example, likes to think of herself as a "sports . . . person—*not* as a woman—and *not* as disabled." She adds, "It's *very* hard work, but I like to feel strong and powerful and that's how I win gold medals—in the same way able-bodied people do."[1] The Major League Baseball (MLB) pitcher Jim Abbott reportedly once said, "I never told myself that I wanted to be the next Pete Gray [a physically impaired outfielder who played one season in 1945]. I always said I wanted to be the next Nolan Ryan."[2] This revelation compelled one baseball historian to explain that Abbott's comment was not meant as an insult to Gray but was a statement of Abbott's desire to be seen as a "ballplayer—not a 'one-armed' ballplayer."[3] While on the surface these admissions may seem innocuous or even empowering, a testament to ideas of "inclusion" and "normalization," I argue that they are a powerful and, in some cases, physically and psychically debilitating form of passing.[4]

"Athlete First" is the title of a recent monograph on the history of the Paralympics (Steve Bailey, *Athlete First: A History of the Paralympic Movement* [Hoboken, N.J.: John Wiley and Sons, 2008]). My subtitle is (I hope) an obvious play on Erving Goffman's universally influential study *Stigma: Notes on the Management of Spoiled Identity* (New York: Simon and Schuster, 1963).

In this essay, I analyze the experiences and utterances of elite dis-abled athletes in a variety of historical settings and social and geo-graphic locations as a means of theorizing (and problematizing) our understanding of passing.[5] The goal of the essay is not to "out" disabled athletes or undermine their achievements. Whether they have com-peted with their nondisabled peers or exclusively in what we might call disabled sport, athletes with disabilities have made tremendous gains both individually and collectively in securing a place on the world stage for themselves and for disabled people generally.[6] While the early his-tory of modern sport contains many stories of disabled athletes, it has only been since the end of World War II, and even more recently, since the United Nations General Assembly declared 1983–1992 the Decade of Disabled Persons, that disabled sports such as wheelchair basketball, road racing, track and field, tennis, and wheelchair rugby (known also as murderball), as well as many other winter sports, have become global events attracting thousands of athletes and spectators. The Summer and Winter Paralympics have become huge sporting festivals in recent decades. Advances in sporting technology are making ever more diffi-cult athletic feats attainable, which will no doubt continue to enhance the integration of disabled athletes into nondisabled sport and increase the popularity of disabled sport among the nondisabled. Every year, the number of disabled athletes competing at the highest levels grows. These tremendous gains have affected (however unevenly) the lives of all disabled people in what most observers consider positive ways—increased awareness, access, and legitimacy, increased acceptance and inclusion, and a generally more positive public attitude toward disabil-ity and disabled people. Yet I would like to suggest that all of this new-found notoriety and acceptance has come at a high cost not only for disabled athletes but also for all of those non-sporting individuals living their lives with impairment. It is the former and not the latter that I will speak to in this essay.

For some elite athletes, especially those who have been marginal-ized in other ways, through their race, class, gender, or the "severity" of their disability, the climb to the pinnacle of the sporting world has required the public erasure of significant aspects of their personal iden-tity. They have been forced to pass. As the following venture into dis-ability, sport, and passing will show, passing need not always involve the act of physically concealing one's impairment, but rather depends on how well one can approximate the gendered, white, heterosexual, nondisabled norm and meet societal expectations for conduct, competition, appearance, and performance. It is too simplistic to think of passing strictly in terms of "visibility" as in Tobin Siebers's assertion that "the more visible the disability the greater the chance the person will be repressed from public view and forgotten."[7] As Dominika Bednarska has argued, very little is ever actually explained or revealed by the visibility of one's disability.[8] "Crips" of all stripes constantly have to decide whether to "out" themselves as they move through the nondisabled world. Wheelchair, amputee, and blind athletes are no different.[9] Their impairment is readily apparent for the world to see. Yet they are able to present a public self that greatly minimizes or in some cases erases their impairment in the eyes of the dominant culture. As a result, they are valorized and held up as "normal." Some even achieve celebrity status. In short, they are allowed to pass.

To Pass or Not to Pass

The concept of passing has its own genealogy. Historically, passing has had very specific connotations and almost always manifested in discussions or cultural articulations of race, specifically in the United States, of blacks passing for white. Early scholars of passing who took a largely psychoanalytic approach attributed such negative motivations as shame, guilt, and envy to those individuals who sought to pass. Passing has become much more complex in the post-civil rights, postcolonial, postmodern world of identity politics, multiculturalism, and political "correctness." More recent explorations of passing that have moved beyond rigid definitions of identity and essentialized notions of a "true self" increasingly have looked at various religious and ethnic groups, and sex, sexuality, and gender, as well as race. These studies have revealed the fluidity of subjectivity and the messiness of all socially constructed categories of human difference.[10] The philosopher Anna Camaiti Hostert asserts in her work on passing that "by passing, individuals travel through fluid, multifaceted phases of their existence, experiencing an interdimensional identity as a remedy against forms of indifference or hostility towards the other."[11] She refers to passing as a "metaphor of subjectivity," as the "act of one creating or choosing an identity" and argues that passing takes place wherever and whenever the politics of identity are at work, which for Hostert and most other scholars seems to be all of the time and in every human interaction. As Mattilda (a.k.a.

Matt Bernstein Sycamore) has noted, "We're all caught in a passing net even in our attempts to challenge, subvert, and dismantle this tyranny."[12]

In the disabled context, passing traditionally has been seen as the ability to conceal one's identity or to mask or cover impairment. Siebers has also introduced the notion of the masquerade in which (like camp in gay male culture) disabled people flaunt or play up various aspects of their impairment for different ends: for survival and legitimacy; to defuse tension, anger, and hostility; or to "fit in."[13] Although some initial attempts have been made both to theorize and to historicize the relationship between passing and disability, surprisingly little work has been done in this area.

Exploring the experiences of elite disabled athletes and the history of the rise of modern disabled sport offers an excellent opportunity further to enrich our understanding of passing, because it forces us to think about blurring the lines between disabled and nondisabled and to think critically about the fluidity and contingency of social constructions of normality. It enables us to consider what is happening when athletes are not allowed to pass (because of race, gender, class, or the "severity" of their disability), or can no longer pass (usually because of age), or choose not to pass (deaf sport). It forces us to explore the moments in between, the liminal spaces, and to consider both the psychic and physical trauma of passing (or not passing). Passing can be as Brooke Kroeger, a writer and professor of journalism, argues, "subversive and amusingly mischievous."[14] It can also be deadly serious. If we are going to develop a theory of passing as it relates to disability, it must engage with the negative effects of passing, as well as its more subversive, irreverent, or sheltering elements. A close reading of the experiences of elite disabled athletes and the rise of modern disabled sport has the potential to achieve this goal.

Although he did not specifically analyze it in terms of "passing," Harlan Hahn was among the first scholars in any field to analyze disability sport as a means of achieving both status and social acceptance.[15] In a brilliant essay written nearly thirty years ago, Hahn recognized what he referred to as an increased emphasis on the body that went beyond any fitness craze. "In many respects," Hahn declared, "popular concerns about physical prowess and 'the body beautiful' seem to have reached a peak unparalleled in recent history."[16] This focus on the body, at least in part, compelled many disabled people to make "extraordinary attempts" to compete on an equal basis with the nondisabled as a "socially acceptable method" of "'adjusting'" to life with a disability. Evidence of these extraordinary attempts at social adjustment had become an "integral feature of cultural folklore." Hahn observed that "books, even autobiographies, about disabled people are replete with 'success stories' in which they strive to achieve status in society by 'overcoming' their disabilities."[17] Many of these "success stories" involved sport. In 1981, for example, the Reagan administration chose to highlight a group of disabled people climbing Mount Rainier as the focal point of the United Nation's International Year of the Disabled. The significance of this public display of disability and sport was not lost on Hahn; nor should it be lost on current scholars attempting to think about passing and sport and their relationship with disability.

Throughout the thirty years since a group of disabled climbers garnered worldwide attention, media and much of the general public continued to portray disabled athletes as "courageous" and "inspiring" individuals who had "overcome" their disability. Sport, especially elite sport, seemed to offer a means through which disabled people could leave their disabled bodies and at least metaphorically walk among their able-bodied peers. As one MLB pitching coach said of Jim Mecir's disability, "It's just not a factor with him. It really isn't a limitation. He's turned it into a non-factor." Through "courage," "guts," and "perseverance," Mecir had rhetorically and metaphorically "overcome" his disability.[18] Similar overcoming narratives can be found in mainstream media coverage of the Paralympics. In their study of British newspaper coverage of the 2000 Paralympic Games, Nigel Thomas and Andrew Smith found that nearly one-quarter of articles described athletes as "victims" or people who "suffer[ed]" from "personal tragedies" and who demonstrated "great dedication and courage . . . despite [the] hurdles or misfortune put in their way." Yet reporters also admitted that spending time in the presence of Tanni Grey-Thompson, one of Britain's most accomplished disabled athletes, enabled them to ignore the "ravages of spina bifida." Other articles conveyed the message to readers that sport released certain disabled runners from the "solitary confinement of autism" and freed disabled swimmers from the "chrysalis of a broken body."[19] According to one wheelchair basketball coach in the United States, sport had the capacity to transform disabled people into "just an athlete, no limitations."[20] Although she did not analyze it as "passing," Karen DePauw has referred to this erasure of disability as the "(in)Visibility of disAbility in sport."[21]

The simplistic and misleading notion that one can overcome a disability through athletic competition remains a powerful part of our collective consciousness and our public discourse. One way to combat the violence of this overcoming narrative is to think of disabled people—in this case, elite disabled athletes—as engaging in a complex form of passing rather than overcoming. Words like "adjusting," "overcoming," or the more powerful "triumphing" convey a sense of finality and permanence, a sense that one has somehow (usually through the force of one's own will) left his or her disabled identity and disabled body behind and entered the ranks of the "normal." It seems that some disabled people can—in the rhetoric of the dominant culture—"transcend" impairment in much the same way that African Americans were once able to "transcend" race. Yet people living with impairment know that their lives are neither this simple nor this tidy. Impairment is always present, even in its absence, and the material effects of living a life with impairment remain pervasive and persistent, despite often well-intentioned efforts at "inclusion." In the end, erasing disability through the overcoming narrative does little to alter the realities of living a life with impairment and in most cases serves the power of the dominant culture by negating any meaningful collective critique of structural inequalities and second-class citizenship.

If we are going to negate this negation, we must deploy an expanded conceptualization of passing when analyzing the numerous ways in which people living with a broad range of impairments learn to navigate the nondisabled world. Unlike overcoming, passing is transitory. It conveys a sense of *im*permanence. It is also relational and socially situated. The act of passing is rooted in a seemingly infinite number of specific sociocultural locations and historical moments. It is a never-ending, and ultimately debilitating, process that all disabled people experience and that in nearly every situation gets played out within and through their impaired bodies. Replacing the overcoming narrative with a discourse rooted in the idea of passing allows us to engage in a sustained analysis of these experiences and of the physical and psychic costs of living with a "double consciousness"—in this case, living as an elite athlete and as a disabled person.[22] Confronting these passing moments head on will enable us to use disability and our impaired bodies to challenge the ubiquitous social and structural inequities of the nondisabled world.

Although it can be argued that everyone's social identity and, ultimately, everyone's ability to pass is located in both time and space and constrained and defined by their body/embodiment, this is especially true for people living with impairment and disabled athletes. As the feminist sports scholar Jennifer Hargreaves has argued, "Embodiment has a poignancy when applied to disabled people because they are looked upon, identified, judged and represented primarily through their bodies, which are perceived in popular consciousness to be imperfect, incomplete and inadequate. Because the lack of physical impairment is treated as the norm, the impaired body immediately and conspicuously signifies difference and abnormality. Thus the disabled body is tied to self and identity in a most intense and evocative way."[23] Disabled people invariably find themselves living within the tense and often perilous space between the perfect and the imperfect body. We know from feminist and queer theorists such as Judith Butler and Robert McRuer that the "perfect body" is a fiction, an unattainable social construction.[24] Yet its idealization remains incredibly powerful, especially in the lives of those individuals living with impairment. Disabled people feel a tremendous pressure to appear as nondisabled as possible and whenever possible to mask the extent of their impairment(s).[25] For disabled athletes, especially those competing at the elite level, the pressure to mask impairment and master their own body is remarkably keen.

But how can someone who is markedly (visibly) disabled and competing in elite sport mask impairment? To begin to unpack this question, we must abandon any positivist notions of embodiment and take a flexible, social, postmodernist approach to studying the body and embodiment—what some scholars might call a "social semiotic interactionist" approach—which will enable us to analyze athletes as "reflexive agents" in the relational process of identity formation.[26] Through this approach, we can begin to think of the body as a story, or a narrative, with its own biography. We can begin to think of embodiment as relational and of the body as both subject and object. We both create and interpret meaning through our bodies/embodiment. Athletes perform sport (and ultimately their own embodied identity) in a staged setting that involves elaborate displays of physicality and, perhaps more important, dominant notions of heteronormative nondisabled masculinity and femininity. Those athletes who most closely approximate the norm are allowed to pass—others, like some women and many of the most "severely" disabled competitors, have been systematically forced out of the ranks of the elite athletes.[27]

As the next section will show, the history of disability and sport in the United States and the United Kingdom is littered with elaborate passing narratives that have revealed themselves in interesting and informative ways. What follows is not a comprehensive overview of these experiences but, rather, a series of brief glimpses at pivotal moments—moments in which, to use a bit of the language from Butler's work on gender and sex, a "sedimentation" of bodily norms occurred, a solidification that over time produced a set of "corporeal styles," which in their "reified form" came to appear as the "natural configuration" of able or "normal" bodies.[28]

Passing and the Elite disAbled Athlete

Any theory of passing as it relates to disability must emerge out of an analysis of what recent Marxist scholars of sport have referred to as the "concrete reality of actual history."[29] Thankfully for our purposes, the history of elite sport is riddled with athletes fighting to pass as nondisabled (or less disabled). In this section, I use two brief case studies to show, first, how employing the concept of passing can force us to reconsider some of our commonly held cultural assumptions concerning the "overcoming" narrative; and second, the extent to which passing is embedded in the institutionalization of modern disabled sport's premier showcase, the Paralympics.

Consider first a case that initially may not appear to be a passing narrative: that of the Hall of Fame Major League Baseball player Mickey Mantle. Perhaps one of the greatest baseball players of all time, and certainly one of the most beloved big league sluggers, Mantle played his entire career on two bad legs. Mantle, who played for the New York Yankees from 1951 through 1968 and held numerous records, had contracted osteomyelitis (a bone infection) early in life, after injuring his shin playing high school football. At one point doctors considered amputating the impaired limb but were eventually able to eradicate the infection with the newly introduced wonder drug, penicillin.[30] Although he had been "cured," Mantle would be plagued with various injuries and ailments in his legs for the rest of his life.

Overt references to Mantle's impairment are nearly nonexistent, but those who knew him best and shared the baseball field with him have left us with brief insights into what it was like for Mantle to live with his impairment. The author Bill Liederman, a friend of Mantle's, recalled simply that "Mickey had bad legs most of his career" and that a "freak ailment, a hip infection" had "knocked" Mickey out of the home-run race with Roger Maris in 1961. Mantle lay in a hospital bed crying when Maris hit home run number sixty-one off the Boston Red Sox pitcher Tracy Stallard.[31] The baseball player and Yankees broadcaster Jim Kaat recalled, "Sometimes when he [Mantle] would hit one and you would see him jogging around the bases in pain from his leg, you couldn't figure out how he could do it."[32] Ralph Kiner, a former National League home-run leader (1946–1952), remembered watching Mantle's powerful swing during batting practice and hearing him groan after almost every effort. "I think Mickey was hurting a good part of his career," Kiner recalled.[33] When asked to provide a memory of Mantle, the baseball player and broadcaster Tim McCarver recalled "those terrible grunts and groans as [Mantle] swung the bat, the terrible pain he was in playing the game with those painful knees and bad legs."[34] We may never know for certain the extent of Mantle's impairment—he died in 1995, and few sources refer directly to his "bad legs"—but I think we can safely argue that Mantle spent a good part of his adult life passing.

Thinking of Mantle as passing enables us to ask a new set of questions about his life and about the era in which he played baseball. For example, was his alcohol use a form of self-medicating? Were his well-known off-field antics a form of "masquerade"—a means of deflecting attention away from his ailing body? Mantle's experience and others like it also allow us to think more broadly about pain and pain management and about masculinity and disability in the post–World War II period; about the powerful compulsion to conform to increasingly rigid, narrow definitions of normality and manhood. Openly acknowledging and addressing the erasure of Mantle's "bad legs" in our collective consciousness will help us begin to analyze the powerful role of impairment in shaping not only individual lives, but also social structures and shared perceptions, memories, and values.

In the second case, I will briefly explore the ways in which disabled sport itself became a means of passing in the late capitalist era. In the same years that Mantle was chasing Babe Ruth's home-run record, athletes with other impairments, primarily in the United Kingdom and the United States, were busy laying the foundation for the modern-day Paralympics. Modern disabled sport was born in the wake of a world war that left many soldiers impaired and searching for a way to "re-enter" civilian life.[35] In both the United States and the United Kingdom, disabled sport began as a means of "rehabilitating" disabled veterans of World War II. In the United States, it began amid the cornfields of Illinois and was led by Timothy J. Nugent. In the late 1940s, Nugent, a veteran (though not disabled), formed a wheelchair basketball team for disabled male former GIs attending the University of Illinois, Urbana-Champaign. In 1949, Nugent and the University of Illinois hosted the first Wheelchair Basketball Tournament, which at that time was a small local competition. The following year, Nugent formed the National Wheelchair Basketball Association, which he led until 1973.[36] In England, disabled sport began in much the same way. At the end of World War II, Ludwig Guttmann began using sport as a means of "rehabilitating" and "reintegrating" former servicemen (and a few servicewomen) with spinal injuries. The first disabled sporting event, held at the National Spinal Injuries Unit at Stoke Mandeville Hospital in Buckinghamshire, coincided with the opening ceremony of the Olympic Games in London in 1948, an intentional bit of foreshadowing on Guttmann's part.[37]

For the remainder of the twentieth century and into the first decade of the twenty-first century, elite disabled sport grew from these modest beginnings to what it is today—an international community of more than one hundred countries and thousands of athletes competing at the highest levels. The first sporting competition at Stoke Mandeville, which took place on July 28, 1948, was an archery competition involving a mere sixteen competitors. Word spread quickly among disabled vets and hospital staff, however, and the following year, sixty competitors from five hospitals participated in the second annual Stoke Mandeville Games. Throughout the 1950s, the games became increasingly international, with nearly ten countries participating by 1957, including France, Israel, Finland, the Netherlands, Canada, the United States, and Australia. By the end of the 1950s, participants informally dubbed the Stoke Mandeville Games the "Paralympics," initially because of the large number of spinal-injured (paraplegic) competitors. The name stuck, despite the expansion of the games to include competitors with other types of impairment, in part because the Greek preposition "*para*" means "beside" or "alongside," and it had always been the intent of the game's organizers to have them occur alongside the Olympics.[38]

Although complications arose, usually around issues of physical access, the future of the Paralympics appeared promising in 1959—the year organizers formed the International Stoke Mandeville Games

Committee. The Paralympics took place with the Olympics in Rome in 1960 and in Tokyo in 1964. The fate of the Paralympics relied solely on the goodwill of host cities and local sponsors, however, and following the games in Tokyo in 1964, one Olympic city after another refused to host the Paralympics. It would not be until 1988, twenty-four years after Tokyo, that disabled athletes would compete in an Olympic host city. In 1984, the United States agreed to host the Paralympics, but not in the host Olympic city of Los Angeles. Instead, the games took place in Uniondale, New York, and after the University of Illinois withdrew its bid to host, at Stoke Mandeville in England. Established in 1976, the Winter Paralympic Games fared little better than the Summer Paralympic Games. They did not take place in the host Olympic city, either, and in most years they did not even occur in the same country as the Winter Olympics.[39]

Determined to propel disabled sport into the realm of elite competition, the overwhelmingly male, nondisabled leaders of the Paralympic movement began during the early 1980s to intensify their organizing efforts and re-brand their sporting event. One of their first moves was to build a permanent "Olympic Village" near the Ludwig Gutt mann Sports Stadium for the Disabled at Stoke Mandeville in 1981, which physically separated the sporting facilities from the hospital and, in the words of one history of the Paralympics, physically separated disabled sport from the "notion of 'illness'" itself.[40] Over the course of the next decade, organizers and athletes consolidated their power and refined their sporting identity. In 1982, several sports organizations joined forces and formed the International Coordinating Committee of the World Sports Organizations (ICC), giving the disabled sports movement a unified voice for the first time in its history.[41] The final phase of the institutional development of disabled sport occurred in 1989, with the establishment of the International Paralympic Committee (IPC).[42] Throughout the next ten years, the IPC would work out a formal relationship with the International Olympic Committee (IOC) that included, among other arrangements, a lucrative financial agreement.[43] By 2001, the IPC and the IOC had formulated a "one city, one bid" policy, which compelled potential host cities to construct a comprehensive plan that would fully accommodate both the Paralympics and the Olympics.[44]

An important part of the organizing of elite disabled athletics that took place during the 1980s and 1990s involved the formal integration of people living with various types of impairment into the Paralympic movement. Beginning in 1972, Paralympic organizers gradually allowed the inclusion of a broader range of disabled people in many of the sports included in the games. Women in the United States, for example, had been barred from participating in the all-male National Wheelchair Basketball Association (NWBA) until 1975.[45] In 1988, at the Seoul Paralympics, leaders ratified the participation of all physically impaired groups, including those with spinal injuries, amputees, the blind, and athletes with cerebral palsy.[46] Interestingly, in preparation for the summer games in Barcelona in 1992, often considered a watershed moment in the Paralympic movement, the organizing committee decided to reduce the number of events to fifteen, highlighting the most popular wheelchair events, and refused to allow cognitively impaired athletes to participate in the games. Spectators, who were allowed free admission to the games, and the significant number of television viewers around the world would not know that cognitively impaired athletes had traveled to Spain to participate in the Paralympics.[47] Faced primarily with pressure from within the disabled community, the Paralympic organizers haltingly incorporated cognitively impaired athletes into the games in Atlanta in 1996.

Although the Paralympics had been formally integrated by the mid-1990s, the mostly male, mostly nondisabled leaders of the Paralympic movement did little to change the hypermasculine wheelchair-oriented culture that had been highlighted in Barcelona and Atlanta and had been a critical part of disabled sport since its founding in the immediate post–World War II period. As two Paralympic athletes later stated, the policies of the IPC worked "in favor of increasingly limiting the opportunities of currently active women and severely disabled athletes."[48] The numbers seem to bear this out. There were 3,020 competitors from eighty-two countries at the Barcelona Paralympics in 1992, and only 697 were women—23 percent of the total. At the Paralympics in Atlanta in 1996, only 24 percent, or 780, of the 3,195 competitors were women.[49] Although the number of female athletes participating in the Paralympics remains disproportionately low, it has inched up in recent years. Approximately 3,013 male (74.7%) and 1,019 female (25.3%) athletes from 122 countries participated in eighteen events at the 2000 Paralympic Games in Sydney. In 2004, Athens hosted 3,806 disabled athletes from 136 countries, with a total of 1,160 female competitors—31 percent of the total number of athletes. The reasons for the low numbers of women and "severely" disabled competitors in the Paralympics are varied and complex and extend well beyond the official policies of the IPC. Yet one cannot deny that in branding and marketing their product to the world, the leaders of the Paralympic movement created (perhaps inadvertently) what one study has referred to as an "acceptability" hierarchy—or what we might call a passing hierarchy—within elite disabled sport.[50]

The creation of a passing hierarchy in disabled sport can be seen in the mainstream media coverage of the Paralympic games. A series of studies conducted between 1997 and 2001 found that female athletes with disabilities were given proportionately less media coverage than their male counterparts, and athletes with cerebral palsy and learning disabilities were given less coverage than athletes with other types of impairment. Male wheelchair athletes consistently attracted the most mainstream media attention.[51] This focus on male disAbled bodies is not surprising. Recent sport scholars have argued, and history has shown, that organized sport, especially at the elite level, often acts as a conservative and not a radical, liberating, or transformative social force.[52] In this case, the largely nondisabled male leaders of the Paralympic movement created their sporting festival in the image of its nondisabled counterpart, thereby socially and culturally—and, in some cases, structurally—excluding a broad range of disabled athletes from competition and international recognition. It can be argued that Paralympic organizers, sponsors, host cities, and modern media have prohibited certain athletes from passing, because these athletes exist outside the bounds of a newly defined "normal." They are not athletes first. They are disabled.

In the last two sections, I further analyze the connections among passing, disability, and sport by looking more closely at two Paralympic athletes as distinct but related examples of elite athletes who have "overcome" their disabilities and pass as "normal," but who, like many disabled people, have also fashioned powerful and sophisticated critiques of the overcoming narrative. Because passing, athleticism, and, ultimately, any critique of overcoming manifest themselves in distinctly gendered ways, I will consider the experiences and utterances of Mark Zupan and Aimee Mullins, perhaps two of the most easily recognizable disabled athletes in North America.

Masculinity, Passing, and disAbled Sport, or I Want to Be Like Zupan

Anyone older than twenty most likely remembers the famous Nike slogan "I want to be like Mike," which, of course, referred to Michael Jordan, the National Basketball Association guard who "transcended" his race and became one of the greatest and most admired basketball stars in the history of the game. In the early 2000s, disabled athletes and sports fans around the world found their "Mike." His name is Mark Zupan.

Perhaps the most iconic figure in the short history of disabled sport, Mark Zupan for many disabled athletes and nondisabled observers has become the embodiment of the idealized, masculinized sporting persona. With his shaved head, goatee, and colorful "ink," Zupan carves a formidable and memorable path both on and off the rugby court. Zupan achieved his fame through his central role in *Murderball* (2005), the candid documentary about the members of the United States quad (or wheelchair) rugby team and their quest for Paralympic gold. Since the release of *Murderball*, Zupan has toured the world, speaking about disability and promoting quad rugby. He has appeared on *The Tonight Show* with Jay Leno and *Larry King Live*.[53] He has published a memoir, *Gimp* (2006), and was featured as a customer on the Learning Channel's television series *Miami Ink*. He even appeared in the farcical daredevil film *Jackass, Number Two* (2006). In 2008, Zupan led the U.S. quad rugby team to Olympic gold in Beijing.

In many ways, Zupan offers an ideal opportunity to explore not only the ways in which the elite athlete is gendered male, but also the contradictions and conflicts disabled people experience when they attempt to pass in the nondisabled world. In *Gimp*, Zupan asks readers to "forget everything [they] think they know about quadriplegics, and just think of [him] as a human being and a competitor, because that's exactly what [he is]."[54] Simply stated, he wants to pass. Later, however, Zupan declares that living with a spinal-cord injury and using a wheelchair make him "a member of a secret club," complete with its own "special handshake."[55] Here he is clearly "othering"—and, I argue, empowering—himself. This "secret club" is a restricted social and cultural space that only a select few can enter. This, moreover, is a place where one's embodiment is not negated, denied, minimized, ignored, loathed, or disparaged. Rather, it is a place were one's body takes on very real and salient dimensions.

This complex embodiment can be seen in *Gimp*.[56] When writing about his initial efforts to "overcome" his newly acquired impairment and run and play soccer again, Zupan admits that he ultimately reached a point at which he realized that he was "fighting an impossible battle, one that was beyond [his] ability to win." He writes, "I chose instead to focus on the life that was within my grasp, and that life happened to be in a chair."[57] This was when Zupan entered the "secret club"—not when he became injured but several years later, when he embraced his disabled body. He writes of experiencing clarity and closure in that moment and admonishes his reader: "You can say I was surrendering to my injury, but I choose to look at it another way. I was surrendering to my desire to live a happy, fulfilling life."[58] Coming to this realization enabled Zupan to "align [his] expectations with [his] abilities." He realized that "most roadblocks existed only in [his] mind," but that his "physical limitations were different. They were real."[59] They were something that would never go away, something that could never be overcome.

The realization of his embodiment compelled Zupan to put his own spin on the overcoming narrative. His is a message of triumph tempered by the very real material effects of living life with impairment. "By accepting [physical limitations], I wasn't admitting defeat," he writes. "In fact, I was doing the exact opposite. I was realizing I had done everything in my power to overcome them. And if I related all this back to my old ideas of winning and losing, I guess I was declaring myself a winner once and for all. It had just taken me some time to recognize what victory was going to look like for me."[60] For Zupan, "victory" or "overcoming" or "passing" meant becoming a star athlete on the U.S. quad rugby team. But it also meant living as a man with a spinal-cord injury—as "a quad."

Zupan's insight into becoming both "a quad" and a world-class athlete captures neatly and succinctly the dilemma all disabled people face when they attempt to reconcile their public self (the self they deploy to pass in the nondisabled world) and their private self, or the person who is the member of the secret club, which is an identity that for many disabled people has become increasingly politicized and in some cases more militant in the wake of the disability rights movement. Disabled people, especially those who have come of age in the post–Americans with Disabilities Act (ADA) world are very much aware of the social and cultural currency of passing, as well as the power that comes with claiming a disabled identity and participating in the disability subculture—even if they do not articulate it in those specific terms. Disabled people's savvy and their insights become readily apparent when one reads the articles in magazines such as *Sports 'n Spokes, New Mobility, Disability Rag,* and *Mouth,* which are deeply rooted in the disabled subculture and provide a safe space for disabled people to offer their own critiques of the dominant culture. Through their commentary, disabled people articulate both the costs and the benefits of passing in a nondisabled world.

Zupan also tackles this deceptively complex dilemma in *Gimp*. Like Mickey Mantle, Zupan plays hard both inside and outside the arena—so hard that he passes for "normal" in the minds of many nondisabled observers. In his memoir, Zupan makes a point of noting that he often reads about himself that he plays quad rugby with "so much intensity" that people "forget" he is disabled. Unlike Mantle, who played baseball in the 1950s and 1960s, Zupan became both disabled and a sports star in a post-civil-rights, post-disability-rights, postmodern world of identity politics and is able to admit to readers that this "bothers [him] a little bit." He then goes on to reveal the double consciousness that develops in many disabled people as they learn to pass in the nondisabled world. "I get what they are trying to say," Zupan writes, "and thank them for the compliment, but the two concepts [disabled and intense athlete] aren't mutually exclusive. That's like saying that Denzel Washington is such a good actor that you forget he's black. I can be disabled and still play really fucking hard."[61] In his own gendered way, Zupan has grasped the bind that all disabled people find themselves in, and he challenges his nondisabled readers to grapple with it, as well. To live normally, one must overcome one's impaired body. Yet Zupan and every other person living with impairment realizes early on the impossibility of escaping one's own embodiment. So we "choose" to pass.

For their part, the nondisabled prefer—or, perhaps, feel compelled—to disregard Zupan's message and instead choose to continue to bask in the glow of the overcoming narrative. They idolize and idealize the public Zupan while simultaneously ignoring or dismissing Zupan the "quad." To do any less would surely jeopardize the very ideals that undergird much of American life. Fancifully overwrought notions of courage, bravery, individualism, and self-reliance would be replaced with interdependence (on technology and one another), accommodation, and adaptation, and the fierce competitiveness of elite athletes would be replaced with the collectivism, comradeship, and solidarity of the "secret club." As long as Zupan plays "really fucking hard," he passes in the nondisabled world. The moment he stops playing, he ceases to be "Mark Zupan" and becomes simply "a quad." The effects of this remain to be seen, both in the specific case of Zupan and in the broader cultural sense. Studies of aging athletes, and especially of aging disabled athletes, are virtually nonexistent. What happens when disabled athletes can no longer pass?

Despite decades of struggle by disability rights activists, disability studies scholars, and some disabled athletes to undo this oppression, a particular masculinized overcoming narrative shows no signs of abating. Its latest iteration can be seen most vividly in current attempts to "rehabilitate" America's most recent cohort of "wounded warriors" and disabled veterans. Since the early 2000s, the U.S. military has "rededicated" itself to the original mission of the immediate post–World War II Paralympic organizers. In 2003, the U.S. Olympic Committee (USOC) formalized its Paralympic Military Program, officially reconnecting the Paralympics and elite disabled sport to its original goal. The result has been the creation of the "Warrior Games," an elite sporting festival open to disabled soldiers. As Charlie Huebner, chief of the Paralympics for the USOC, notes, "Using sport as part of their [disabled veterans'] rehabilitation is why we exist."[62]

In the rhetoric of military leadership, and much of the rest of society, disability remains something to be "overcome" through individual "will" and "determination." Huebner explains that the Warrior Games have an "inspirational component" that allows people who are already "motivated to get healthy" and "motivated to get back to their jobs, whether that's serving their country or just returning to their community," to "jump back into an active lifestyle."[63] U.S. Army Brigadier General Gary Cheek adds, "Every soldier is unique, but it is interesting to note that those with their own personal will and desire can really accelerate their healing process and get back into life."[64] At the opening ceremony of the Warrior Games in May 2010, General Victor E. Renuart described the disabled competitors as an "inspiration." According to Renuart, their "resolve and desire to improve their lives is an inspiration for the nation, and is in keeping with the military community's goal to build resilience among its members." Renuart continued that the "games are a testament of the influence of sports and proof of what one can accomplish through determination and will power." Governor Bill Ritter of Colorado hailed the troops as heroes and role models, calling them "the pride of America" for volunteering to serve and for their ability to "triumph over adversity." Juan M. Garcia III, the U.S. Navy's assistant secretary for manpower and reserve affairs, "lauded" the troops for their "willingness to compete and to never give up on themselves and their nation." Garcia characterized them as "men and women who suffered injuries both physical and mental [but] . . . refuse[d] to be defeated."[65] According to a reporter who covered the event, U.S. Navy Admiral Mike Mullen of the Joint Chiefs of Staff told the disabled competitors in a video message aired during the games' closing ceremony that their "willingness to participate in the games and ability to overcome adversity [could] inspire others to do the same." General Renuart encouraged competitors to help teach other injured troops how to "properly heal themselves" and "find closure in their injuries." Renuart, who is not disabled, then informed his disabled audience that "overcoming adversity is more than simply healing physical wounds. It involves accepting new challenges and taking risks, pushing the limits of your disabilities."[66]

Through the overcoming narrative, military officials are continuing and updating an older individualized and internalized measure of success that emerged in the wake of World War II. Among other things, the unrealistic, masculinized calls for self-reliance evoked by the messages of militarily leaders swiftly and powerfully forestall any type of collective criticism of military and Veterans Administration policy and practices and greatly limit any meaningful or transformative (for disabled veterans) response to the trauma of wartime injury. Within this stifling context, any deviation from the norm, any overt attempts not to pass, become a sign of weakness and individual moral failure. The pressure to conform or to pass becomes almost insurmountable, despite the pronouncements of athletes such as Zupan, who openly acknowledge the reality of living life in an impaired body. The result is that many disabled veterans are left feeling alienated, marginalized, and in some cases abandoned by the government and citizenry they initial sought to serve. In reporting on the Warrior Games, one publication highlighted the story of U.S. Army Sergeant Monica Southall, who despite extreme pain from two torn rotator cuffs did not stop pedaling her hand-cycle through a hazardous May snow shower that brought freezing temperatures and slippery roads. She later admitted that she wanted to stop, but "soldiers don't quit, and I wasn't going to quit."[67] Disabled veterans like Southall are responding not only to their own internalized sense of what they must do to appear "normal" but also to pressure from peers, military leaders, and the larger nondisabled society to "triumph over adversity" through "determination and will." In this masculinized, militarized culture, Southall must "play really fucking hard" to pass, even if that means living life with two torn rotator cuffs.

Aimee Mullins and the Feminine Critique

Although she is an accomplished elite athlete, Aimee Mullins is best known for her achievements outside the arena. As a prospective Paralympian (Atlanta in 1996) Mullins set world records in the 100 meter, 200 meter, and long jump. While a student at Georgetown University in the mid-1990s, Mullins became the only double-below-the-knee amputee to compete on a Division I track team and the first disabled competitor in National Collegiate Athletic Association history. In 1997, USA Track and Field named Mullins "Disabled Female Athlete of the Year."[68] Yet these accomplishments might have gone unnoticed and unheralded had Mullins not posed seductively in 1998 in a Nick Knight photo shoot for the fashion magazine *Dazed and Confused*.[69] Shortly thereafter, Mullins garnered more media attention when she sauntered along a London catwalk in hand-carved wooden prostheses for Alexander McQueen's 1999 spring–summer collection. A few years later, Mullins appeared in the American artist filmmaker Matthew Barney's *Cremaster 3* (2002), solidifying her, as one visual studies scholar has put it, as the "Cyborgian sex kitten" of the new millennium.[70]

The revealing images of Mullins's body produced during this period have since become the focus of criticism and critique among feminist scholars in various fields, including disability studies.[71] Yet surprisingly little has been written about Mullins as a historical actor. Scholars seem content with deconstructing the visual representations of her body without engaging in any meaningful analysis of her as a middle-class white college graduate, world-class athlete, model, actor, advocate, popular motivational speaker, or disabled person. This reluctance to deal with what Siebers might call Mullins's "complex embodiment" has done little more than further objectify her and alienate her within certain segments of the larger disabled and feminist communities. In the

remainder of this chapter, I use popular press accounts, scholarly inter-
pretations, and Mullins's own utterances in an effort to disentangle the
complicated threads of her recent past—threads that, I argue, reveal
the many conflicts and complications that arise when a politicized disabled person attempts (or, some might say, is forced) to pass in the
nondisabled world.

When one first encounters Aimee Mullins, it appears as though she
wants little more than to pass.[72] This becomes clear in the way she has
presented her public self. Tall and thin, with long blond hair and hazel-
brown eyes, Mullins looks like any other "model-actress." Even when
she was a serious athlete and a "fierce" competitor on the track, she
made it a point to appear "feminine" off the track.[73] In more recent
interviews, Mullins admits to being prone to vanity—a trait she says
she shares with millions of women around the world.[74] Mullins speaks
of her twelve pairs of prosthetic legs as if they were shoes and in casual
conversation has compared her love of footwear to that of the fictional
character Carrie Bradshaw (played by Sarah Jessica Parker in the television series *Sex and the City*) and the nonfictional Imelda Marcos.[75]
In an appearance on *The Today Show,* Mullins declared, "The best thing
I'll ever do for people with disabilities is by not being thought of as
one." In the same interview, Mullins stated that her ultimate hope was
"that I am finally Aimee Mullins, . . . and my legs are not the most interesting thing about me."[76]

It seems that many people in the nondisabled world want Mullins
to pass, as well. In 1999, *People* magazine named her one of the "50
Most Beautiful People in the World." Four years later, *Rolling Stone* put
Mullins on its annual "Hot List."[77] When Mullins appeared recently on
The Colbert Report, Stephan Colbert referred to her as "smoking hot."[78]
In her *Today Show* interview, Mullins stated, "People say to me, 'You're
so beautiful, you don't look like you're disabled.'"[79] Like Zupan, Mullins
has "transcended" or "overcome" her disability and entered the ranks of
the "normal." And like Zupan, she has achieved her "normal" status in
very gendered ways: by using her normative sexual allure and, more
important, her disabled body to brand and market herself and ultimately build a lucrative career.[80]

This, however, does not tell the whole story of Aimee Mullins. Born
in 1976 into a comfortably middle-class family in Allentown, Pennsylvania, she came of age in a post–Title IX, post–Individuals with Disabilities Education Act, post–ADA world, in which she was able not

only to achieve her goals, but also to forge a powerful and sophisticated disabled identity, which in turn has enabled her to construct her own feminine critique of the overcoming narrative. Although both her disabled identity and her critique of overcoming are deeply rooted in her experience as a normatively attractive, white, heterosexual, middle-class woman, they are not any less important, radical, or transformative than any other standpoint. As long as we remain mindful of the powerful role of Mullins's social and class status and her historical location, hers is a critique worth noting. As she continually reminds her audiences, she *is* an amputee. No amount of "overcoming" or photographic sleight of hand will ever change that reality.

While the notion that Mullins appears to be passing in plain sight may be true, this certainly is not how she perceives her own embodiment. Mullins admits to going through a phase (during her early teens) when she desperately wanted "human" legs, when she wanted to feel the grass and sand on her toes. She states that later in her life, in her mid-twenties, she came to the realization that given the opportunity, she would not "trade in" her prosthetic limbs. She has no desire for a "cure." Impairment is a very real part of Mullins's embodiment. This becomes readily apparent when she discusses "overcoming adversity," by which she really means "overcoming impairment." One can easily substitute "impairment" for "adversity" in the following excerpt from one of Mullins's talks, given in 2009, and see that for her, impairment is ever present and a critical part of her identity:

> People have continually wanted to talk to me about overcoming adversity and I am going to make an admission, this phrase never sat right with me, and I always felt uneasy trying to answer people's questions about it—and I think I'm starting to figure out why . . . implicit in this phrase of overcoming adversity is the idea that success or happiness is about emerging on the other side of a challenging experience unscathed or unmarked by the experience; as if my successes in life have come about from an ability to sidestep or circumnavigate the presumed pitfalls of a life with prosthetics or what other people perceive as my disability, but in fact we are changed, we are marked . . . by a challenge, whether physically, emotionally or both, and I'm going to suggest that this is a good thing; adversity isn't an obstacle that we need to get around in order to

resume living our life. It's part of our life, and I tend to think of it like my shadow; sometimes I see a lot of it, sometimes there's very little but it's always with me.[81]

Like Zupan, Mullins is upset by people insisting that she has "overcome" her impairment, and she challenges her audience to struggle with the reality and the permanence of impairment. For Mullins, challenging and changing dominant paradigms of impairment is

> not about devaluing or negating these more trying times as something we want to avoid or sweep under the rug, but instead to find those opportunities wrapped in the adversity. . . . The idea I want to put out there is not so much overcoming adversity as it is opening ourselves up to it, embracing it, grappling with it . . . maybe even dancing with it. . . . If we see adversity as natural, consistent, and useful, we're less burdened by the presence of it.[82]

Mullins is clearly attempting to negate the erasure of impairment in the popular imaginary by reinscribing a new understanding of impairment and the disabled body in the minds of her audience.

For Mullins, impairment is permanent and an impaired body is a beautiful body. While addressing the comment that she does not "look disabled," Mullins noted that such statements were "very telling to me about two things: number one, what people thought people with disabilities looked like, and number two, what people thought beautiful women should look like."[83] Although she has vigorously pursued a normative standard of beauty, Mullins remains rhetorically and ideologically committed to pluralism and to deconstructing conventional heteronormative understandings of beauty and desirability. This, and not simply her impaired body, is the paradox of Aimee Mullins.[84]

Mullins, like many young disabled people who have grown up in the era of "inclusion," remains wary but hopeful for an even more equitable future—one in which empowered disabled people can begin to forge their own reality. From her standpoint,

> The conversation with society has changed profoundly in this last decade [1998–2008]. It's no longer a conversation about overcoming deficiency; it's a conversation about augmentation;

it's a conversation about potential. A prosthetic limb doesn't represent the need to replace loss anymore. It can stand as a symbol that the wearer has the power to create whatever it is that [she or he] want[s] to create in that space. So people that society once considered to be disabled can now become the architects of their own identities and indeed continue to change those identities by designing their bodies from a place of empowerment.[85]

Although steeped in the rhetoric of neoliberal individualism and late capitalist consumption and branding, Mullins assertion that the material conditions under which certain disabled people (white middle-class or upper-class Westerners or Northerners) live have changed significantly during her lifetime is a valid one. For people with means and access to resources, the opportunities to pass in the nondisabled world are abundant. But what happens to all those people who cannot or choose not to pass? It is clear from this brief encounter with Mullins that her critique of overcoming, which she couches in the language of "empowerment" through consumption, need not and should not be the end of the conversation.

Largely because she is concerned with passing (and making a substantial living), Mullins's activism has taken the form of "motivational speaking," which, of course, remains fraught with sentimental appeals to personal transformation rather than a serious discussion of systemic or structural inequalities. Part of Mullins's activism is also rooted in mentoring and speaking to young girls, because, as she said more than a decade ago, she wants to live in a world where she is "seen as beautiful because of [her] disability, not in spite of it."[86] Mullins's work with young people is done primarily through sport. In 1998, she co-founded Helping Others Perform with Excellence (HOPE), which her online biography describes as "a non-profit organization to provide means, training, and opportunity for persons with disabilities to compete in sports."[87] Mullins served as the president of the Women's Sports Foundation in 2007 and 2008.[88] What, then, are we to make of Mullins as a disabled person and a historical actor? And how can her feminine critique of the overcoming narrative inform our theories about passing?

Mullins, like most disabled people living in the twenty-first century, lives simultaneously in two worlds. She wants to pass. Yet passing upsets her. She wants to be accepted as "normal." Yet she has forged a very real and very powerful disabled identity. She has formed a critique of dominant notions of beauty. Yet she clearly has worked hard to achieve those very same standards. She recognizes gains that have been made by disabled people but realizes that much work remains. She wants to work within the late capitalist neoliberal system but knows that the current state of social relations can be both damaging and disempowering, especially to people living with impairment. So she engages in a one-woman consciousness-raising effort. While vitally important, this type of individual activism is not only physically and mentally exhausting, but it ultimately will serve to perpetuate, and possibly exacerbate, longstanding divisions both within the disabled community and between certain segments of "the disabled" and "the rest of society." Mullins, like Zupan, is able to disrupt popular discourse and provide a counter to the overcoming narrative precisely because she passes as "normal." This, I think, is one of the intriguing conundrums facing scholars and activists alike.

Conclusion

It is clear sixty-five years after the introduction of modern disabled sport to the United States and the United Kingdom, and forty years after the rise of the modern disability rights movement in those countries, that the overcoming narrative remains a powerful and pervasive part of our popular culture. We live in an era where, at least in the West (or global North), "inclusion" and "empowerment" have become watchwords, and the state, prodded by movement participants, has gone to great lengths legally to enfranchise its citizens. Ours is an age in which, at least rhetorically and ideologically, everyone has the right to "succeed" and "flourish," largely through the force of their own will and through their participation in the private market economy. Under this regime of power-knowledge, we all possess the ability to "overcome" whatever "deficiencies" may characterize our state of being in the world, regardless of our class, race, sex, gender, sexuality, or disability status. In this sense, the neoliberal, late capitalist subject position has come to embody a new norm, a powerful yet equally oppressive standardized corporeality that remains forever haunted by muted but ever present markers of diversity. Put simply, we are all forced to "overcome" to "thrive" in the modern world. Yet none of us can actually "overcome" the realities of our own embodiment. So in the end, many of us "choose" to pass. For some of us, especially certain disabled athletes such as Mullins and Zupan, the realization that we all participate in "overcoming" causes a significant amount of unease, which we attempt to articulate through a counter-narrative that validates our own bodies and the material realities that shape our lives. Too often, however, this alternative discourse gets ignored, negated, or marginalized by the dominant culture, which instead clings to "inspiring" and "heroic" tales of "overcoming."

One way to move beyond the overcoming narrative is to recognize it for what it really is—passing—and to acknowledge that "choosing" to pass is a direct violation of our civil and human rights.[89] When we replace ideas about overcoming with a more expansive understanding of the concept of passing, we open ourselves to a new set of powerful analytics, pedagogies, epistemologies, and activist strategies that we can begin to deploy in our efforts to dislodge the cruel grip of the new normality. Impaired Major League Baseball players and Paralympic athletes, reality television stars, children learning in "inclusive" classrooms, professors living with psychiatric diagnoses, and pipefitters with "bad backs" all make many daily decisions about when and where and how to pass in the "nondisabled world" about how best to appear "temporarily able-bodied" in the minds of their peers and within the values of the dominant culture. Over the days, months, and years, enormous amounts of time and energy are spent minimizing the extent of the impairments that affect all our lives, which can be both physically and psychically debilitating. In the end, we must choose not to pass and to build a well-articulated and accessible critique of the capitalist, patriarchal notions of "productivity," "independence," and "beauty" that undergird many of our social relations. We must also act together to effect change. Only then will we be able to cast off the tyrannical net of the overcoming narrative.

Notes

1. Jennifer Hargreaves, "Impaired and Disabled: Building on Ability," in Jennifer Hargreaves, *Heroines of Sport: The Politics of Difference and Identity* (London: Routledge, 2000), 203.

2. Rick Swaine, *Beating the Breaks: Major League Ballplayers Who Overcame Disabilities* (Jefferson, N.C.: McFarland, 2004), 24, 25.

3. Ibid., 24–25.

4. Writing in a different context, the legal scholar Kenji Yoshino argues that when viewed from the dominant culture, passing becomes covering. Yoshino

argues that everyone covers; that it is a form of assimilation; and that it is a direct assault on our civil rights. The idea that we all cover is indeed a powerful and provocative assertion and one that should be explored in future work. In our present state, however, such a claim has the potential to dilute the concept of passing, with all of its inherent contradictions and complexities, to a point of near-meaninglessness. For this reason, and because I am focusing on the often fraught relationships among disabled athletes and the dominant culture, I will use the term "passing," not "covering," throughout this essay: see Kenji Yoshino, *Covering: The Hidden Assault on Our Civil Rights* (New York: Random House, 2007).

5. I will use evidence from the history of elite disabled athletes in both non-disabled or "mainstream" sport and in disabled sport, mostly during the post–World War II period, in both the United States and the United Kingdom.

6. The experiences of those few disabled athletes who have managed to compete with their nondisabled peers at the highest levels are informative and will be taken up in this discussion, but the main focus of this analysis will be on disabled athletes who compete in what we might call disability-specific sports—those sporting events in which all of the competitors are disabled. I will refer to this as elite disabled sport, or simply disabled sport.

7. Tobin Siebers, *Disability Theory* (Ann Arbor: University of Michigan Press, 2008), 103.

8. Dominika Bednarska, "Passing Last Summer," in *Nobody Passes: Rejecting the Rules of Gender and Conformity,* ed. Mattilda [Matt Bernstein Sycamore] (Emeryville, Calif.: Seal Press, 2006), 73.

9. I purposely did not include deaf athletes here because historically they have chosen not to pass. Deaf sport has a longer history than other disability sport, and most deaf athletes have chosen not to "mainstream." For more on deaf sport, see David A. Stewart, *Deaf Sport: The Impact of Sports within the Deaf Community* (Washington, D.C.: Gallaudet University Press, 1991).

10. Anna Camaiti Hostert, *Passing: A Strategy to Dissolve Identities and Remap Differences,* trans. Christine Marciasini (Madison, N.J.: Fairleigh Dickinson University Press, 2007); Brooke Kroeger, *Passing: When People Can't Be Who They Are* (New York: Public Affairs, 2003).

11. Hostert, *Passing,* 80.

12. Mattilda, "Reaching Too Far: An Introduction," in Mattilda, *Nobody Passes,* 13.

13. Siebers, *Disability Theory.*

14. Kroeger, *Passing.*

15. Harlan Hahn, "Sports and the Political Movement of Disabled Persons: Examining Non-disabled Social Values," *Arena Review* 18, no. 1(1984): 1–15.

16. Ibid., 3.

17. Ibid., 6.

18. Swaine, *Beating the Breaks,* 110–111.

19. Nigel Thomas and Andrew Smith. "Preoccupied with Able-bodiedness? An Analysis of the British Media Coverage of the 2000 Paralympic Games," *Adapted Physical Activity Quarterly* 20 (2003): 172–173.

20. Corey Inscoe, "Hoop Dreams," *Sports 'n Spokes,* September 2010, 52.

21. DePauw considered the erasure of disability in sport to be an incomplete but largely positive advancement for disabled people because it indicated a certain level of equality among nondisabled and disabled athletes: Karen P. DePauw, "The (In)visibility of disAbility: Cultural Contexts and 'Sporting Bodies,'" *Quest* (1997): 49, 424.

22. Here I am borrowing and modifying the notion of "double consciousness" articulated by W. E. B. Du Bois in his classic essay "Of Our Spiritual Strivings," in W. E. B. Du Bois, *The Souls of Black Folk* (Mineola, N.Y.: Dover, 1994).

23. Hargreaves, "Impaired and Disabled," 185.

24. Judith Butler, "Bodily Inscriptions, Performative Subversions," in *Feminist Theory and the Body: A Reader,* ed. Janet Price and Margrit Shildrick (New York: Routledge, 1999), 420–421; Robert McRuer, "We Were Never Identified: Feminism, Queer Theory, and a Disabled World," *Radical History Review* 94 (Winter 2006): 148–154; Robert McRuer, *Crip Theory: Cultural Signs of Queerness and Disability* (New York: New York University Press, 2006).

25. Hargreaves, "Impaired and Disabled," 185.

26. Dennis Waskul and Phillip Vannini, eds., *Body/Embodiment: Symbolic Interaction and the Sociology of the Body* (Aldershot: Ashgate, 2006).

27. For the exclusion of women and "severely" disabled, see Hargreaves, "Impaired and Disabled."

28. Butler, "Bodily Inscriptions," 420–421.

29. Toby Miller, "Michel Foucault and the Critique of Sport," in *Marxism, Cultural Studies, and Sport,* ed. Ben Carrington and Ian McDonald (London: Routledge, 2009), 198.

30. Swaine, *Beating the Breaks,* 196.

31. Bill Liederman and Maury Allen, *Our Mickey: Cherished Memories of an American Icon* (Chicago: Triumph Books, 2004), xii.

32. Jim Kaat, quoted in ibid., 141–142.

33. Ralph Kiner, quoted in ibid., 149.

34. Tim McCarver, quoted in ibid., 154.

35. Deaf people around the world had been engaging in competitive organized sport since the late nineteenth century and had formed the International Committee of Sports for the Deaf in 1924. They held the first International Silent Games the same year, attracting athletes from ten European countries and marking the beginning of the World Games for the Deaf, later recognized as the Deaflympics by the International Olympic Committee. For reasons that fall beyond the scope of this essay, deaf athletes and organizers chose not to integrate deaf sport into the "mainstream" sporting world. For more on deaf sport, see Stewart, *Deaf Sport.*

36. John W. DenBoer and Sigmund Hough, "Nugent, Timothy J. (1923–) Disability Activist," in *Encyclopedia of American Disability History*, ed. Susan Burch (New York: Facts on File, 2009), 666–667.

37. John R. Gold and Margaret M. Gold, "The Paralympic Games," in *Olympic Cities: City Agendas, Planning, and the World's Games, 1896–2012* (London: Routledge, 2007), 84–99.

38. Ibid., 84–99.

39. Ibid.

40. Ibid., 90.

41. The organizations that joined forces were the International Stoke Mandeville Wheelchair Sports Federation, the International Sports Organization for the Disabled, the International Blind Sports Federation, and the Cerebral Palsy International Sport and Recreation Association. These organizations were later joined by the International Committee of Sports for the Deaf and the International Sports Federation for Persons with Mental Handicap—later changed to Intellectual Disability: Gold and Gold, "The Paralympic Games," 90.

42. Based in Bonn, Germany, the IPC serves as the umbrella organization for 162 National Paralympic Committees, five regional organizations, and four international disability-specific sports federations. It also acts as the international federation for thirteen of the twenty-four Paralympic sports: Gold and Gold, "The Paralympic Games," 93.

43. Ibid.

44. Ibid., 94.

45. Hargreaves, "Impaired and Disabled," 184.

46. Ibid., 183.

47. Overall responsibility for the Barcelona games was given to the Organizing Committee of the Barcelona Games. The International Sports Federation for Persons with Mental Handicap held its own games in Madrid following the Paralympics in Barcelona; 1,400 athletes from 73 countries participated in the event: Gold and Gold, "The Paralympic Games," 93–94.

48. Hargreaves, "Impaired and Disabled," 209.

49. Ibid., 206.

50. Although they were not writing about disability and sport, I found the following essays in Carrington and McDonald, *Marxism, Cultural Studies, and Sport*, helpful in thinking about the commodification of sport in the late capitalist era: David L. Andrews, "Sport, Culture, and Late Capitalism"; Alan Baimer, "Re-appropriating Gramsci: Marxism, Hegemony, and Sport"; and Miller, "Michel Foucault."

51. Thomas and Smith, "Preoccupied with Able-bodiedness?" 169.

52. Gail Bederman, *Manliness and Civilization: A Cultural History of Gender and Race in the United States, 1880–1917* (Chicago: University of Chicago Press, 1996); Carrington and McDonald, *Marxism, Cultural Studies, and Sport*; Michael Oriard, *Reading Football: How the Popular Press Created an American Spectacle* (Chapel Hill: University of North Carolina Press, 1998); Karen P.

DePauw, "The (In)Visibility of DisAbility: Cultural Contexts and 'Sporting Bodies,'" *Quest* 49 (1997): 416–430.

53. Leno jokingly called Zupan a "big asshole," which he thought was "hilarious," and King apparently became incredulous when Zupan and his rugby teammates said they would not want to be "cured" because there was nothing wrong with them that needed to be "cured": Mark Zupan and Tim Swanson, *Gimp: When Life Deals You a Crappy Hand, You Can Fold—or You Can Play* (New York: HarperCollins, 2006), 269.

54. Ibid., 6.

55. Ibid., 193.

56. Siebers uses the term "complex embodiment" in *Disability Theory.*

57. Zupan and Swanson, *Gimp,* 199.

58. Ibid.

59. Ibid.

60. Ibid., 200.

61. Ibid., 7.

62. Nicholas Brown, "Disabled Soldiers and the Warrior Games," *Athletic Business,* August 2010, available online at http://athleticbusiness.com/articles/article.aspx?articleid=3596&zoneid=11 (accessed January 3, 2011).

63. Ibid.

64. Michael J. Carden, "Warrior Games Seek to Inspire Disabled Warriors," American Forces Press Services, U.S. Department of Defense, April 13, 2010, available online at http://www.defense.gov/news/newsarticle.aspx?id=58717 (accessed January 3, 2011).

65. Michael J. Carden, "Disabled Vets, Troops Compete in First Warrior Games," American Forces Press Services, U.S. Air Force, May 11, 2010, available online at http://www.af.mil/news/story.asp?id=123203958 (accessed January 3, 2010).

66. Michael J. Carden, "The Will of a Warrior," *Sports 'n Spokes,* July 2010, 15–19.

67. Ibid., 16.

68. "Biography of Aimee Mullins," available online at http://www.allamericanspeakers.com/speakerbio/Aimee_Mullins.php (accessed January 25, 2011).

69. The issue's guest editor was the fashion designer Alexander McQueen.

70. Smith did not intend this moniker to be a compliment. In fact, she remains critical of Mullins. I will engage with some of this criticism in this final section. See Marquard Smith, "The Vulnerable Articulate: James Gillingham, Aimee Mullins, and Matthew Barney," in *The Prosthetic Impulse: From a Posthuman Present to a Biocultural Future,* ed. Marquard Smith and Joanne Morra (Cambridge, Mass.: MIT Press, 2006), 47.

71. Ibid.; Rosemarie Garland Thomson, "Integrating Disability, Transforming Feminist Theory," in *The Disability Studies Reader,* ed. Lennard J. Davis (London: Routledge, 2006), 257–273.

72. Thomson argues that Mullins refuses to "normalize or hide her disability in order to pass for nondisabled." While it may be true that Mullins refuses to "hide" her disability, I have been arguing here that we need to adopt a more complex and capacious notion of passing that goes beyond merely "hiding" one's disability. I argue, moreover, that Mullins has done everything within her power to "normalize" her disability: ibid., 270–271.

73. "Aimee Mullins Amputee DBK Taking Off Prosthetic Legs," video clip, February 20, 2009, YouTube.com, available online at http://www.youtube.com/watch?v=LKpRPo4cN8s&feature=related (accessed January 23, 2011).

74. Smith, "The Vulnerable Articulate," 58–59.

75. "Aimee Mullins on *The Colbert Report*," video clip, YouTube.com, available online at http://www.colbertnation.com/the-colbert-report-videos/271372/april-15-2010/aimee-mullins (accessed January 23, 2011).

76. *The Today Show* is a nationally syndicated morning talk show in the United States: "Aimee Mullins on *The Today Show*," video clip, YouTube.com, available online at http://www.youtube.com/watch?v=51ybBLEav-M&feature=related (accessed January 23, 2011).

77. "Biography of Aimee Mullins."

78. "Aimee Mullins on *The Colbert Report*." Smith recognizes this passing when she argues that Mullins's "'becoming visible' as an eroticized Cyborgian sex kitten, while significant for the public presence of differently abled bodies in our visual culture, takes place at the expense of her identity as an amputee—in fact, requires the very negation of her figural condition as an amputee." What is Mullins's "identity as an amputee"? Can Smith claim to be privy to that identity by poring over a few photos and a single film appearance? Is there an "amputee identity" to which Mullins must aspire? Are we to read this public proclamation of Mullins's sexual appeal as a "negation" of her identity as an amputee? Or is Colbert merely a "devotee"? Either stance does little more than negate and delegitimize Mullins's agency in forming her own sexual identity and her own voice: see Smith, "The Vulnerable Articulate," 58.

79. "Aimee Mullins on *The Today Show*."

80. As a public speaker, Mullins commands $10,000–$20,000 per appearance: "Biography of Aimee Mullins."

81. Mullins gave her talk at TEDMED in San Diego in October 2009. As its website describes, TEDMED is a speaker series that was created by Marc Hodosh and Richard Saul Wurman. It "celebrates conversations that demonstrate the intersection and connections between all things medical and healthcare related: from personal health to public health, devices to design and Hollywood to the hospital. Together, this encompasses more than twenty percent of our GNP in America while touching everyone's life around the globe": TEDMED 2010, available online at http://www.tedmed.com/what (accessed January 30, 2011). Aimee Mullins, "The Opportunity of Adversity," video clip, YouTube.com, http://www.youtube.com/watch?v=dTwXeZ4GkzI&feature=channel (accessed January 23, 2011).

82. Mullins, "The Opportunity of Adversity."

83. "Aimee Mullins on *The Today Show.*"

84. I diverge slightly here from Thomson, who argues that Mullins is an "embodied paradox" because she is "legless and beautiful," and thus her body possesses "inherently disruptive potential." It is not necessarily Mullins's body—which in many ways fits conventional notions of beauty—that is disruptive; but her agency as a historical actor, although even that is problematic, as I have stated: see Thomson, "Integrating Disability," 271.

85. Aimee Mullins, "How My Legs Give me Super Powers," video clip, You Tube.com, available online at http://www.youtube.com/watch?v=JQ0iMulicgg (accessed January 23, 2011). For an insightful analysis of bodily augmentation, see Sander L. Gilman, *Making the Body Beautiful: A Cultural History of Aesthetic Surgery* (Princeton, N.J.: Princeton University Press, 1999).

86. Mullins, quoted in Hargreaves, "Impaired and Disabled," 188.

87. "Biography of Aimee Mullins."

88. "Former Presidents," Women's Sports Foundation, available online at http://www.womenssportsfoundation.org/About-Us/Who-We-Are/Past-Presidents .aspx (accessed January 25, 2011).

89. Yoshino calls this "covering" and argues, as the title of his book states, that it is a "hidden assault on our civil rights": Yoshino, *Covering.*

8 The Sociopolitical Contexts of Passing and Intellectual Disability

ALLISON C. CAREY

INDIVIDUALS WITH DISABILITIES face an environment fraught with contradictions regarding whether one should try to pass as non-disabled, develop disability pride and resist passing, or deconstruct and disregard the binary construction of disability–ability altogether. The study of passing is often approached from the perspective of social psychology, involving a consideration of why and how individuals engage in the active manipulation of their identity. However, the very notion of passing, and thereby individuals' experiences with and decisions regarding passing, are shaped by the larger sociopolitical context and the way in which identity categories are socially constructed on a macro level. By developing and applying a structural model of identity and passing, we come to a greater understanding of the meanings of, the incentives for, and the likelihood of passing for people with intellectual disabilities in various time periods.

In the early twentieth century, eugenicists feared that the "feeble-minded" would pass and spread an epidemic of mental degeneracy throughout the nation. They constructed categories of "feebleminded" and "fit" that were sharply demarcated, with rigid expectations regarding the behavior and abilities of people with disabilities, static views of disability that denied its dynamic nature, and intense inequality, all of which heightened the relevance of passing. To then prevent passing, they relied heavily on extensive systems of identification and segregation. Unlike eugenicists who saw normality as an impossible achievement for the feebleminded, parents in the 1950s and '60s walked a far subtler line in recognizing the differences of their children and families while striving to pass as "normal," or some approximation of it. Today, the system is fraught with contradictory messages about passing. Models of self-advocacy and empowerment suggest that human variations should be respected and valued. The proliferation of disability identity constructions that are gradational, fluid, dynamic, and equal lessen the incentives to pass, as well as the meaning of passing. However, typical patterns of socialization emphasize that value in American society is tied to one's status as a contributing, productive citizen, and many people truly want to conform to that standard to the best of their ability. Still more problematic, extensive specialized systems, including special education, sheltered workshops, and segregated recreation, continue to create sharp distinctions between the able and the disabled, heightening the tensions around passing and removing people's choices about how to identify.

Historical Analysis

Eugenic Anxiety and the Panic over Passing

Much academic literature has tied the rise of eugenics and the associated panic regarding feeblemindedness to increasing anxiety over status provoked by the social transformations that occurred in the late nineteenth century and early twentieth century, including industrialization, urbanization, and immigration.[1] In the midst of these social transformations, eugenics—a pseudo-scientific endeavor to improve population quality—quickly became a tool to reinforce social stratification.[2] Eugenicists rooted social problems of the day in individuals' biology and claimed that defective people caused poverty, crime, and the moral decline of society generally. Based on this position, they commonly advocated measures to enforce social control and limit social change, such as the restriction of immigration, the prohibition of miscegenation, and the valorization of traditional gender roles.[3] As the eugenics movement grew, it increasingly focused attention on the threat of the feebleminded and advocated social policies such as institutionalization and sterilization to prevent feeblemindedness.[4] Feeblemindedness served as a conceptually advantageous focal point for the politics of the eugenics movement for several reasons: it was widely assumed to be rooted in genetics and biology; it indicated biological, social, and moral inferiority; and it justified medical treatment or control and legal and social restrictions. By using an expansive and flexible definition of feeblemindedness, eugenicists could exercise tremendous control over a wide variety of socially marginalized populations.[5]

As a mechanism to enforce control, eugenicists constructed the identity category of feeblemindedness in particular ways to emphasize the clear demarcations between the "feebleminded" and the "fit" and to enforce the consequences associated with feeblemindedness. First, they drew thick boundaries around the categories of feebleminded and fit citizens, depicting the feebleminded to be fundamentally different from other citizens. Sharply bounded categorical constructions portray the people within identity categories as totally different *kinds* of people, compared with quantitative constructions that assume a continuum of humanity so that differences are of degree, not kind.[6] According to eugenicists, the feebleminded lacked rationality, moral judgment, and the ability to achieve self-sufficiency; as such, they were at best a "burden" or a "dead load," and at worst, they were a "social evil," a "danger," and a "menace."[7] Some eugenicists relied on war metaphors to heighten the "otherness" of the feebleminded, while others compared them to a biological epidemic.[8] Thus, the proclamation by Alexander Johnson, a leader in the field of social work and director at the Training School at Vineland, New Jersey, that feebleminded women constituted a "graver danger to the prosperity of the state than a foreign war or a native pestilence" is illustrative of eugenic rhetoric rather than exceptional in its fervor."[9]

Moreover, eugenicists depicted these identity categories as rigid, static, and of singular importance.[10] Rigid constructions, versus malleable ones, constrain the content of the categories, offering narrow views of the behavior, attitudes, and lifestyles associated with an identity. Thus, eugenicists argued that the feebleminded were necessarily immoral and unproductive and would fare best among their own kind rather than imagining a population with diverse interests, abilities, and potential lifestyles. Not only was the content of the identity rigid, it was also static—or, in other words, unlikely to change over one's lifespan. Presented as a genetic disorder that impaired one's overall mental and moral functioning, feeblemindedness was seen as without hope of cure or improvement. Along these lines, Henry Goddard, director of research at the Training School at Vineland, argued that environmental programs could not improve the deficient nature of the feebleminded; education would be lost on them, and model housing would be turned into slums "because we have these mentally defective people who can never be taught to live otherwise than as they have been living."[11] With no hope of cure, social control and prevention were perceived as the only effective answer. Feeblemindedness was therefore also imagined as the identity characteristic of singular importance—a "master status"—that trumped all other identities, such as gender, race, profession, or regional demographics, in shaping one's interactions and opportunities.

These characteristics of identity construction heightened the likelihood that human variation would be perceived as "passing." Because these identity categories were seen as bounded, rigid, and static, there was no room to be both able and disabled. If one acted able, it was understood as a transgression and defined as "passing."[12] In fact, Edgar Doll and Joseph Jastak, leading psychologists in this field, argued that people with mental deficiency could never be socially successful; successful social adaptation defied the very definition of mental deficiency.[13] Therefore, social success indicated deception (passing) on the part of the person with a disability or misdiagnosis by experts. Given the prestige conferred on medical professionals, the more common assumption was deception. The person may seem to be successful, but passing was certain to end in failure due to his or her inherent limitations.

Eugenicists also explicitly tied the construction of feeblemindedness to the distribution of privilege. Feeblemindedness was not a neutral descriptive category; it was laden with value and tied to a system of norms, resources, and privileges.[14] People labeled as such were potentially subject to a pervasive system of medical, legal, and social control.[15] While some medical institutions offered treatment based on this diagnosis (and therefore the label or identity of feeblemindedness connected one to a resource), most medical institutions operated as a form of social control and physical segregation in which inmates experienced neglect, abuse, and social, and civil "death."[16] Outside the medical institution, too, people labeled feebleminded experienced restrictions on the rights to marry, bear children, enter contracts, and vote.

Categorical constructions that enforce inferior access to power and privilege likely magnify the incentives for passing.[17] Because of the incentives to pass and the desire to preserve the exclusive privileges conferred on those defined as fit, we see tremendous anxiety about and fear of passing expressed by professionals and elites. This fear of passing is ironic given that eugenicists argued that sharp distinctions between the disabled and the fit existed, yet they bemoaned the difficulty of distinguishing able from disabled and warned of the common practice of passing especially among those with greater skill levels, whom they referred to as "morons" or "high-grade feebleminded." For example, Seth Humphrey, an avid eugenicist, warned that the high-grade feebleminded person wreaks havoc on communities because he or she appears able and thereby evades social-control mechanisms:

> The helplessly idiotic and the insane are fairly taken care of, but the numerous class variously known as "high-grade imbecile," "defective delinquent," "moron," "borderliner" is left in the community,—the man, shifty, alcoholic, thieving, unworkable, habitually in jail; the woman, with enough wit to make a dissolute living but not enough wit to avoid child-bearing, the prolific mother of incapables,—what of her? . . . Society does its very best for her at the particular moment when she is doing her worst for society—and then turns her adrift again, because "she can take care of herself!"[18]

The institutional superintendents George Bliss and Walter Fernald similarly criticized the practice of allowing "high-grade" feebleminded individuals to live in the community.[19] Bliss cautioned, "He may have the physical appearance of a well developed individual, may even be what is called handsome in person and face. Those not informed will hardly ever believe the kind of immoral acts, and the sort of anti-social conduct, that is possible with such an individual."[20] Thus, the problem of passing as presented by eugenicists was rooted in the necessary failure of it; because the feebleminded were distinctly different from and inferior to other citizens, they could not actually succeed, and opportunities to try to do so were destined to end in ruin for the individual and for society.

Ironically, although the feebleminded were presented as distinctly and qualitatively different from and inferior to fit citizens, the so-called defining traits were largely invisible. Visibility is not simply a natural phenomenon; it, too, is culturally produced, and feeblemindedness had to be made visible through systems of diagnosis, registration, and segregation.[21] According to Martin Barr, chief physician at a Pennsylvania training school, "There must be permanent sequestration, otherwise the trained imbecile is a greater menace to society than is the untrained, in that, with latent powers and talents developed to the point of concealing defects, he is no longer recognized, and has opened to him a larger field for indulgence of emotional or criminal instincts."[22] The IQ test, implemented systematically in the school systems, became central to the project of making the invisible visible and the ambiguous identifiable and bounded.[23] Segregation through institutionalization and in educational settings also provided visible markers of one's identity and associated status. Systems of registration for all feebleminded individuals were promoted to enable easy identification and the corresponding denial of rights and privileges.[24] Exclusion from education and typical social experiences further made disability visible by increasing the likely presence of associated indicators such as illiteracy, atypical behavior, and poverty.

Given the tremendous disadvantages tied to a label of feeblemindedness, and the absence of a community that proposed a positive disability identity,[25] most advantages were staked to passing as a "normal" citizen and avoiding a label of feeblemindedness. When we try to consider how common passing was or was not, it seems that there was little reason to claim an identity of "feebleminded." The choices were to accept a stigmatizing label that provided few advantages, led to segregation and exclusion, and offered little to no sense of alternative community acceptance and belonging *or* participate in the community the best one could and risk being accused of passing and thereby of deceiving and threatening society. This situation offered people with intellectual disabilities lose–lose options. Failure to achieve the typical norms and values of society served as evidence of disability, whereas success was presented by eugenicists as deception and a threat. To note, because identification as feebleminded typically led to the denial of resources and privilege and few people voluntarily took this label, there was little fear of "fit" citizens passing as "feebleminded." However, some evidence indicates that reverse passing did occur on rare occasions. For example, in her study of sterilization practices in North Carolina (published in 1950), Moya Woodside mentions that some women sought a diagnosis of feeblemindedness to gain access to sterilization, a procedure that otherwise would have been too expensive for them.[26]

Hence, in the early twentieth century, eugenicists created sharply demarcated identity categories and encouraged the fear that the feebleminded would pass and spread an epidemic of mental degeneracy throughout the nation.[27] Passing was an act to be prevented, and the extensive systems of identification and segregation were encouraged. This sociopolitical context offered people the choices of passing or accepting a social position as non-citizens. However, so great were the negative consequences of receiving a label of feeblemindedness that the very push to prevent passing presumably created in many individuals so labeled, or potentially so labeled, the desire to hide their disability and pass.

Claiming Difference in the Pursuit of Passing

Unlike eugenicists who saw normality as an impossible goal for the feebleminded, parents and professionals in the 1950s worked to soften the boundaries between the categories of able and disabled, expand the rigid, narrow range of behavior and choices conceived as possible for those now labeled "mentally retarded" and to criticize unequal access to resources and services based on disability labels. Whereas eugenicists tended to portray "feebleminded" and "fit" as sharply bounded categories, parents in the middle of the century challenged these distinctions and created softer, more inclusive categories based on gradational or continuous differences. According to the emerging parents' movement, all children were similar in nature, but some children needed *more* attention and support than others. This theory gained professional credence with the "developmental approach," developed by the psychologist Edward Zigler, who proposed that retarded children proceeded through the same sequences of development as other children but required additional time and learning opportunities to do so.[28] Expressed politically in "A Bill of Rights for the Retarded", the National Association for Retarded Children (NARC) argued that children with mental retardation had "in general all the needs of other children," yet were "exceptional, not because they differ from us in having these needs, but because they have additional or exceptional needs over and above the needs common to the majority."[29] The new term "mental retardation" was intended to suggest slowed development rather than a different type of person. Thus, parents portrayed their children as children just like other children but with *additional* or *special* needs. Because disabled children were just like "normal" children in so many ways, disability no longer needed to be seen as a master status of singular importance that constrained all of their options. With support, disabled children could be children first and pursue the typical range of children's experiences, such as sports, school, friendships, and a fulfilling home and family life.

While on the one hand, parent activists sought to portray their children as "normal," on the other hand, they also demanded acknowledgment of and support for their differences. Typically, the recognition of normality and difference went hand in hand; parents fought for the recognition of difference to receive the services and support that would allow their children and families to function as expected and pass as typical. Put in terms of visibility and invisibility, parents and professionals sought to make disability visible ideally to make it invisible, or as invisible as possible.[30] The NARC argued, for instance, that community services would "enable [children with disabilities] to become acceptable members of their families and neighborhoods," strengthen the family unit, and allow families to thrive in their communities.[31] The recognition of difference to support the goal of normality was most commonly found in the way parents of this era justified a variety of services, especially education. In the fight for education, parents first established a similarity across children: all children could learn and had the right to education.[32] Then parents explained the different resources and strategies necessary to educate children based on their needs, such as adapted curriculum, teachers trained in special needs, and additional years of education. They then argued that through the accommodation and support of difference, education could foster mainstream American goals, such as socialization, self-sufficiency, and citizenship, in a way that was inclusive of people with disabilities and, it was hoped, erased the signs of disability.

Professionals, even more than parents, stressed the provision of services to foster normality and the achievement of mainstream American values and goals. Professionals, for example, claimed that special education could prepare thousands of mentally retarded children "to be responsible, contributing citizens and in no sense a burden to family or community."[33] Structuring services to replicate and produce normality became a philosophical cornerstone in the 1970s with the emergence of "normalization." Developed by scholars including Bengt Nirje and Wolf Wolfensberger, the principle of normalization advocated that services make "available to the mentally retarded patterns and conditions of everyday life, which are as close as possible to the norms and patterns of the mainstream society."[34] Normalized social services, according to this philosophy, would best enable people with mental retardation to become well-adjusted members of society.[35] Success therefore was clearly defined in terms of meeting the expectations of mainstream society by passing for or becoming "normal".

Disability, though, proved difficult to erase or hide. In *The Cloak of Competence* (1967), the sociologist Robert Edgerton found that recently deinstitutionalized adults with intellectual disabilities internalized the pressing desire to appear normal and considered passing among their highest priorities. According to Edgerton, these adults recognized that society put forth various markers of competence, such as employment and intimate relationships, and they strove to attain these markers and visibly display them as their "cloak of competence." Unfortunately, their attempts to pass were often thwarted by their lack of skills and resources, leading Edgerton to write, "The cloaks that they think protect them are in reality such tattered and transparent garments that they reveal their wearers in all their naked incompetence."[36] The systems that had so long marked them as disabled had long-lasting, embodied effects on their skills, appearance, behavior, and access to resources, while social supports located in the community continued to impose constrained disability identities on them.

Stigma and passing were concerns related not only to the individual with a disability; eugenic theories of heredity heaped disgrace on the entire family. Recalling her experiences in the 1940s, a sibling stated, "Eugenics was popular at the time. We weren't just a family, we were a family with a disability; it defined our history, it defined our story."[37] Parents vigorously sought to dispel the negative stereotypes of the family promoted by eugenics. For example, in an article in the *Saturday Evening Post,* Eunice Kennedy Shriver stated, "Mental retardation can happen in any family. It *has* happened in the families of the poor and the rich, of governors, senators, Nobel prizewinners, doctors, lawyers, writers, men of genius, presidents of corporations—the president of the United States."[38] Similarly, the Pulitzer Prize winner Pearl Buck wrote, "The old stigma of 'something in the family' is all too often unjust."[39] Both Shriver and Buck criticized the association between disability and social maladaptation and stressed the moral and genetic neutrality of disability. Disability could happen in any family, even socially valued ones; thus, the presence of disability could not serve to measure the genetic or social worth of a family.

As they dispelled theories of genetic taint, parents criticized long-standing professional theories that disability was both caused by and caused family dysfunction. Parents stressed that, like other families, they had strong, loving ties to one another that included their disabled child. One couple wrote about their relationship with their disabled son, "We enjoy everything about him. . . . It's as if because we love him so devotedly and so specially, and because we know we will not always have him with us, that we are somehow closer to our baby and he to us than is normally the case."[40] Another parent wrote, "I'd say we're as happy a family as there is in the Borough of Queens." This parent continued his discussion, saying that his disabled son had "drawn us all closer together," strengthening rather than weakening family ties.[41] Instead of marking one as a bad parent, parenting a child with a disability transformed one into the quintessential parent who offered endless selfless love and care. Through these writings parents presented themselves as meeting the standards of the good family. Moreover, they resisted the very idea that they needed to "pass" as good families and instead offered themselves as the model for which other parents should strive.

As the historian Katherine Castles found, the quest for normality had a double edge. While some families sought to integrate their disabled children into their home and community in typical ways and create inclusive ideal families, others saw institutionalization as the only feasible way to pass as a typical, functioning family, given the expectations of the day.[42] One parent explained that if the disabled child had been kept at home, "We should have to curtail normal family activities. . . . [W]e would have to devote the major part of our time to her, leaving her little brother to develop as best he could."[43] Parents felt tension particularly in their responsibility to care adequately for multiple children with competing needs and abilities: "It seemed we were being forced to make a choice for either the normal or the subnormal child. There wasn't much choice, stated that way, so we had this relative fill out the necessary papers for her application for admittance to the State School for the Retarded."[44] Thus, when parents felt that they could not pass as good families with their disabled children at home, institutionalization seemed to offer an alternative.

Rather than the fear of passing expressed by eugenicists, it seems that passing had become the goal. But had it really? Despite parents' and professionals' focus on normality, the goal of passing was systematically and purposefully undercut in the development of the service system, including the expansion of institutions and community-based services. Like eugenicists, parents and professionals in the mid-twentieth century deeply feared the negative consequences of passing on the part of people with disabilities. Whereas eugenicists stressed that attempts at passing would hasten the biological and moral degeneration of society, parents in the mid-twentieth century expressed more personal concerns. They worried that failed attempts to pass would harm their children and families. For example, although parents wanted their children to have access to an appropriate and accommodated education, they worried about the pressure, bullying, and social exclusion that might occur in integrated educational settings. One parent wrote, "We know that our handicapped child would be miserable if he had to compete, though it might be only on the playground, with normal children. He has the right to be among his own kind, where he need face no unfair competition."[45] Another parent expressed similar fears of exclusion and resolved them through institutionalization: "At the school [the institution], he is just as good as the next fellow, and considerably better than some! It is not a case of sitting on the sidelines, as he did at home, watching the others do things he could not enter into, and consequently becoming more and more passive."[46] Professionals also worried about the failure of passing, particularly as it might lead to lower success rates for their services, increased liability, and community backlash if people with disabilities who lived in the community lacked supervision and got into trouble. To minimize the negative effects of failure, professionals developed the "continuum of services" through which people earned (potentially, at least, albeit rarely) placement in the community by first succeeding in supervised programs.[47] Sheltered workshops, for example, would serve as a training ground for work in the community.[48] Ultimately, parents and professionals in this time period typically wanted to see people strive to fulfill their potential but lacked confidence that most people with mental retardation could meet the American norms of a self-sufficient, independent, sexually responsible citizen.

Rather than integration, parents and professionals sought to protect people with disabilities, families, professional services, and communities from the negative ramifications of the failure to pass. They designed a paternalistic service system in which "normalization" occurred in protected, safe spheres, ultimately making passing for "normal" impossible. The categories that parents had worked to soften became hardened again as they were institutionalized within a service system, bounded by IQ, rigid in their assumptions about the appropriate lives of people with retardation, and constrained in the choices offered to them. For example, children were to be given education, but their disability label would determine their school, program, and even transportation (e.g., the infamous "yellow bus"). In institutions, group homes, sheltered workshops, and special educational programs, disability was always at the forefront of interactions and identity politics, making disability a master status that also determined one's peers, access to leisure, access to worship, and all of the activities of daily living. Through the extensive system of services (some of which actually served and some of which did not), disability became *more* visible than it had been. More children were identified as disabled and channeled into often segregated services. The channeling of people with intellectual disabilities into segregated and inferior educational, work, and housing options perpetuated their inequality by limiting their access to freedom, rights, and resources. Thus, individuals diagnosed with mental retardation were expected to want and try to pass, yet they were typically offered false approximations for normality—segregated group homes rather than participation in the community, sheltered workshops rather than competitive work experiences—so that their attempts were systematically undermined by separate and protected spheres that largely assumed their failure and were designed instead to protect them, their families, the service providers, and society from such a failure to pass.

Thus, in the 1950s, parents and professionals worked to soften the boundaries between the categories of able and disabled, expand the range of behavior and choices possible for those now labeled "mentally retarded," and criticize the unequal access to resources and services based on disability labels. They made disability visible in the hope that attention to difference could eventually erase such differences and support their children in passing or even in becoming "normal." Passing seemed to become the goal, but fears associated with the possible negative consequences of passing led parents and professionals to create a paternalistic system that they claimed approximated normality yet actually subverted it.

Disability Pride, Person First Pride, and Challenges to the Act of and the Concept of Passing

The emergence of the disability rights movement in the 1970s and the self-advocacy movement in the 1990s provided a framework, culture, and community that encouraged the development of a positive disability identity and, correspondingly, a resistance to the expectation that one must strive to "pass" to feel valued. Carol Gill's theory regarding disability identity suggests that a sense of belonging in the disability community, among other things, may lead to "coming out"—or, in other words, comfort and pride in expressing one's self and disability, regardless of environment.[49] According to the historian Paul Longmore, a positive disability identity is important not merely for one's psychological well-being but also for social justice. The pursuit of normality serves the interests of the nondisabled; therefore, disability rights activists must resist the "ever-elusive carrot of social acceptance" and instead articulate a collective process of self-definition rooted in disability values.[50] In doing so, activists heighten the visibility of disability not to demean it, but to show the value of disability and of people who have disabilities.

In creating valued identities, activists have fought to blur the boundaries between able and disabled. First, disability rights communities challenged the historically dominant constructions of disability that presumed boundedness, rigidity, singularity, and staticity and instead offered positive depictions of disability that allowed for fluidity and stressed the multidimensionality of people with disabilities. They have argued that people with disabilities can be disabled *and* beautiful, powerful, sexual, and politically active. The very act of self-advocacy positioned people with intellectual disabilities in a role that had previously been denied to them because of their presumed incompetence. Moreover, activists debunked the "myth" of the able-bodied, rational, autonomous citizen. All people, according to disability activists, experience interdependence and require support. People could simultaneously experience being caregiver and care receiver, expert and learner, and worker and dependent. Rather than occupying one pole in a mutually exclusive construct, individuals were better able to move nimbly across identity categories, incorporating multiple intersecting identities into their self-presentation rather than adhering to or resisting constraining categories. Blurring these boundaries does more than simply make passing less attractive; to the extent that one can be simultaneously disabled and able, the meaning of passing is obscured and the necessity for it is diminished.

Given the recent emphasis on disability pride and self-acceptance rooted in these movements, it is perhaps not surprising that self-advocates with intellectual disabilities list as some of the most valuable aspects of the movement the opportunities to challenge the constraints of traditional disability identities and instead build positive identities rooted in disability that offer them flexibility, pride, and empowerment. In particular, self-advocates express that they have learned not to be ashamed of asking for assistance or pursuing their particular needs and interests; they no longer have to hide their disability. According to the self-advocate Marvin Moss, self-advocacy is about "speaking up for myself and asking for help if I need it."[51] The self-advocate Linda Kunick explains that, because speaking up for oneself gives one power, it also creates a sense of pride: "because I have power now, and if we have power over our life and what we want to do, we will feel good."[52] Liz Obermayer specifically challenges the traditional rigidity of disability identity when she demands to have choices in life, saying, "If people with disabilities can live with everyone else, then why can't I make choices like anyone else?"[53] Certainly, these presentations of self offer a more flexible and positive interpretation of disability than the constructions typical in earlier eras. Disability activists have fought to make disability visible not to demean it or erase it, but to find value in it.

Power is a key factor in the shifting sociopolitical context. In addition to fostering visible, flexible, and positive disability identities, disability rights activists have secured an impressive array of legislative victories designed to dismantle the long history of stratification and discrimination tied to disability identification while encouraging the growth of advantages tied to disability identification. These political and legal advances fundamentally alter the calculus regarding whether to claim a disability identity. People with disabilities now have some protection from discrimination and may even gain advantages based on their identity. Once the disadvantages of an identity are lessened and advantages connected to the same identity are created, the reasons to try to hide one's disability and pass as "normal" potentially become nonexistent.

The disability rights community became an attractive community that welcomed people with disabilities and encouraged disability pride and empowerment. In fact, access to this community was at times tied to one's willingness to actively display a positive disability identity. For example, in their discussion of the rise of activism among people with autism, Joyce Davidson and Victoria Henderson argue that creating a positive public image and treatment of people with disabilities requires that activists purposefully self-identify as disabled and express disability pride.[54] This self-identification demands respect from the public and offers a community by which others with disabilities can come to appreciate their differences and identify with disability pride. Disability communities may therefore enforce sanctions against those who try to pass, accusing them of the pursuit of individual advantage at the expense of the broader community. Therefore, the rise of disability communities increases the advantages associated with a disability identity and stigmatizes the decision to pass as conforming to hegemonic ableism, thereby creating a very different calculus for decisions regarding passing.

Although disability pride and self-definition have become more readily available options, concerns about passing have not simply disappeared. Instead, concerns about passing transform with the rise of the disability rights movement. First, the emphasis on disability pride has in some ways contradicted the project of categorical blurring because it potentially reifies the boundaries between able and disabled and thereby perpetuates the relevance of passing. Once we tie the exhibition of disability pride to the formation of a positive disability identity, the decision to obscure, hide, or de-prioritize one's disability can correspondingly be viewed as an indication of shame, a malformed identity, and, worse yet, an act of betrayal against one's community. Of those who minimize or hide their disability to be accepted in the community, the self-advocate Chester Finn states, "We can do more damage to ourselves when we deny who we are and deny fighting for what we want. When we do that, it's almost like giving up, and say[ing], 'Yes, cuff our hands, tie our feet, drag us back, throw us in the institutions.' . . . So we've got to work with the young people."[55] Now, in addition to those privileged by their able-bodied status fearing passing by people with disabilities, activists with disabilities also come to fear and reject passing as a threat to their collective power and identity and potentially interpret behavior or attitudes that seems to fit within the mainstream as harmful acts of passing. While this stance makes political sense, it is problematic for the ultimate liberation of people with disabilities. The notion of disability pride assumes a priori the relevance and importance of disability for identity, and for this reason, it potentially loses its ability to accommodate the complexity, intersectionality, and fluidity of identity and behavior. Disability may not be relevant to every interaction or may not form a key part of every disabled person's identity; however, the mandate of disability pride imposes disability identity and defines as failure any interaction without evidence of disability identification. Hence, the acceptable range of attitudes, behavior, and identities is narrowed once again for people with disabilities.

Second, many of these hard-won rights and accommodations are tied to disability identification, and these, too, may harden the boundaries of able and disabled at the same time that they seek to dismantle stratification. For example, one must typically prove one's disability to gain access to the rights provided under the Americans with Disabilities Act and the Individuals with Disabilities Education Act.[56] In *Littleton v. Wal-Mart* (2005), an Alabama court decided that Charles Littleton, a young man labeled mentally retarded by both the school district and the Social Security Administration, was insufficiently disabled to qualify for job accommodations through the ADA. The court used Littleton's successful adaptation and his own pride regarding his skills and abilities against him to disqualify him from claiming a disability identity and corresponding ADA rights.[57] In his appeal two years later, Littleton was then forced to highlight his incapacities and publicly display his disability (defined by the court as incapacities) in his efforts to secure job accommodations.[58] Rather than making disability identification irrelevant or fluid, the courts' handling of rights legislation has retained the relevance of a disability identity and heightened the difficult decision regarding passing for individuals with disabilities. Because the disabled and the able are enmeshed in the law as categorically distinct beings, indications of ability can be used to disqualify people from the rights provided to the disabled, while indications of disability can be used to disqualify people from typical civil rights.[59]

Third, as disability increasingly has been connected to some privileges, concerns about identity gatekeeping have also increased and inverted; in addition to concerns about the disabled passing as able, we increasingly see concerns that the able are passing as disabled. For example, recent news stories accuse wealthy students and their families of obtaining "questionable diagnosis of learning disabilities to secure extra time to take the SATs," and websites such as BustaThief.com contain pages of entries in which individuals accuse their neighbors and colleagues of fraudulent receipt of disability benefits.[60] Accusations of passing are also commonly hurled against self-advocates. Because many people assume away the ability of people with developmental disabilities to advocate for themselves, successful self-advocates face challenges regarding whether they "really" have developmental disabilities and therefore whether they can legitimately speak for this population and its interests. These challenges hark back to Doll and other professionals who argued that success was an indication of misdiagnosis or deception, so that successful self-advocacy must reveal the misapplication of a label or fraud.

To add to the complexity, although claiming a disability identity is becoming more advantageous in some ways, stigma and discrimination based on disability continues to exist, and the choice to identify as disabled still increases one's vulnerability to oppression. Children with disabilities are still the butt of jokes and are bullied and abused at school. Employers are still hesitant to hire people with obvious disabilities. The paternalistic systems developed in the 1960s, '70s, and '80s still exist, and they continue to thrive on disability identification. Thus, people with disabilities are in a Catch-22 position. If they identify as disabled, they may gain the advantages of the identity, such as belonging to a disability culture and gaining access to accommodations, but they also expose themselves to the stigma, segregation, and discrimination that still widely exists. This tension may be particularly challenging for people with intellectual disabilities. The self-advocate Tia Nelis says, "I think it is really hard for people who have a label of developmental disabilities to . . . stand up and say, 'I am retarded and I am proud' because of all the [bad] stuff that goes on with it. Society labels us something different. And the stuff you have gone through, put in institutions, kids not liking you, hit, called names, spit at, beat up because of a label."[61] Thus, despite the rise of disability pride, there are still many reasons to hide or try to discard the label of retardation.

In fact, given the persistent onslaught of stigma and discrimination, acting in typical ways might actually be a form of resistance rather than conformity. For example, when a person with an intellectual disability seeks to perform well in an integrated class, she or he may be challenging the dominant stereotypes that assume his or her academic inferiority rather than (or simultaneously) conforming. As another example, as self-advocates engage in activism, they often do so in extremely typical ways: they hold meetings in conference rooms, proudly use Robert's Rules of Order, take minutes, and vote. Is this "passing" an act of conformity or an act of resistance against the stereotypes that deny them political and organizational agency?

Perhaps more pressing, is "passing" still a relevant conceptualization? Once we question the dichotomy of disabled and able, the notion of passing and the imposed responses of conformity or resistance become a potentially oppressive framework for analysis. All individuals create identities in response to the relational environment in which we are socialized, simultaneously conforming to and resisting various expectations; yet those in privileged statuses are not subject to the constant questioning of their behavior as acts of passing or resisting. While the psychological drive to hide part of one's identity is problematic, the accusation of passing when engaging in typical behavior is also damaging, as can be the alternative positioning of resistance. Either way, the behavior of people with disabilities is analyzed as if those people necessarily and uniquely exist outside the system and respond to an external and coercive system with the only options of passing or resisting (or passing as resisting). Their potential insider status is denied, as is their agency to express themselves in ways that exist in complex interaction with social norms and feel not like passing nor resisting but like just being.

One of the most important tenets of the self-advocacy movement is to respect people as people first—not necessarily as disabled people, not necessarily in any predetermined fashion, but as self-defined beings with a full range of interests, motivations, and needs. Self-advocates recognize that building a positive disability identity is crucial to the task of helping people define and pursue their goals; however, gaining a sense of comfort with one's disability is different from embracing a category or label, and the self-advocacy movement has worked strenuously to resist the labels, which, they argue, are themselves a form of discrimination. Several key initiatives in the self-advocacy movement have focused on the issue of respecting the person while discarding negative labels, including use of the slogan "Label Jars, Not People"; the person-first language campaign and the use of the associated name "People First" for self-advocacy groups; and the movement to end the use of the "r-word."[62] Self-advocates teach that one should never be ashamed of one's disability, but that does not mean that disability is a priori *the* defining part of one's identity. One might be an artist, a soccer fan, a great sister, and a person who needs support in particular tasks.

These acts of resistance are not primarily about establishing disability pride or passing. They seek to establish the right to be respected as complete people who need neither to display their disability, if that is undesirable or unnecessary, nor to hide it. Nelis explains, "I think one of the things that the self-advocacy movement does is to be accepted for who you are. It doesn't look into disability. It looks at the person.

You are not called 'consumer' and you are not called 'client.' You are called by your name." She continues to say that people may not be "proud" to be labeled "retarded" but, instead, may root their pride in their accomplishments.[63] The self-advocacy movement therefore strives to allow for a gradational, fluid, flexible understanding of identity. Success is not necessarily measured by the creation and display of a disability identity (and thereby resistance to passing) or proving that one is able (passing). Ideally, self-advocacy supports people in exploring and developing who they are, what they want, and how to obtain it—in other words, pursuing individual interests, perhaps with a broader sense of collective well-being and social justice.

Conclusion

The understanding and relevance of "passing," as well as the desire and ability to "pass," is structured by the sociopolitical environment and shifts through time. In the early twentieth century, eugenicists feared passing and attempted to prevent it by establishing extensive systems of identification and segregation. Unlike eugenicists who saw normality as an impossible achievement for the feebleminded, parents in the 1950s and '60s strove for "normality" while subverting it through paternalistic policies. Today, we claim to value human diversity but simultaneously tie disability identification to accommodations, services, and even rights, thereby again limiting the identities to which people with disabilities have access. In general, throughout the past century the creation of sharp boundaries between the able and disabled, rigid expectations regarding the behavior and abilities of the disabled, static views that deny development and the dynamic nature of disability, and intense inequality all served to heighten the relevance of passing. However, gradational, fluid, dynamic, and equal constructions of identity lessened the incentives to pass, as well as the meaning of passing. While at a micro level, Gill claims a positive culmination of identity development to be a self that feels no need to pass, perhaps at a macro level, a positive culmination of social justice movements would be a society that resists sharp demarcations of identity and related resources and instead meets the individualized needs of its people without imposing bounded identities on them, thereby removing the structural constraints that shape individuals' choices regarding, and understandings of, passing.

Notes

1. See, e.g., Edwin R. Black, *War against the Weak: Eugenics and America's Campaign to Create a Master Race* (New York: Four Walls Eight Windows, 2003); Daniel J. Kevles, *In the Name of Eugenics: Genetics and the Uses of Human Heredity* (New York: Alfred A. Knopf, 1985); Diane Paul, *Controlling Human Heredity* (Atlantic Highlands, N.J.: Humanities Press International, 1995); James W. Trent Jr. *Inventing the Feeble Mind: A History of Mental Retardation in the United States* (Berkeley: University of California Press, 1994).

2. Thomas C. Leonard, "Protecting Family and Face: The Progressive Case for Regulating Women's Work," *American Journal of Economics and Sociology* 64, no. 3 (2005): 1–35.

3. For a discussion of eugenics and immigration, see Douglas C. Baynton, "Disability and the Justification of Inequality in American History," in *The New Disability History: American Perspectives,* ed. Paul K. Longmore and Lauri Umansky (New York: New York University Press, 2001), 35–57. For a discussion of eugenics and miscegenation, see Lisa Lindquist Dorr, "Arm in Arm: Gender, Eugenics, and Virginia's Racial Integrity Acts of the 1920's," *Journal of Women's History* 11, no. 1 (1999): 143–166. For a discussion of eugenics and the valorization of traditional gender roles, see Wendy Kline, *Building a Better Race: Gender, Sexuality, and Eugenics from the Turn of the Century to the Baby Boom* (Berkeley: University of California Press, 2001).

4. Nicole H. Rafter, *White Trash: The Eugenic Family Studies, 1877–1919* (Boston: Northeastern University Press, 1988).

5. Phillip R. Reilly, *The Surgical Solution: History of Involuntary Sterilization in the United States* (Baltimore: Johns Hopkins University Press, 1991); Trent, *Inventing the Feeble Mind,* 166–183.

6. Licia Carlson, "Docile Bodies, Docile Minds: Foucauldian Reflections on Mental Retardation," in *Foucault and the Government of Disability,* ed. Shelley Tremain (Ann Arbor: University of Michigan Press, 2005), 133–152. In this work, Carlson discusses the notion of sharply bounded versus gradational differences in terms of qualitative versus quantitative constructions, so that qualitative constructions assume a different kind of person and quantitative constructions assume a continuum of humanity.

7. In describing the "feebleminded," Joseph Byers uses the terms "burden" and "social evil"; Henry Wellington Wack uses "burden"; Seth Humphrey uses "dead load" and "menace"; Alexander Johnson uses "a danger"; and Martin Barr uses "a menace": Joseph P. Byers, "A State Plan for the Care of the Feeble-Minded," *Proceedings of the National Conference of Charities and Corrections* (1916): 223–239; Henry Wellington Wack, "Rational Eugenics," *Lawyer and Banker* 6, no. 1 (1913): 143–150; Seth K. Humphrey, "Parenthood and the Social Conscience," *Forum* 49 (1913): 457–464; Alexander Johnson, "The Case of the Nation versus the Feebleminded," *Survey* 34, no. 6 (1915): 136–137; Martin W.

Barr, "The Prevention of Mental Defect: The Duty of the Hour," *Proceedings of the National Conference of Charities and Corrections* (1915): 361–367.

8. Gerald O'Brien, "War and the Eugenic Control of Persons with Disabilities: Metaphor, Rationalization and Point of Contrast," paper presented at the Annual Meeting of the Society for Disability Studies, Washington, D.C., 2006; Wendell Oliver Holmes, "Opinion of the Court." *Buck v. Bell* 274 U.S. 200, 1927. O'Brien examines the use of war metaphors in discussions of feeblemindedness, while Holmes offers a primary source comparing the feebleminded to a biological epidemic.

9. Johnson, "The Case of the Nation versus the Feebleminded," 137.

10. Charles B. Davenport, *Heredity, in Relation to Eugenics* (New York: Henry Holt, 1913); Walter E. Fernald, "State Care of the Insane, Feeble-minded, and Epileptic," *Proceedings of the National Conference of Charities and Corrections* (1915): 289–297.

11. Henry H. Goddard, *The Kallikak Family: A Study in the Heredity of Feeblemindedness* (New York: Macmillan, 1912), 71.

12. Elaine K. Ginsberg, "Introduction: The Politics of Passing," in *Passing and the Fictions of Identity,* ed. Elaine K. Ginsberg (Durham, N.C.: Duke University Press, 1996), 1–18.

13. Edgar A. Doll, "What Is a Moron?" *Journal of Abnormal and Social Psychology* 43, no. 4 (1948): 495–501; Joseph Jastak, "A Rigorous Criterion of Feeblemindedness," *Journal of Abnormal and Social Psychology* 44, no. 3 (1949): 367–378.

14. Fiona Kumari Campbell, "Legislating Disability: Narrative Ontologies and the Government of Legal Identities," in Tremain, *Foucault and the Government of Disability,* 108–130.

15. Allison C. Carey, *On the Margins of Citizenship: Intellectual Disability and Civil Rights* (Philadelphia: Temple University Press, 2009).

16. Burton Blatt and Fred Kaplan, *Christmas in Purgatory: A Photographic Essay on Mental Retardation* (Syracuse, N.Y.: Human Policy Press, 1974); Philip M. Ferguson, *Abandoned to Their Fate: Social Policy and Practice toward Severely Disabled People in America, 1820–1920* (Philadelphia: Temple University Press, 1994); Erving Goffman, *Asylums* (New York: Anchor Books, 1961).

17. Ginsberg, "Introduction"; Julia Stern, "Spanish Masquerade and the Drama of Racial Identity in Uncle Tom's Cabin," in Ginsberg, *Passing and the Fictions of Identity,* 103–130.

18. Humphrey, "Parenthood and the Social Conscience," 461.

19. George S. Bliss, "The Danger of Classifying Merely Backward Children Who Are Feeble-minded," *Proceedings of the National Conference of Charities and Corrections* (1916), 263–266; Fernald, "State Care of the Insane," 289–297.

20. Bliss, "The Danger of Classifying Merely Backward Children," 263.

21. Carlson, "Docile Bodies," 133–152.

22. Barr, "The Prevention of Mental Defect," 364.

23. JoAnne Brown, *The Definition of a Profession: The Authority of Metaphor in the History of Intelligence Testing, 1890–1930* (Princeton, N.J.: Princeton University Press, 1992).

24. F. V. Willhite, "Program for the Social Control of the Mentally Deficient," *American Association of Mental Deficiency* 42 (1937): 95–100.

25. Despite the dramatic changes they proposed to the understanding of intellectual disability, eugenicists faced little challenge regarding their construction of feeblemindedness. While some groups challenged eugenic policies such as compulsory sterilization, they tended to be philosophically, politically, or religiously opposed to state intervention in reproduction and bodily integrity rather than supporters of a positive disability identity and disability rights. Neither parents nor people with disabilities had yet developed political movements capable of challenging the dominance of medical discourse.

26. Moya Woodside, *Sterilization in North Carolina* (Chapel Hill: University of North Carolina Press, 1950).

27. To add to the complexity, although the dominant eugenic narrative presented the identity categories as bounded, rigid, and static and warned of passing, this was not the only construction they offered. Sometimes, for some purposes, eugenicists offered far more flexible and dynamic versions. For example, B. W. Baker explained, "Sometimes those persons who we think should succeed fail. Those whose failure we have reason to expect sometimes surprise us by success": B. W. Baker, "Parole and Sterilization," *Training School Bulletin* 35 (1929): 177–179, 185. Similarly, George Skinner showed that 35 percent of inmates in Kentucky "could be safely released in good times, and could make their own way": George T. Skinner, "A Sterilization Statute for Kentucky?" *Kentucky Law Journal* 23, no. 1 (1934): 174. These more positive, dynamic constructions were typically developed not to create a positive disability identity but (like the rigid and static constructions) to serve the interests of professionals. Professionals used flexible constructions of identity particularly when they were interested in promoting parole and the expansion of community services. Nothing "natural" or even scientific supported these identity constructions; they were rooted in the interests of professionals and created the context for decisions regarding passing. See James W. Trent Jr., "To Cut and Control: Institutional Preservation and the Sterilization of Mentally Retarded People in the United States, 1892–1947," *Journal of Historical Sociology* 6 (1993): 56–73.

28. Edward Zigler. "Developmental versus Difference Theories of Mental Retardation and the Problem of Motivation," *American Journal of Mental Deficiency* 73 (1969): 536–556.

29. Richard H. Hungerford, "A Bill of Rights for the Retarded" (1952), reprinted in *American Journal of Mental Deficiency* 63 (April 1959): 937.

30. For arguments that disability policy has often sought to provide supports insofar as disability could then be erased, see Marta Russell, *Beyond Ramps: Disability at the End of the Social Contract* (Monroe, Me.: Common Courage

Press, 2002); Henri-Jacques Striker, *A History of Disability* (Ann Arbor: University of Michigan Press, 2000).

31. Education Committee of the National Association for Retarded Children, "Day Classes for Severely Retarded Children: A Report of the Education Committee of the National Association for Retarded Children," *American Journal of Mental Deficiency* 59, no. 1 (1954): 357.

32. For examples, see Norma L. Bostock, "The Parent Outlook," *American Journal of Mental Deficiency* 63 (January, 1959): 511–516; Steven M. Spencer, "Retarded Children Can Be Helped," *Saturday Evening Post,* vol. 225, no. 5, 1952, 25–26, 107–108, 110–111.

33. Kenneth Robb, "Planning for the Feebleminded," *Today's Health,* vol. 35, 1952, 55.

34. Bengt Nirje, "The Normalization Principle and Its Human Management Implications," in *Changing Patterns in Residential Services for the Mentally Retarded,* ed. Robert B. Kugel and Wolf Wolfensberger (Washington, D.C.: President's Committee on Mental Retardation, 1969), 181.

35. To deal with the argument that normalization imposed mainstream expectations on people with disabilities and therefore served to legitimate an oppressive system, Wolfensberger later developed the theory of "social role valorization" to analyze why particular people are devalued, the effects of devaluation, and how social services can support people in gaining the roles that are of value to them: Wolf Wolfensberger, "Social Role Valorization: A Proposed New Term for the Principle of Normalization," *Mental Retardation* 21, no. 6 (1983): 234–239.

36. Robert B. Edgerton, *The Cloak of Competence: Stigma in the Lives of the Mentally Retarded* (Berkeley: University of California Press, 1967), 217–218.

37. Susan Schwartzenberg, *Becoming Citizens: Family Life and the Politics of Disability* (Seattle: University of Washington Press, 2005), 8.

38. Eunice Kennedy Shriver, "Hope for Retarded Children," *Saturday Evening Post,* vol. 235, 1962, 72.

39. Pearl S. Buck, *The Child Who Never Grew* (1950), repr. ed. (Bethesda, Md.: Woodbine House, 1992), 48.

40. "Not Like Other Children," *Parents Magazine,* vol. 18, October 1943, 99.

41. Frank Piccola, "We Kept Our Retarded Child at Home," *Coronet,* vol. 39, November 1955, 49–50.

42. Katherine Castles, "'Nice, Average Americans': Postwar Parents, Groups and the Defense of the Normal Family," in *Mental Retardation in America,* ed. Steven Noll and James W. Trent Jr. (New York: New York University Press, 2004), 351–370.

43. "We Committed Our Child," *Rotarian,* vol. 67, August 1945, 20.

44. Lucille Stout, *I Reclaimed My Child* (Philadelphia: Chilton, 1959), 10.

45. "Not Like Other Children," 100.

46. "School for a Different Child," *Parents Magazine,* vol. 16, March 1941, 81.

47. Steven J. Taylor, "Caught in the Continuum: A Critical Analysis of the Principle of the Least Restrictive Environment," *Journal of the Association for the Severely Handicapped* 13, no. 1 (1988): 41–53.

48. Max Dubrow, "Sheltered Workshops for the Mentally Retarded as an Educational and Vocational Experience," *Personnel and Guidance Journal* 38, no. 5 (1960): 392–395.

49. Carol J. Gill, "Four Types of Integration in Disability Identity Development," *Journal of Vocational Rehabilitation* 9 (1997): 39–46.

50. Paul K. Longmore, "The Second Phase: From Disability Rights to Disability Culture," in *Why I Burned My Book and Other Essays on Disability*, ed. Paul K. Longmore (Philadelphia: Temple University Press, 2003), 221.

51. Marvin Moss, "Oral History," in *Leaders with Developmental Disabilities in the Self-Advocacy Movement*, Regional Oral History Office, Bancroft Library, University of California, Berkeley, 2007, available online at http://bancroft .berkeley.edu/ROHO, 16.

52. Linda Kunick, "Oral History," in ibid., 19.

53. Liz Obermayer, "Choices," in *"Community for All" Tool Kit: Resources for Supporting Community Living* (Syracuse, N.Y.: Human Policy Press, 2004).

54. Joyce Davidson and Victoria Henderson, "Coming Out on the Spectrum: Autism, Identity, and Disclosure," *Social and Cultural Geography* 11, no. 2 (2010): 155–170.

55. Chester Finn, "Oral History," in *Leaders with Developmental Disabilities in the Self-Advocacy Movement*, 59.

56. Leslie Pickering Francis and Anita Silvers, eds., *Americans with Disabilities: Exploring the Implications of Rights for Individuals and Institutions* (New York: Routledge, 2000); Ruth O'Brien, ed., *Voices from the Edge: Narratives about the Americans with Disabilities Act* (New York: Oxford University Press, 2004).

57. *Charles Irvin Littleton Jr. v. Wal-Mart Stores, Inc.,* U.S. District Court for Northern District of Alabama (April 12, 2005), available online at http://www .ca11.uscourts.gov/unpub/ops/200512770.pdf (accessed May 10, 2009).

58. *Charles Irvin Littleton Jr. v. Wal-Mart Stores, Inc.,* Appeal, U.S. District Court of Alabama (May 11, 2007), available online at http://www.ca11.uscourts .gov/unpub/ops/200512770.pdf (accessed May 10, 2009).

59. Allison C. Carey, "Beyond the Medical Model: A Reconsideration of 'Feeblemindedness' and Eugenic Restrictions," *Disability and Society* 18, no. 4 (2003): 411–430; Francis and Silvers, *Americans with Disabilities*; O'Brien, *Voices from the Edge*.

60. Jake Tapper, Dan Morris, and Lara Setrakian, "Does Loophole Give Rich Kids More Time on SAT?" *Nightline,* March 30, 2006, available online at http://abcnews.go.com/Nightline/story?id=1787712&page=1 (accessed July 20, 2010); "Disability Fraud–Disability Scam," available online at http://www.Busta Thief.com/disability-fraud-disability-scam (accessed July 20, 2010).

61. Tia Nelis, "Oral History," in *Leaders with Developmental Disabilities in the Self-Advocacy Movement,* 25–26.

62. David Finnegan, "Label Jars, Not People," no. 25, Action Research Centre for Inclusion, Bolton Institute of Higher Learning, Bolton, U.K., 1995.

63. Nelis, "Oral History," 27.

Growing Up to Become Hearing
*Dreams of Passing
in Oral Deaf Education*

KRISTEN C. HARMON

*"Now she is deaf, and it doesn't seem real; it doesn't seem like
these results are accurate. I just sat there kind of numb and,
OK, now I know that my child can't hear me, can't hear
anything, what do I do? I really didn't react at that point
because I just felt that I needed to get as much information
as possible and then I went home and cried my brains out."*
   *Segue to dreamy black and white shot of a breezy meadow,
with tall grass swaying in the sun.*
                    —Parent of a deaf toddler, in Oberkotter Foundation,
                              Dreams Spoken Here (1998)

SOME YEARS AGO, my mother and I were talking about what it
meant for us that I had been educated and raised in the "pure oral
method."[1] At that time, I was in graduate school at a large Mid-
western university and supporting myself through a teaching fellow-
ship. Even when my students—all hearing, all polite—sat in a circle and
raised their hands when they wanted to talk, I guessed at what they
said and stammered my way through the lesson. When they frowned
as though they could not quite trust that I knew what I was doing,
I knew I had to stop faking it. They knew I did not "hear well," but to
confess to *deafness* rather than *hearing impairment* is to enter a completely different cultural conversation.[2]

This work was partially supported by National Science Foundation grant SBE-1041725.

I consulted with my graduate teaching mentor about how to handle disclosures of "serious" disability, of vulnerability, in the hearing classroom. We discussed the intricacies of the situation and strategized for possible reactions and scenarios. Barely out of school myself, I had reached the end of what was possible with just my hearing aid, my careful speaking and lip-reading abilities, and nothing else. Standing at the chalkboard instead of sitting in a seat at the front of the classroom, I had ended up at the end of the road of almost passing for hearing.

Before then, I had been an "oral deaf education success story," occasionally written up in school and city newspapers when there was a lull in the news. Like many other "oral deaf" adults, I depended on one-on-one interactions or carefully controlled small groups for my carefully fenced-in successes. I had parlayed this laborious work—in reading context clues, drawing on a large vocabulary, using prior knowledge and prediction skills, the management of visual and auditory information, careful memorization of my voice's location in chest and nose, and expert co-dependence on technological devices—into a carefully polished series of achievements. But I was tired and had weirdly real dreams of coasting to a stop in a car that had run out of gas. This "success" also came with constant pressure to "pass" as hearing and to act "as if" hearing, and doing so comes with a social, emotional, psychological, even spiritual price to pay. I knew that I did a pretty good job of conveying myself through my voice, but I had become frustrated by the linearity of this communication. You understood me, but what were *you* saying?

"You make funny squeaky noises when you yawn," my sister said.
"You're talking through your nose," my speech therapist said.
"Simply don't tell them you're deaf," my career counselor said.
"Pretend like you're singing the songs in church," my grandmother said.
"What country are you from?" German tourists asked.
"You look like you don't really know what's going on, but you're being nice about it," a fellow graduate student said.

If the goal of passing is "to be seen as unmarked in one's class, racial, sexual, or religious identity,"[3] then deafness becomes the marked and stigmatized identity, one that must be elided, denied, and suppressed. As much is possible, *hearingness* is the goal. As a Public Law

94-142 "first-generation" student, I had been told that sign language, such a clearly visible symbol of social stigma,[4] was an option only for the "oral failures." So we persevered, my family and I, along a path that from was bound to wash out sooner or later.

"I know it sounds so silly now," my mother—the young and brave champion of my early education—said, "but you did so well that I think, on some level, we all thought you would grow up to become hearing." We sat back in our chairs, stunned by our mutual complicity in this dead-end story. Soon after, I began coming out as a deaf person by taking American Sign Language (ASL) classes, going to a local deaf club, and later, becoming a faculty member at a deaf university. Like many others in this situation, I became *visibly* deaf and, in the process, stopped living a shadow life.

This notion of a deaf child who effectively grows up to become hearing is a compelling cultural fantasy, one that appears in the subtext of much of the discourse surrounding educational approaches for deaf children. For one, the continuing development of ever smaller and more powerful hearing devices (surgical and non-surgical) means that these are held out as the promise of an eternally deferred, *just about hearing without actually being hearing*, future.

The other aspects of this construction of the deaf child with a presumed hearing and speaking future are discursive, performative, and linguistic in nature. The ideological constructions that make this strangely recuperative and endlessly rehearsed future possible depend on successful "passing" and the convincing presentation of an identity that is also tied up with discourses of socioeconomic class and American identity, not only for the deaf child but also for the family as a whole. Even the metaphors we use to describe deafness are dismayingly embedded within already conceived notions of ability and humanity. To be deaf is to be "stone deaf," to turn a deaf ear, to have information fall on deaf ears, to be deaf and dumb.

Little wonder, then, that hearing parents interviewed in expository documentaries on deaf education—such as the *Dreams Spoken Here* and *Dreams Made Real* series that the Oberkotter Foundation produces— express such sentiments as this one: "And it's awful. You realize that she is completely deaf, and still it gets you. . . . You *don't know what you can expect*."[5] In response, the reassuring and authoritative voice narrating the two *Dreams Spoken Here* films says, "Every parent has dreams for their child, *dreams of what they might do, dreams of who they might become*. For many parents who are told that their child is deaf, suddenly, in a single moment, their *visions are shattered*. But for parents who want their child to speak and listen *there is hope. . . . Dreams Spoken Here . . .* a documentary about teaching deaf children to speak and listen."[6] The Oberkotter Foundation is one of several major organizations that disseminates material on what is known as auditory-verbal therapy (AVT). Auditory-verbal therapy facilitates the

> optimal acquisition of spoken language through listening by newborns, infants, toddlers, and young children who are deaf or hard of hearing. Auditory-Verbal therapy promotes early diagnosis, one-on-one therapy, and state-of-the-art audiologic management and technology. Parents and caregivers actively participate in therapy. Through guidance, coaching, and demonstration, parents become the primary facilitators of their child's spoken language development. Ultimately, parents and caregivers gain confidence that their child can have access to a full range of academic, social, and occupational choices throughout life.[7]

This philosophy is consistent with the history of oral deaf education in America, which owed much to the efforts of those who worked to find "the most effective ways to help these children acquire the skills necessary to succeed in a world where listening and spoken language are the norm."[8] However, even the house journal for the Alexander Graham Bell organization, the *Volta Review,* noted in a review of the literature that "few empirical studies have evaluated the communication and academic outcomes of children who have participated in this [AVT] approach. . . . Furthermore, studies examining the social functioning, self-perception, and personal adjustment of children participating in AVT are virtually non-existent."[9]

Most parents are likely to have had little to no experience with deaf people, so to receive the diagnosis of deafness is to receive a frightening abstraction. Parents then fall back on conceptual systems—stereotypes, prototypes, image schemas, frames, and conceptual metaphors—to understand the sudden specter of deafness in the home. Shaken out of the trajectory of their lives before diagnosis, the parents are searching for a new script for how to shape and understand deafness—and, importantly for them, how to proceed from that initial state of shock, incomprehension, and fear, to *knowing what to do next, what to do with a deaf kid.*" For those hearing parents who cannot yet imagine the possibility of self-actualized, independent, and successful deaf children and adults in the context of their heretofore "hearing lives" and family unit, feelings of devastation and confusion are natural.[10] "For a long time," one parent said, "I just thought *I'm going to wake up and this is not happening.*"[11]

In answer, the Oberkotter Foundation's films and related print materials make the overall rhetorical case that can be compressed into the following metaphorically constructed claim:

> Upon receiving the diagnosis of deafness, parents feel as though they have entered a dream with qualities of nightmare or unreality, but with medical intervention, guidance, and the map to the road of oralism, they—along with the teachers and medical paraprofessionals in the child's life—begin the journey of "teaching the deaf child to learn to listen and speak"; in order to achieve goals or "dreams," this journey requires time, energy, and investment of considerable emotional and time resources. Then, and only then, at the end of this lengthy process, can the child be "free to dream any dream,"[12] i.e., be able to speak and join the mainstream.

A number of conceptual systems are at work here, and like any other situation in which metaphors are used to compelling effect, particular metaphors are preferred in specific situations because they "provide satisfactory mappings onto already existing cultural understandings . . . [also referred to as a] cultural model."[13]

Cultural models are "everyday theories (i.e., storylines, images, schemas, metaphors, and models) about the world that tell people what is typical or normal, not universally, but from the perspective of a particular [d]iscourse . . . ; [a] cultural model is an often tacit theory or story about how things work in the world."[14] These models result in conceptual metaphors—or can produce such metaphors—and these discursive lines of thinking become embedded within and reiterative of individual, familial, organizational, and cultural thinking. As such, these systems of thought reveal "expressions of universal principles at work in individual cognition *and* as properties of an underlying, 'institutionalized' cultural 'world view.'"[15]

As the narrator of the most recent *Dreams Spoken Here* reminds us:

Narrator: [A.] was born profoundly deaf, but now at age four, [A.] can do something that you may find very hard to believe. [Child on-screen hugs and snuggles with a white teddy bear.]

Woman: Can you say your name again? [Subtitles read, "(A.) deaf since birth."]

[A.]: My name's [A.].

Narrator: She can hear some sounds.

[A.]: I'm four.

Narrator: She can speak and sing.

[A.]: Twinkle, twinkle, little star.

Narrator: And she can dream.

[A.]: Up the sky. Twinkle, little star.[16]

The elements of achieving this "dream" for a deaf child are laid out with startling clarity: she can "dream" if she can speak and sing and hear some sounds. Then and only then is becoming mainstream possible.

To be "mainstream" is to suggest any number of ideas about normality, fitting in, not standing out, sensory integrity in an able-bodied setting. As one parent said,

> You know, mainstreaming is more than just mainstreaming in the school. One of the things I was worried about with [her son] was his social life. And he's proven me to be wrong, which is nice. . . . He's got lots of things going on: sports and school and friends coming in and out. . . . For the parents who are getting ready to mainstream, be brave. . . . And challenge—challenge your fears. Sometimes you just feel like, you know, I'm just so tired. You just have to have that little push. *Follow your dreams, 'cause reality is right there.*[17]

The producers—and parents—of the Oberkotter Foundation's films draw on different senses of the word "dream" for talking about, presenting, and understanding the deaf child in a hearing family. The first sense of dreams, as expressed by the parent cited below, functions more like a semantic frame[18]—or a prototypical description of a scene—that in turn provides elements for the mapping of the primary conceptual metaphor used here in the films, related to the parents' experience on discovering their child is deaf. For the parents shown in the films, and for the personae who narrate, deafness is initially conceptualized as a nightmare, a new and surreal reality in which the center does not hold; the parents are caught up in a waking dream, grieving lost dreams of and for their (heretofore presumed hearing) child. One parent says what others in the film series echo: "I think you go through a lot of different stages of feelings when you first initially find out about the deafness. . . . One of them is shock, you know, and *not wanting to believe and really thinking this is all a dream.*"[19]

Dreams and their obverse, nightmares, can and do mean any of the following (as defined by the online edition of the *Oxford English Dictionary*) for the parents and narrators of the Oberkotter Foundation's expository documentaries:

a. An oppressive fear; a frightening experience or thing;
   a source of fear or anxiety;
b. Having the quality of a nightmare; extremely distressing;
   fraught with difficulty;
c. To behold or imagine in sleep or in a vision;
d. To think or believe something to be possible;
e. A visionary anticipation, a reverie, a "castle in the air,"
   a day-dream;
f. An ideal or aspiration.

Deafness is experienced and understood, alternatively, in terms of a surreal and nightmarish state, a reverie, aspirations and goals, and journeys. These alternations between different senses of the word "dreams" effectively elide or gloss over deafness.

Deafness is first presented as a nightmarish or surreal new reality facing the parents in the aftermath of a diagnosis; later, a second sense of the word comes into play: "dreams" becomes hopes, goals, even fantasies, for the deaf child who is "learning to listen and speak." The first sense—or, rather, frame—relating to dreams is mostly presented by the parents, and the second sense is primarily, but not exclusively, used by the narrator of the films. By borrowing the goal-oriented sense concerning dreams (a popular American cultural model) to talk about possible futures, the producers make it possible for the parents to transfer the content of the "dreams as goals" cultural model onto the oral education/AVT method. This narrative—or, rather, new script—ostensibly provides a way out of the "bad dream" that descends on the parents when they are formally told of their child's diagnosis.

As one parent of a newly diagnosed deaf child said in *Dreams Spoken Here*, "I remember the worst part was about three days into it. At that point, I hadn't really told anybody except immediate family, and my husband told this lady who likes to tell everybody everything. I just felt, god, you know it's like—you're in this little cocoon . . . and it's just like, now, it's out, everybody knows, and *that good world is gone*."[20] Parents in this situation, the film implies, lack a script, or a narrative, for understanding the deaf child in the midst of a family newly stigmatized, a family suddenly made anomalous.

Another important sense of the word "dreams" comes into play in the films, and this third usage goes beyond cultural models, venturing into cultural stereotypes. This overarching sense of "dreams" has more to do with ideas concerning the all-American family living the American dream. In this larger slice of American mythology, to live the "American dream" is to believe that everyone can participate equally; everyone can start over; there is a reasonable expectation of success; said success results from actions and traits under one's own control; and people who fail are presumed to lack talent or will—success is associated with virtue.[21] In this frame, the bourgeois American family is idealized as being representative (i.e., "all-American"). However, when deafness is discovered, as one parent says, "that good world"—and all of its overtones suggesting a particular construction of a family identity—is gone for these parents. What parents seem to lose (and what they hope to regain, with help) when they find out about the diagnosis is a dream of a "good world" that seems particularly tied to socioeconomic status (all families in the film are dressed well and shown in settings in keeping with middle-income to upper-middle-income status).

"In the last five years," states the narrator of the original version of *Dreams Spoken Here*, "incredible advances in technology and oral education mean that even profoundly deaf children can learn to listen and talk and even sing." Shortly after that statement, a young couple, parents of a deaf toddler, say, "I think that's when we really got our signs of hope is when we walked [into a school that uses AVT]. I mean, it's amazing to see all these kids here who are communicating. They're talking. You can tell that there is something a little off in their speech, maybe their tones aren't quite right, but they're communicating just like any child is, and they're playing just like any child is, and you start to realize, well, they are just like any child is—it's just that they just can't hear."[22]

"Passing" for hearing—or close enough, in the case of the Oberkotter Foundation's films—is both a goal and a byproduct of the reconceptualizations of deafness dramatized in the films. Hearing status, and deafness in particular, is both highlighted and glossed over in many of the performances of listening and speaking" shown in the film. Many of the children look hearing, even sound hearing to a certain extent (although others are speaking with a "deaf voice"). Passing is conditional and generally dependent on the silent practices of lip reading and observing (strategies that are commonly called "learning to listen" in AVT), but for limited moments during the interviews, some children do look down and listen through cochlear implants and hearing aids. In those moments, the children could pass as hearing children.

Therein lies the "problem" of identity, "a problem to which passing owes the very possibility of its practice, is predicated on the false promise of the visible as an epistemological guarantee."[23] It is only when a mother repeats herself, or a child's friend taps her on the shoulder, or a father uses gestures—or even when a child uses gestures herself—to enhance meaning that it becomes clear that the successful performance is of that moment but not, perhaps, the next. Passing "is only successful passing."[24] Here, passing is conditional, temporary, always contextual, and always shifting.

It may seem odd for some readers to see "passing" discussed in relation to hearing status in people who are not elderly, but "'passing' has been applied discursively to disguises of other elements of an individual's presumed 'natural' or 'essential' identity, including class, ethnicity, and sexuality, as well as gender."[25] Passing signifies "the risk of identity in that the practice has social, economic, and even physical consequences."[26] To use deafness in this context is to assert that it is possible to "pass"—however provisionally—for hearing and then to "come out" as deaf. This, in turn, has the powerful effect of claiming visual orientation as part of human biodiversity. In effect, this is a reclamation and recuperation of what Alexander Graham Bell once pejoratively called "a deaf variety of the human race.[27]"

My mother told me once, "I don't know if you remember, but I used to tell you that your ears were a little bit broken."

For as long as I can remember, I have slept on my stomach, face down, with my "good ear" (the ear that I wore a hearing aid in) up and my other ear in the pillow—just in case there was a sound in the night that I needed to sense. After all those years of being pressed into the pillow, my left ear is flatter, closer to the skull, than my right.

Even today, my ears are a little bit bent.

Our "conceptual system, in terms of which we both think and act, is fundamentally metaphorical in nature," according to the linguists George Lakoff and Mark Johnson, "and our conceptual system thus plays a central role in defining our everyday realities."[28] Because of their role in cognition, metaphors "structure how we perceive, how we think, and what we do."[29] We act according to our perceptions, and this has profound implications for the hearing parents who seek a relationship with their child and for the deaf person who is being acted on. Both internalize these ways to see deafness and possibilities for self-actualization.

As the cultural anthropologist Naomi Quinn suggests, "Metaphors, far from constituting understanding, are ordinarily selected to fit a preexisting and culturally shared model," which "underlies and gives coherence to the various metaphors" used.[30] The differing senses of "dreams" used in the films suggests that the underlying value system is centered in the concept of "normality" as it is understood by the hearing parents and by the larger social structures at work here.

The distinctly different uses of "dreams" allow parents to map different ontological correspondences related to "dreams" onto knowledge about deafness. The physiological and emotional experience of dream states are transformed into a conceptual metaphor when parents use this metaphorical construct to call up a system of knowledge organized around dreams to reframe and understand deafness. Metaphors become "conceptual" when a particular concept—one understood in terms of another concept—becomes pervasive in thought and language.[31] Examples of such conceptual metaphors include "love is a journey" and "argument is war."[32]

Even though this chapter focuses primarily on the use of the word "dreams" in several different conceptual systems, other conceptual metaphors are present.[33] Parents experience the news as a devastating physical loss. The loss of their previous hopes and "dreams" for their child is experienced as a loss of possessions, as an existential disconnect, or even as a kind of deprivation of participation in the conceptual metaphor LIFE AS A GAME:

- *Father:* Oh, I cried, yeah, it seems like *I lost everything,* and as a father I *hope to give him a fair chance* to face the world and equal opportunities just like any other kid.
- *Father:* But these *hopes, gone, completely gone.*
- *Father:* You start thinking about the smallest details of your life and of your day, and you're thinking, *how can I share this* with her now?

Our embodied experiences structure our thinking in ways that are pre-conceptual and as such influence and shape our metaphors. These metaphorical orientations are based in our physical and cultural experiences; happy is "up," sad is "down," and so forth.[34] Metaphors are motivated by a larger structure of experience that is also intricately tied up with the body: the image schema. Schemas are "structures that organize our mental representations at a level more general and abstract than that at which we form particular mental images."[35] They "are a primary means by which we *construct* or *constitute* order and are not mere passive receptacles into which experience is poured."[36]

Thus, image schemas exist as "continuous and analogue patterns beneath conscious awareness."[37] For example, we conceptualize of much of our lives around the "container" image schema, which allows us to conceive of boundaries, of *in* versus *out.*[38] Both the container and the "source-path-goal" image schemas are most relevant here in this scripted presentation of *where to go, what to do* with deafness. The basic logic of the container schema is that we experience our bodies both as containers and as things in containers. As a result, structural elements include an interior, boundary, and exterior.[39] Parents are "in" a bad dream.

The network of conceptual metaphors presented through the domains related to dreams is grounded and constrained by the "path" schema. The internal structure of this schema has "1) a source, or starting point; 2) a goal, or end-point; and 3) a sequence of contiguous locations connecting the source with the goal."[40] Because of this consistent internal structure, schemas function as gestalts; they "generate coherence for, establish unity within, and constrain our network of meaning."[41]

With the source-path-goal image schema, "Every time we move anywhere there is a place we start from, a place we wind up at, a sequence of contiguous locations connecting the starting and ending points, and a direction."[42] Purposes are then understood in terms of directions; the source-path-goal image schema both structures and is used to structure the parents' experience of deafness (outlining a path from diagnosis to "success"). In the films, this image schema undergoes what is known as an "end-point transformation": The path becomes focused on the end of the journey, a revealing insight into the dynamics at work here in the families. Certainly, the end of the journey is where the parents are focused. Success is ostensibly located there.[43]

The driving conceptual metaphor at work here could be described as something along the lines of *discovery of deafness has qualities of or feels like a bad dream.* Parents note first that "this is all a dream" or this "doesn't seem real." This sense of the word is followed by a second, incongruent, but related sense, when parents talk about "waking up," stating that "this is not happening." If discovery of deafness is the abstract target domain for this conceptual metaphor, and "bad dream" is the source, then information in that domain becomes part of how deafness is understood. The conceptual metaphor of nightmare clearly becomes a mode for thinking about deafness; parents feel they need help moving beyond that "bad dream," and as they do so, they recover and return to their previous equilibrium.

Metaphors draw on frame-based knowledge, or idealized cognitive models (ICMs),[44] and frames function as the background knowledge necessary for understanding the relations between words. Frames are conceptual underpinnings for words and thus are inference generating. If a frame structures and organizes a particular—and thereby proto-typed—scenario, the frame then structures the word meanings that arise from that prototypical situation; words from within that frame evoke the frame.[45] As such, frames provide a kind of script or proto-typical scenario, with slots for participants. Important for our purposes here, not only do metaphoric mappings "preserve frame relations and inferences,"[46] they also function in ways that inform the psychology of making a choice.[47] A decision maker must first conceive of a problem that must be solved; then he or she then must consider possible out-comes or consequences for acts. This is where frames help to structure the decision maker's sense of the situation. In other words, frames "select and call attention to particular aspects of the reality described, which logically means that frames simultaneously direct attention away from other aspects."[48] This particular metaphor mapping—*the discovery of deafness has qualities of or feels like a bad dream*—draws on literal frame-based knowledge about physiological dreams and the dream state; elements from this frame then help structure the metaphor.

With the dream frame, the metaphorical mapping carries over into the frame's prototypical scenario and relations between elements. Entities related to this scenario for deafness (i.e., hearing parents; deafness as a little understood and, for these parents, disturbing phenomenon; movement into a new and surreal "reality" after the diagnosis) have ontological correspondences to entities in the domain of dreaming (sleepers, a sudden and incomprehensible situation presents itself, waking up to the aftermath of the nightmare). When the parents say, "I'm going to wake up, and this is not happening," "It doesn't seem real," "This is all a dream," "You don't know what you can expect," they are using their experiences of bad dreams and nightmares as the closest analogous experience to what they are feeling when they discover their child is deaf.

These sets of correspondences allows us to analyze the frame elements at work with the two senses of dream/nightmare and the related conceptual metaphor:

DREAM/NIGHTMARE	DISCOVERY OF DEAFNESS
Sleeper/dreamer	Hearing parents
Dreams are unpredictable	Deafness removes the usual sense of process; no script for how to proceed
Overwhelming experience	Parents feel overwhelmed
Dreams could become nightmares	Parents are grieving; they feel loss
Bad dreams are not real	Parents feel that the experience is unreal
Bad dreams are temporary	Parents are looking for answers
Bad dreams are not really real	Situation feels surreal; what is deafness?

Thrown out of the trajectory of their cultural life scripts,[49] these parents—as do many hearing parents with deaf children not portrayed in these films—struggle to understand this new event in their collective life story as an individual family.

As a film series that is presented in documentary format—yet that clearly is heavily edited with a particular agenda in mind—*Dreams Made Real* presents a series of portraits of *ideal cases*,[50] success stories of deaf children and their families that are meant to be "real" for all or most deaf children who enter AVT programs. These ideal cases are meant to illustrate the narrator's assertion that "for babies who are diagnosed with a hearing loss, the future has never sounded so hopeful."[51] The families then become paragons for *how to have a deaf kid, what to do with a deaf kid.* They become cognitive reference points for other parents of deaf children, who then compare or judge themselves and their families in relation to what they see on-screen.

When I was born two months early at the tail end of a muggy Louisiana summer, the doctors told my young parents to prepare themselves for my death or, if I lived, devastating disability. My young father, his hairline just beginning to slide back on his forehead, listened to his mother as she tried to offer comforting words at the hospital, words along the lines of "God gives; God takes, and perhaps it would all be for the best if . . ."

My father had snapped at her: "We want her no matter what shape she's in."

Later, when I grew into an awkward and antagonizing adolescence, he became worried and cross, and we struggled with what it was I was supposed to do, what I needed to learn, how I should behave to survive in the hearing world.

When I was fourteen, he brought home from his office applications for secretarial jobs completed by young women with careful, round handwriting. He told me that with my attitude, he would not hire me—not to mention the deaf thing, he did not say, but I knew he thought.

Through the presentation of "success stories" in the Oberkotter Foundation's films, the prototyping process results in powerful alternative and recuperative cultural scripts for hearing families with deaf children, who in turn, internalize, reiterate, or resist these culturally grounded and shared life scripts (which, after all, largely depend on *seeming as hearing as possible* and therefore are not all that different from the previous life script—just reincorporated and rehabilitated).

By cultural life scripts, I mean a "series of events that take place in a specific order and represent . . . a prototypical life course within a certain culture."[52] This is in keeping with passing as "a performance in which one presents oneself as what one is not, a performance commonly imagined along the axis of race, class, gender, or sexuality."[53] Because life scripts help structure individual life stories by providing a general template for a life's trajectory, most "culturally expected transitional events are considered positive and important," while a traumatic event is "almost by definition a life script deviant experience."[54]

These parents clearly feel shaken out of their understanding of how things are and should be and are instead grappling with the social stereotypes that their heretofore prototypical all-American families now face—for example, the "special ed kid," the "deaf kid," the deeply loved but also potentially embarrassing child who makes them *all* different. As one parent said, "When I first found out that she was deaf, I didn't think she'd be able to go to our neighborhood school. I really thought she'd be in special classes, be, you know, the kid that everybody kind of—Oh, she's a little different."[55]

Once, during an argument we had when I was thirteen, my mother startled me into silence when she told me that my being deaf was harder for her than it was for me. I understand now that she meant the experience expressed by the parents with older deaf children in the films— that it takes hours and hours, but then "you start to see the hard work pay off with little victories. She'll alert to her name or know that a sound is happening and it starts here."[56]

But then I watch the children at my son's ASL-English bilingual school and see how effortlessly young signing deaf children—especially those who started signing very early in their lives—pick up their two languages, without prompting and with seamless monitoring and reinforcement from their parents. They are performing largely at grade level in their classes, and they communicate with sophistication about books they read, movies they saw, activities in which they participated the weekend before with friends and families. It makes me wonder how much frustration could have been saved for everyone if bilingual ASL-English or bilingual-bimodal programs were the norm.[57] For those who would like to try both sign and speech, many ASL-English bilingual schools for deaf children also offer speech therapy for students with hearing aids and cochlear implants. Why not take advantage of the ease of language input through a sighted deaf child's eyes? After all, it is the fact of a language foundation that correlates with speech skills,[58] and the brain processes spoken and signed language in the very same brain tissue.[59] And importantly, proficiency in ASL has been found to correlate with development of literacy skills in English.[60]

In the Oberkotter Foundation's films, medical professionals punctuate the parents' initial, bewildered observations with authoritative sounding commentary and enjoiners about the "hard work" and miracles of AVT approaches. Investing "a lot of hard work" and dedication, the various medical professionals and teachers say in the films, "will pay off." The alternation of grief and medical remediation with parents' expressions of relief serves to ritualize the cultural model—and resulting script—expressed in these films. "All it takes," the narrator's voice intones, "is hard work and a dream—the dream of teachers and therapists whose dedication make it possible for deaf children to speak and listen."[61]

In an important shift, dreams are used to suggest that "to think or believe something is possible," and that is the overriding concern of all of these materials. In short, if dreams are achievable with hard work and focus; if dreams require investment; if dreams can sour if they are thwarted; if dreams are a uniquely American striving and thus a unique feature of American cultural identity, then this cultural model both underlies and gives coherence to the narrative that the Oberkotter Foundation uses to structure the *Dreams Spoken Here* films.

The initial, nightmarish, sense of the dream frame and conceptual metaphor is then transformed into a kind of daydream, or reverie, about the child's possibilities, and from there it is transformed into goals and hopes by means of the cultural model concerning the notions of self-actualization implicit in such *constructions* as to "achieve your dreams."

The Oberkotter Foundation's *Dreams Spoken Here* film series uses multiple senses of the word "dream" in the hope that the parents will transfer the content of that "dream" frame onto the oral educational method. Oral education is then explicitly tied into this conceptual system in that "one of the goals of [this educational philosophy] is to support deaf children so they can succeed in most mainstream environments."[62] By means of the components of oral education—use of residual hearing, speech and "listening" therapy, specialized teaching instruction, and so forth—success may be possible.

Cultural models are passed on "through shared stories, practices, and procedures that get newcomers to pay attention to salient features of prototypical cases in the domain—the ones that best reflect the cultural models."[63] Parent interviews are used to quite powerful effect in this way in the Oberkotter Foundation's films. As one parent said, "*I had the dream, and now it's reality.* She's hearing things . . . that she's never heard before and responding to sounds in ways that she never responded before."[64] Another parent said, I am so much happier emotionally, because *the future is not so scary.* It's still challenging. She probably works harder than the average kindergartener, but we are doing what we set off to do."[65]

The scripting of hearing families' process through diagnosis to a "hopeful future" demonstrates a canny manipulation of the frames and metaphors first expressed by parents. It is unclear how much of the parents' commentary is spontaneous and how much of it is guided or scripted, but it certainly is edited with a clear overall rhetorical message in mind. The more dramatic commentary is repeated and echoed throughout the different filmed products. As one mother said: "I think my dreams were the same as any parent. You want to see them grow, be independent, to be happy, to do what they want to do. It's amazing to see that happening. Their deafness will not stop them from doing anything. And if someone had told me that nine years ago, when we found out about [R., one of her two deaf children], I wouldn't have believed them. She's worked so hard, as has [A., the mother's other deaf child], to get to where they are. And now they can do anything. [The mother has tears in her eyes.] And they do."[66] Equation with the average becomes important here. As one parent of a six-year-old with a cochlear implant says, "To think back then that he would be where he is today, I could not even have imagined. To see him running around the playground with hearing peers and feel like he's their equal, there's nothing that they could do that he couldn't do—is just an incredible thing to feel and know."[67]

Mainstreaming, then, is meant and presented quite literally "in the middle." One parent noted, "Mainstreaming was an important goal for our family, because life is mainstreaming, and I feel mainstreaming in a classroom with all hearing children is what life is. That was my dream, to have her ready to mainstream at kindergarten."[68] Mainstreaming thus suggests the ordinary; nothing is out of place. However, the parent's and the child's hard work behind the scenes is extraordinary: "I think for me, *I just appreciate the ordinary,*" a parent says. "We can be driving in the car, and she's sitting in the back with a couple of friends just chatting and laughing, and I'm sitting in the front seat with tears going down my face *because the ordinary is so wonderful.*"[69]

Tellingly, being "ordinary" plays out into having a future; the future of a deaf child is now open to being scripted in ways that the parents were not able to imagine before, when they were thrown out of their cultural life script for themselves and for their children. When they grow up, the children want to become teachers, pilots, veterinarians, baseball players . . . But what is unusual is that the narrative asks viewers again and again, "How is this possible?" The narrator reminds viewers that "the answer to these questions is oral education."[70] All that aside, the notion of possible futures is typically tied into socioeconomic status and gender stereotypes, and this intersects in interestingly complex ways with deafness.

Throughout junior high, the deaf and hard-of-hearing program—all five of us—met with the deaf education teacher in what used to be a janitor's closet. As we progressed through the grades and closer to high school, the teacher prepared us for life beyond. One afternoon, she asked us to imagine what we would like to become once we finished high school.

For me, at fourteen, the future had to involve writing and reading and some kind of professional career that required people to look professional and carry nice leather briefcases. One by one, we shared our dreams. The only boy in the class said he wanted to be a car mechanic. Two girls, sisters, said they wanted to be teachers of the deaf. My fellow deaf classmates were congratulated and applauded. Then it was my turn to share.

"A lawyer," I told everyone.

The teacher paused, a look of annoyance on her face. She turned to the last of my classmates, a sweet girl whom everyone at the school liked, known as much for her warm smile as for her gorgeous mane of thick auburn hair. I never knew whether I should feel jealous of the smiles and attention she got from our hearing classmates, girls who spent hours brushing out and braiding my deaf classmate's hair.

My classmate said, "A hairdresser."

That was the correct answer. The teacher applauded her and said, "That's it! Go after your dream"—cutting hair and sweeping it up in grotesque piles on the floor afterward, little animal deaths.

I shrank back in my cold desk chair and stared out the small square window of Texas sun, counting down the minutes until the bell rang and I could be sprung from this little closet smelling of chemicals.

That was a different era in a part of the country known for conservative politics, but even so, twenty years later it is telling that none of the little boys in the Oberkotter Foundation's films want to be teachers; only the girls do. When asked what they want to do when they grow up, the boys rattle off gender-typed professions; they want to be pilots, baseball players, and the like.

As a means to an end, voices become almost totemic in their elemental qualities. The spoken word becomes a powerful entity, something that is "had," something that maps the known world of the parents:

- *Mother:* When it does start sinking in and you think, well, she's *not going to have her first word. She doesn't know my name, she doesn't know* . . . she doesn't know mommy, daddy, kitty, *simple simple things.*
- *Father:* The hardest thing for me, I was thinking *she is never going to hear me say I love you, or I'm proud of you.*
- *Mother:* So for a child to be able to say more, or she'd say "ooce"—and, oh, you want some juice, and her face would light up, and it seemed like those *first little words were so powerful.*

The spoken word becomes a fraught element in an exchange between adult and child, with emphasis on kinship words and other words that delimit family units. At this point, the word rests almost entirely on the naming level. In addition, this stress on naming also implies an Adamic element to the family unit. (Religious overtones already exist in some of the materials, with allusion to making a "joyful noise" in the handbook in the Oberkotter Foundation's parent kit.)

With naming, the child enters into the prototypical family economy, a place where there are clear sociocultural scripts to be followed. The presence of a deaf child unsettles the prototypical family because, as the narrator in *Dreams Made Real* repeatedly suggests, how is it *possible* for a deaf child to fit with the rest of the family? Hence, stress is placed on an approach that teaches a child to "listen and speak and to dream." The word must be had, at all costs.

Words—and most often, single words, not sentences—become the currency of exchange between family members and the deaf children portrayed in the films. Parents of the girls more often talk about their children speaking individual words, and these more typically include relational terms to describe kinship; parents of the boys are shown more often talking about voice as a gateway to "membership" in a "larger" society; the male child is more often talked about in terms of the "world" and in terms of economic exchanges. Although both male and female children are shown in the act of listening, female children are shown this way more often.

This understanding of a voice as something that is "had" becomes very important for the parents' vision of their child at a later age, when he or she must leave the immediate family unit and enter into economic exchanges. Voices become a commodity necessary for participation within the consumer-oriented capitalist economy here, and the family unit is the microcosm for the capitalist economy:

> *Mother:* Why was it so important for him to learn to speak? . . . One of the main reasons is that we . . . really wanted [A.] to be able to interact with the rest of the world. . . . I wanted him to go to McDonald's and ask for his hamburger and French fries. I wanted to go to the bank and go to any store and be able to ask for what he wants and ask for what he wants vocally. It is very important to me that [A.] get out and communicate. Our family is just very noisy. Our family is . . . all we do is talk . . . and I wanted him to be a part of that.[71]

This sentiment is echoed in *Dreams Made Real* in a scene showing a mother and her young daughters in a fast-food restaurant:

> *Mother:* One of the goals that we've always had for the girls was that they would be able to be independent citizens. [The daughters grin as they approach the microphone and the clerk.]
> *Daughter 1:* I'll have a small vanilla cone dipped in chocolate.
> *Daughter 2:* A small chocolate cone, please.
> *Mother [in close-up outside the restaurant, in a green summer setting]:* They could order their own dinner if they went out to a restaurant, that they could ask for help if they needed help, that they could call home if they were, for some reason, to be lost and to have that sense of independence. [Camera returns to fast-food restaurant, where Daughter 1 is holding money.] And there's really nothing that they see [clerk hands Daughter 1 her ice cream cone] that they can't just walk up and go do. [Close-up of mother.] I mean, they always feel like they belong. [Piano music][72]

Voices also become representative of middle-class, democratic values. The deaf children here, it is implied, are not exceptional. They are mainstream in more ways than one:

- *Mother:* No, you don't have to have money, and you don't have to be Miss America . . . to learn to speak.[73]
- *Teacher in interview:* When you use the words "a deaf child," you think they probably don't function in class well, that you give them separate assignments, that you have to modify a lot of work for them. Maybe a lot of language therapy might be your impression. But with [one particular child in the film], it's not the case. I mean, she's very, very mainstream. . . . And she doesn't let her hearing impairment enable her not to do well.

In a related sense, voices are seen as equating self-expression and self-actualization within a highly individualized American culture. As one oral deaf young adult says, "I have a message for parents that these kids . . . have a voice, and they need to give their children's voices a chance to speak and be exercised to express their feelings with, to cry with, and to laugh with." Voicing is then placed in opposition to sign language, with one denoting success and the other, failure.

One oral deaf adult equates the perceived need for sign language interpretation with failure to succeed in the hearing world, in short, a failure to pass as good enough:

Rebecca: I called my field experience teacher and told her, "Hi, I'm hearing impaired, and I'm going to be in your classroom, and I'm going to gain experience in this education field." . . . Well, she gave me a hard time, She's like, "You're hearing impaired. How can you be with kids? How can you communicate with them? Do you need an interpreter to be with you?" It was really a blow.[74]

"Passing" for hearing—or close enough—holds the social bearings in place and provides one of the cornerstones for the oral deaf approach to education, which provides the metaphorical pathway, the road map, for a culturally constructed and sanctioned passing. The child's once lost future is regained, once again scriptable and scripted.

My father sent me to college with the pointed admonition, "Don't do anything I wouldn't do." He looked at me as if to say, *You know what I mean, and don't.* He did this with my sisters, too, but with me his reminders oxidized with worry that I would mess up when my chances were already slim, or so it seemed.

Understanding the constructions that underlie the discourses at work here in regard to deafness and socioeconomic class allows us to see them as artifacts of a particular value system that in turn serve to perpetuate particular ideologies concerning deafness. Only then can we see other possibilities for envisioning deaf lives, other narratives, *visually centered cultural life scripts.*

Indeed, there is such a script. Ask any freshman at Gallaudet University what her first-year experience is, and often, the answer involves letting go of one life script and falling into, falling in love with, another (shared) story of self within a vibrant and lively sociolinguistic community.[75] Following a decades-old tradition, they shave their heads in tandem with other freshmen and come out as deaf. Those who participate in "Bald Day" usually also put away their hearing aids and cochlear implants. A swagger and confidence enters their walk: "Yes, I'm bald. I have no hardware on my head. I'm here, and I'm a part of this." Or alternatively, the hardware is on full, flamboyant, display, as if to say, "I have nothing to hide. I am still deaf."

Any time deafness is presented as something to "overcome," or a deaf person is presented as remarkable for his or her successes "in spite of" the implicit obstacle of disability, notions of sensory integration and able-bodiedness are reinforced. To assimilate, to "pass" for not deaf, not disabled, is to play into that particular cultural model of what is and what is not "normal." In this model, deafness is an obstacle in the path to normalcy, something that must be conquered. Even the appearance of deafness is often presented as a sign of personal weakness, a character flaw: "are you deaf or something?"

The expository documentary form lends itself to this kind of analysis because as an edited product, the *Dreams Made Real* and *Dreams Spoken Here* series, demonstrate the mechanisms of "discourse as the instrument of the social creation of reality."[76] Discourse used in this way becomes a means to serve the ends of an organization—here, an organization that disseminates information about one of at least two primary models in America of deaf education and language acquisition. Discourse, then, is "the principal means by which organization members create a social reality that frames their sense of who they are."[77] By framing the discussion of deafness and AVT with "dreams," the organization establishes not only a script for understanding deafness but also a value system that, in effect, "enforces normalcy."[78] By emphasizing discursive constructs of learning to listen and speak within a cultural model that effectively erases or makes over deafness, hearing status is revealed to be an unstable identity category. Deafness is presented in ways that allows parents to see their children as "almost hearing."

Through AVT, they become "like any other child," as one parent says. They become functionally hearing through the acts of speaking, listening, and dreaming. They are no longer "disabled," disconnected, when they join the family economy.

> *Father [after entering a preschool for oral deaf children]:* But these kids were hearing. They were hearing and they were talking, and we were looking at each other like, can [our daughter] ... do this and if [she] ... can do this, then, well, she is going to hear me say, "I love you," and "I'm proud of you."[79]

The difficulty inherent in describing a deaf child's actions as hearing or as seeming to be hearing shows up in the awkward ways in which the parents and the children describe deafness: not just as deaf but as different, and so on. None describe deafness as something that forms the basis of an identity that rests outside the family and social structures portrayed in the films.

To act as if hearing, to become hearing, is to dodge assumptions about deafness and to assume the privileges of a spoken life. In this case, passing is not transgressive. It is, instead, a culturally and ideologically motivated performance. It is not the same kind of passing described here, in relation to race: "As the term metaphorically implies, such an individual crossed or passed through a racial line or boundary—indeed trespassed—to assume a new identity, escaping the subordination and oppression accompanying one identity and accessing the privileges and status of the other."[80] Here, passing is meant to escape stigma, to escape a "disabled" and disabling construction of deafness in the minds of many hearing people. After all, able-bodied/hearing people wonder, why would anyone want to be deaf? The notion of disability immediately calls up discourses of correction and cultural narratives of sensory integration.

"Can you hear that?" is the refrain for many young deaf children's lives. "Or that?" Slowly, through those kinds of sessions, a deaf child begins to build a sensory map of what it means to "hear" or not hear. But, then, what is deafness? Where is deafness? What does it mean to be deaf if to be deaf is built on a sequence of binaries, gaps in the sound, gaps in the sightline? Essentially, a deaf child in a hearing environment is asked to build an identity based on lacking something, grasping after something that is sometimes out of reach.

There is little to no discussion in the Oberkotter Foundation's films of using the major sensory advantage that sighted deaf children have: their eyes. Yet nearly all of the families shown in the films show awareness of visuality: they maintain clear sightlines, they gesture toward a child to get his or her attention, they make sure the child can see. They may be different, but they are still deaf.

Identities "are contested public terrain."[81] I wonder how many of the deaf children shown in these and similar films grew up to question the identities that were constructed for them. How many of them grew up to become academically and professionally successful but still felt something was missing? How many learned sign language and took on a more visibly "deaf" identity later? Identities "are contested not just in the sense that there are struggles over the kinds of identities we are allowed to *claim* for ourselves, but there are also struggles over the kinds of identities we can *conceive* for ourselves, and which identities in any system of heteroglossic practice we will strive to establish *in* ourselves."[82]

It is telling that much of the definition of "success" in achieving the goal, in erasing the nightmare and returning to the possibility of "dreams" depends on forgetting or erasing the fact of the child's deafness. As one mother said, "We almost forget that he's a hearing-impaired child is the incredible part of this whole thing." And, as another parent said, "I know that I'm very comfortable with where she's at. Literally, I don't even think about her being hearing impaired."[83] Forgetting, then becomes, a sign of a successful passing, for the moment.

Interestingly enough, the deaf children and young adults in the documentary have a slightly different script for understanding themselves:

> [V., a deaf-blind boy with a cochlear implant]: Well . . . I would say you can do anything well, like, like normal people you can do anything, you can go swimming, you can play drums. I

and speaking children. What about their stories? What was the real story after the hearing aid, the cochlear implant, after college, after the first job?

Yet many oral deaf adults grow up and find other deaf adults, many of whom sign. A bilingual identity is very much part of the territory for older deaf adults who enter the signing community late. For example, Caitlyn Parton, who received one of the earliest pediatric cochlear implants in the United States, is now a young adult. She has told newspaper reporters that she both signs and speaks and "functions in the signing world."[85]

Oddly enough, considering that many parents do "invest" a great deal of time, effort, and probably money in their children, none of the films discusses the advantages of being bilingual—and in this case, being bilingual and bimodal (sign language is visual; spoken language is auditory). Recent research has shown the benefits of spoken-language bilingualism, ASL–English bilingualism, and bimodal bilingualism (sign and speech for young deaf children).[86]

Why is it that, even when the advantages of bilingualism, especially for reading,[87] are becoming well known, not one parent is shown considering the possibility of adding a second language to the home and school environment? There is considerable risk of delay for what is known as a "sensitive period" for language acquisition. Learning a first language later has significant detrimental effects.[88]

Sadly, many of the children shown in the films are in the early days of their "therapy," and they are strikingly language delayed; their speech may have caught up since then, but one does wonder about their later language development and academic achievements. As shown in the films, even preschool to school-age children struggle at the word level ("mmm" becomes "more") rather than at the sentence level. This is in stark contrast to signing deaf settings, where children look and interact, and run and play, with one another in ways that are exactly like hearing children, except that the language is signed, not spoken.

The issue of fully functional fluency in at least one language is rarely addressed, except in relation to citations of the "research": "The research is clear. Early intervention, appropriate treatment, and oral deaf education mean that babies who are deaf can have speech and language development that approximates their hearing peers."[89] Despite repeated admonitions and reminders that early intervention and appropriate technology help a child develop language, the few and repetitive—half-mean it's, like, I'll explain it, it's not like you have a problem. You're just deaf.[84]

Deafness becomes yet another difference in a multicultural society. As one young deaf adult said, "As you get older, it stops, and everybody realizes that everybody's different; it's not so bad to be different; and people notice other differences a lot more, even if its racial or ethnic, people start to accept your differences a lot more. And deafness is just another difference, you know, among many." The documentaries seem to suggest that it does not matter if one is different as long as one speaks the majority language. If one is deaf but one speaks English, this implies, then deafness is only one more element in the great melting pot we call America. Oral deaf education seems to rest on assimilation on a broader scale than just within the family.

Despite the compelling nature of these conceptual metaphors and the schemas used to bring them together to form a coherent script for parents of deaf and hard-of-hearing children, there are a number of troubling gaps in the narrative. Strikingly, no oral deaf adults are interviewed in the most recent documentaries. "Dreams are spoken here" and "dreams are made real" through the AVT approach espoused in the films, but what does this mean to those who have since grown up? To what extent does this trajectory toward "success" hold? There is little discussion of what many oral deaf adults know: that even with mainstream "success" and a more or less prototypical career choice, there is still a price to be paid in terms of other difficult-to-quantify factors—namely, social confidence, self-esteem, and, importantly, self-actualization.

Then there are the other factors not discussed in the films: what happens when oral deaf teenagers or adults start dating, fall in love, eventually leave the family structure? What happens when college professors tell them they do not need support in the classroom because they can read lips? What happens when hearing babies and children are difficult to understand? When hearing spouses become frustrated? Almost without exception, the deaf person is shown only as a child or very young teenager, particularly in the foundation's later films. The 1998 version (but not the 2004 version) of *Dreams Spoken Here* does include a few, short interviews with oral adults; they all talk about their success in terms of struggle. A few talk about the social repercussions; none talk about the lack of easy communication in terms of dating and significant relationships or, later, their own presumably hearing formed, in some cases—utterances made by some of the toddlers and young deaf children shown in the films pale in comparison with the complexity of language use by their ASL-fluent deaf peers. In fact, some of the children in the films seem dangerously close to not having a functional first language at three or four years old. Most of the children shown in the Oberkotter Foundation's films are six to ten years old; the research on language acquisition suggests that there will be a linguistic and therefore academic toll for uneven or inconsistent access to a first language.[90]

And what happened to the children not shown—the ones for whom oral education did not meet its full "potential"? What about those from impoverished backgrounds, from rural country settings, with few immediately accessible services? Instead, the Oberkotter Foundation's films encourage the culture of exceptionalism and individualism that pervades much of oral deaf education: if one "succeeds," it is because he or she (and the parents) has worked "harder" than everyone else.

This rendition of the American dream seems awfully lonely.

Even though I was an "oral success story," by the time I hit my mid-twenties, I was exhausted from the exigencies of lip reading. I was exhausted from "passing," from being close enough to hearing, from being *like* but not quite the *same as*. I wondered what it would be like, what it would feel like, not to have to worry constantly about what word or phrase I was missing, not to have to worry about lighting arrangements and optimal sound arrangements. It took a few more years, but I learned the answer.

It is now 2013. The children and young teens portrayed in the 2004 release of *Dreams Spoken Here* are nine years older. They have found their "voice." What happened to them? Are they like the rest of us "oral deaf successes" who realized that—when deafness is encouraged to be "forgotten"—the price of passing at times was too high? Are they living their own dreams and not one that someone else dreamed up for them?

Notes

1. "Pure oral" is shorthand for an educational approach that focuses on auditory-verbal means for communication. Typically, sign language is discouraged and often presented as appropriate for those who "fail" this approach.

2. Erving Goffman's discussion of stigma and the role of the "discreditable" for the socially discredited is relevant here: Erving Goffman, *Stigma: Notes on the Management of Spoiled Identity* (New York: Simon and Schuster, 1963).

3. Shireen Roshanravan, "Passing-as-if: Model-Minority Subjectivity and Women of Color Identification," *Meridians* 10, no. 1(2010): 8.

4. Goffman, *Stigma*, 43–44.

5. Oberkotter Foundation, *Dreams Spoken Here: Full Version* (60 min.), videocassette, Philadelphia, 1998.

6. Ibid.; Oberkotter Foundation, *Dreams Spoken Here* (20 min.), DVD, Philadelphia, 2004.

7. Alexander Graham Bell Academy for Listening and Spoken Language, "Auditory-Verbal Therapy," available online at http://nc.agbell.org/NetCommu nity/Page.aspx?pid=360 (accessed May 29, 2012).

8. Alan Marvelli, "Highlights in the History of Oral Teacher Preparation in America," *Volta Review* 110, no. 2 (Summer 2010): 110.

9. Alice Eriks-Brophy, "Outcomes of Auditory-Verbal Therapy: A Review of the Evidence and a Call for Action," *Volta Review* 104, no. 1 (2004): 22.

10. Oberkotter Foundation, "Make a Joyful Noise: An Information Kit for Parents of Children who are Deaf and Hard of Hearing," Philadelphia, 2000, 8.

11. Oberkotter Foundation, *Dreams Spoken Here* (1998).

12. Oberkotter Foundation, *Dreams Spoken Here* (2004).

13. Naomi Quinn, "The Cultural Basis of Metaphor," in *Beyond Metaphor: The Theory of Tropes in Anthropology*, ed. James W. Fernandez (Palo Alto, Calif.: Stanford University Press, 1991), 65.

14. Ibid., 40.

15. Beate Hampe and Joseph Grady, eds., *From Perception to Meaning: Image Schemas in Cognitive Linguistics* (Berlin: Walter de Gruyter, 2005), 6.

16. Oberkotter Foundation, *Dreams Spoken Here* (2004).

17. Oberkotter Foundation, *Dreams Made Real: Into the Mainstream*, DVD, Philadelphia, 2004.

18. Frames are "any system of concepts related in such a way that to understand any one of them you have to understand the whole structure in which it fits": Charles Fillmore, "Frame Semantics," in *Linguistics in the Morning Calm*, ed. Linguistic Society of Korea (Seoul: Hanshin Publishing, 1982), 111. Frames are therefore organizing principles for the lexicon called up in a particular scenario and as such provide the details for conceptual metaphors that arise out of this system. Words evoke frames, which in turn outline prototypical scenarios, with slots for participants and entities. Metaphorical mappings are then linked to frame elements: see also Jean Mark Gawron, "Frame Semantics," available online at http://hf.uib.no/forskerskole/new_frames_intro.pdf (accessed April 28, 2010).

19. Oberkotter Foundation, *Dreams Spoken Here* (1998).

20. Ibid.

21. Jennifer L. Hochschild, *Facing Up to the American Dream: Race, Class, and the Soul of the Nation* (Princeton, N.J.: Princeton University Press, 1996), 26–30.

22. Oberkotter Foundation, *Dreams Spoken Here* (1998).

23. Amy Robinson, quoted in Elaine Ginsberg, *Passing and the Fictions of Identity* (Durham, N.C.: Duke University Press, 1995), 4.

24. Valerie Rohy, "Displacing Desire: Passing, Nostalgia, and *Giovanni's Room*," in Ginsberg, *Passing and the Fictions of Identity*, 226.

25. Ginsberg, *Passing and the Fictions of Identity*, 3.

26. Quoted in Brenda Jo Brueggemann and Debra A. Moddelmog, "Coming-Out Pedagogy: Risking Identity in Language and Literature Classrooms," *Pedagogy* 2, no. 3 (2002): 313.

27. Alexander Graham Bell, "Upon the Formation of a Deaf Variety of the Human Race," *Memoirs of the National Academy of the Sciences* 2 (1883): 179–262.

28. George Lakoff and Mark Johnson, *Metaphors We Live By* (Chicago: University of Chicago Press, 1980), 3.

29. Ibid., 4.

30. Quinn, "The Cultural Basis of Metaphor," 60, 63.

31. Lakoff and Johnson, *Metaphors We Live By*.

32. Ibid.

33. Oberkotter Foundation, *Dreams Spoken Here* (1998).

34. Lakoff and Johnson, *Metaphors We Live By*, 14–15.

35. Mark Johnson, *The Body in the Mind: The Bodily Basis of Meaning, Imagination, and Reason* (Chicago: University of Chicago Press, 1987), 24.

36. Ibid., 29.

37. Hampe and Grady, *From Perception to Meaning*, 1.

38. George Lakoff, *Women, Fire, and Dangerous Things: What Categories Reveal about the Mind* (Chicago: University of Chicago Press, 1987), 271.

39. George Lakoff, "Cognitive Semantics," in *Meaning and Mental Representations*, ed. Philip N. Johnson-Laird (Bloomington: Indiana University Press, 1988), 141.

40. Johnson, *The Body in the Mind*, 113.

41. Ibid., 41.

42. Lakoff, *Women, Fire, and Dangerous Things*, 275.

43. I have written a separate analysis of further implications of this particular image schema, and this will be published elsewhere.

44. An ICM is a complex structured whole, a gestalt that draws from Fillmore's ideas about the propositional structure of frames: see Lakoff, *Women, Fire, and Dangerous Things*, 68.

45. Fillmore, "Frame Semantics," 117.

46. Karen Sullivan, "Frame-Based Constraints on Lexical Choice in Metaphor," paper presented at the 32nd Annual Meeting of the Berkeley Linguistics Society, Berkeley, Calif., 2006, available online at http://ssrn.com/abstract =14920263 (accessed April 16, 2012).

47. Amos Tversky and Daniel Kahneman, "The Framing of Decisions and the Psychology of Choice," *Science* 211, no. 4481 (1981): 453.

48. Robert M. Entman, "Framing: Toward Clarification of a Fractured Paradigm," *Journal of Communication* 43, no. 4 (1993): 54.

49. The cultural life script "combines the concept of story scripts . . . with the idea of an age segmentation of the lifespan and culturally sanctioned age norms for salient life events. . . . life scripts are semantic knowledge learned within one's culture. . . . A cultural life script consists of a series of culturally important transitional events that are expected to take place in a specific order in specific time slots in a prototypical life course within a given culture": Annette Bohn, "Normative Ideas of Life and Autobiographical Reasoning in Life Narratives," in *The Development of Autobiographical Reasoning in Adolescence and Beyond*, ed. Tilmann Habermas (San Francisco: Jossey-Bass, 2011), 22. See also Roger Schank and Robert Abelson, "Scripts, Plans, Goals, and Understanding," in *Advance Papers of the Fourth International Joint Conference on Artificial Intelligence, Tbilisi, Georgia, USSR* (Cambridge, Mass.: Artificial Intelligence Lab, 1975).

50. Categories are understood in terms of ideal cases: Lakoff, *Women, Fire, and Dangerous Things*, 87.

51. Oberkotter Foundation, *Dreams Made Real*.

52. David C. Rubin, Dorthe Berntsen, and Michael Hutson, "The Normative and the Personal Life: Individual Differences in Life Scripts and Life Story Events among USA and Danish Undergraduates," *Memory* 17, no. 1 (2009): 55.

53. Rohy, "Displacing Desire," 219.

54. Rubin et al., "The Normative and the Personal Life," 57.

55. Oberkotter Foundation, *Dreams Made Real*.

56. Ibid.

57. See Sharon Baker, "Advantages of Early Visual Language," Visual Language and Learning Research Brief no. 2, January 2011, available online at http://vl2.gallaudet.edu/assets/section7/document104.pdf; Sarah Fish and Jill Morford, "The Benefits of Bilingualism: Impacts on Language and Cognitive Development," Visual Language and Learning Research Brief no. 7, June 2012, available online at http://vl2.gallaudet.edu/assets/section7/document206.pdf; Julie Mitchiner, Debra Berlin Nussbaum, and Susanne Scott "The Implications of Bimodal-Bilingual Approaches for Children with Cochlear Implants" Visual Language and Learning Research Brief no. 7, June 2012, available online at http://vl2.gallaudet.edu/assets/section7/document205.pdf (all accessed December 7, 2012).

58. Baker, "Advantages of Early Visual Language."

59. Laura Ann Petitto, Robert J. Zatorre, Kristine Gauna, E. J. Nikelski, Deanna Dostie, and Alan C. Evans, "Speech-Like Cerebral Activity in Profoundly Deaf People Processing Signed Languages: Implications for the Neural Basis of Human Language," *Proceedings of the National Academy of the Sciences of the United States of America* 97, no. 25 (December 2000): 13961–13966.

60. Michael Strong and Philip M. Prinz, "A Study of the Relationship between American Sign Language and English Literacy," *Journal of Deaf Studies and Deaf Education* 2, no. 1 (1997): 37–46.

61. Oberkotter Foundation, *Dreams Spoken Here* (1998).

62. Oberkotter Foundation, *Dreams Spoken Here* (2004).

63. James Paul Gee, "Discourse Analysis: What Makes It Critical?" in *An Introduction to Critical Discourse Analysis in Education,* ed. Rebecca Rogers (Mahwah, N.J.: Lawrence Erlbaum Associates, 2004), 45.

64. Oberkotter Foundation, *Dreams Spoken Here* (1998).

65. Oberkotter Foundation, *Dreams Made Real.*

66. Ibid.

67. Oberkotter Foundation, *Dreams Spoken Here* (2004).

68. Oberkotter Foundation, *Dreams Made Real.*

69. Ibid.

70. Oberkotter Foundation, *Dreams Spoken Here* (1998).

71. Oberkotter Foundation, *Dreams Spoken Here* (2004).

72. Oberkotter Foundation, *Dreams Made Real.*

73. The reference is to Heather Whitestone, the first deaf Miss America.

74. Oberkotter Foundation, *Dreams Spoken Here* (1998).

75. Most Gallaudet University freshmen come from hearing families, and many were mainstreamed. Many also wear hearing aids and cochlear implants. A significant number arrive either as non-signers or as new signers.

76. Theo van Leeuwen, quoted in Adam Jaworski and Nikolas Coupland, *The Discourse Reader* (New York: Routledge, 2000), 34.

77. Dennis Mumby and Robin Clair, "Organizational Discourse," in *Discourse as Social Interaction,* ed. Teun Van Dijk (London: Sage Publications, 1997), 181.

78. See Lennard Davis, *Enforcing Normalcy: Disability, Deafness, and the Body* (New York: Verso, 1995).

79. Oberkotter Foundation, *Dreams Spoken Here* (1998).

80. Ginsberg, *Passing and the Fictions of Identity,* 3.

81. Jay Lemke, "Identity, Development, and Desire: Critical Questions," in *Identity Trouble: Critical Discourse and Contested Identities,* ed. Carmen Rosa Caldas-Coulthard and Rick Iedema (New York: Palgrave Macmillan, 2008), 32.

82. Ibid., 31.

83. Oberkotter Foundation, *Dreams Made Real.*

84. Ibid.

85. Dan Woog, "The Parton Family Speaks Up," Newstimes.com, available online at http://www.newstimes.com/default/article/Woog-s-World-The-Parton -family-speaks-up-494864.php (accessed September 15, 2010).

86. For an overview of the scholarship, see Kristin Snoddon, "American Sign Language and Early Intervention," *Canadian Modern Language Review* 64, no. 4 (2008): 581–604. See also Mitchiner et al., "The Implications of Bimodal Bilingual Approaches."

87. Ioulia Kovelman, Stephanie Baker, and Laura-Ann Petitto, "Age of First Bilingual Exposure as a New Window into Bilingual Reading Development,"

Bilingualism 11, no. 2(2008): 203–223; Laura-Ann Petitto, "New Discoveries from the Bilingual Brain and Mind Across the Life Span: Implications for Education," *Mind, Brain, and Education* 3, no. 4 (2009): 185–197.

88. See Rachel Mayberry, "When Timing Is Everything: Age of First-Language Acquisition Effects on Second-Language Learning," *Applied Psycholinguistics* 28 (2007): 537–549.

89. Oberkotter Foundation, *Dreams Made Real*.

90. "Between the early pre-school years and adolescence, 62% of deaf children shifted from oral programs to programs with sign support or ASL (Akamatsu et al., 2000). These statistics indicate that the majority of deaf children are deprived of access to a full language when they begin school, and they fall steadily behind their hearing peers through each grade—a conclusion supported by Johnson et al. (1989) and by Kuntze (1998). As a result, deaf students are often transferred for remedial instruction in a signed language environment after losing valuable years of language learning": Snoddon, "American Sign Language," p. 584. See also C. Tane Akamatsu, Carol Musselman, and Avraham Zweibel, "Nature versus Nurture in the Development of Cognition in Deaf People," in *The Deaf Child in the Family and the School: Essays in Honour of Kathryn P. Meadow-Orlans,* ed. Patricia Elizabeth Spencer, Carol J. Erting, and Marc Marschark (Mahwah, N.J.: Lawrence Erlbaum, 2000), 255–274; Robert E. Johnson, Scott K. Liddell, and Carol J. Erting, *Unlocking the Curriculum: Principles for Achieving Access in Deaf Education* (Washington, D.C.: Gallaudet University, 1989); Marlon Kuntze, "Literacy and Deaf Children: The Language Question," *Topics in Language Disorders* 18, no. 4 (1998): 1–15.

 **Contributors**

Dea H. Boster is an instructor at Columbus State Community College and the author of *African American Slavery and Disability: Bodies, Property and Power in the Antebellum South, 1800–1860.*

Jeffrey A. Brune is an assistant professor of history at Gallaudet University and is working on a book manuscript titled *Disability Stigma and the Modern American State.*

Allison C. Carey is an associate professor of sociology at Shippensburg University and the author of *On the Margins of Citizenship: Intellectual Disability and Civil Rights in Twentieth Century America.*

Peta Cox is a tutor and doctoral candidate at the University of Technology, Sydney, Australia.

Kristen C. Harmon is a professor of English at Gallaudet University and the author of several articles and book chapters on deafness and hearing.

David Linton is a professor of communication arts at Marymount Manhattan College and the author of several essays on menstruation.

Michael A. Rembis is an assistant professor of history and the director of the Center for Disability Studies at the University at Buffalo. He is the author of *Defining Deviance: Sex, Science, and Delinquent Girls, 1890–1960*.

Daniel J. Wilson is a professor of history at Muhlenberg College. He is the author of *Living with Polio: The Epidemic and Its Survivors* and *Polio: The Biography of a Disease*, as well as co-author (with Julie Silver) of *Polio Voices: An Oral History from the American Polio Epidemics and Worldwide Eradication Efforts*.

Index

Abbott, Jim, 111
Ableism, 5, 40
Abney, James, 75
American Dream, 174, 193
American Sign Language (ASL), 169, 187;
    bilingualism and, 181, 192
Americans with Disabilities Act (ADA), 5,
    126, 157
Antiracism, 48
Auditory-verbal therapy (AVT), 170, 174,
    175, 180, 182, 189, 191

Barr, Martin, 146
Barrow, Bennet H., 77
Baumgartner, Barbara, 78
Bednarska, Dominika, 113
Bell, Alexander Graham, 175
Bell, Lavinia, 86
Berlin, Ira, 92
Bias, Gail, 24
Black Like Me (Griffin), 7–8, 37, 44, 46–54
Blinded Veterans Association (BVA), 48
Blindness, 5; antiracism and, 48; identity
    and, 43; metaphorical uses of, 49; pass-
    ing and, 36–43, 44–45, 48; slavery and
    feigned, 77
Bliss, George, 146

Boggs, John, 74
Bonazzi, Robert, 44, 53
Brown, Henry Box, 79
Brown, William Wells, 90
Buck, Pearl, 150
Butler, Judith, 9, 102, 117, 118

Campbell, Israel, 79–80
Cartwright, Samuel A., 76
Castles, Katherine, 151
Cheek, Gary, 127
Child, Lydia Maria, 90
Clarke, Milton, 84–85
Cloak of Competence, The (Edgerton),
    150
Cochlear implants, 175, 183, 188, 192
Cognitive-behavioral therapy, 104
Cognitive disabilities, 5, 9
Coleman, J. Winston, Jr., 80
Craft, Ellen, 87–92
Craft, William, 87–92
Cultural life scripts, 179–180, 183
Cultural models, 171, 174, 182, 188

Daggett, Richard, 24
Davidson, Joyce, 155
Davis, Fred, 19–20

Deaf: coming out as, 169, 175, 188; educational institutions for the, 8; oral education and the, 8, 167–168, 170, 174, 182, 183, 184, 186, 187, 191, 192; visibility as, 169

Deafness, 5, 167; conceptualization of, 173, 179; diagnosis of, 170, 171, 173, 176; dreams and, 172–173, 178–179, 182, 184, 189; feigned, 71–73, 87–89; identity and, 190; impact on family of, 174, 176, 183, 185, 189; parents' reaction to child's, 174, 176–177, 179, 181–183, 185–189, 192; passing and, 168, 183, 186–189; reality of, 173; voices and, 186–187

Demps [slave], 77

DePauw, Karen, 115

Depression, 103

Desensitization, 104

Diagnostic and Statistical Manual of Mental Disorders, 101

Disability: advocacy regarding, 9, 50, 52, 133, 153, 154–160; erasure of, 115–117, 126, 132, 156, 158, 190; feigned, 74, 79, 81, 86, 87–92; masculinity and, 122, 127; masquerade and, 73, 106–107, 114; performing, 7, 31–32, 41, 72–73, 80–82, 86, 87–92, 99–102, 189; rights relating to, 51, 53, 60, 129, 153–158; social construction of, 2, 101–102, 142, 160; studies of, 2–4, 54. *See also* Disability identity; Disability passing

Disability identity, 1, 51–52, 117, 131, 142; blindness and, 43; deafness and, 175, 189; intellectual impairment and, 142–143, 144, 154–155, 158–160; pride and, 9, 154–157

Disability passing, 1–2, 116–117, 151–152, 155–156, 158–160, 175; slavery and, 72, 74–76, 86, 87–91; staring and, 47; in texts and public discourse, 36, 49–54

Disabled athletics, 6–7, 112; passing and, 112, 114–116, 119–121, 123, 125, 126, 134–135

Doll, Edgar, 145

Dreams, deafness and, 172–174, 176–179, 183, 184, 189, 190

Dreams Made Real (documentary, 2004), 169, 179, 185, 186, 188

Dreams Spoken Here (documentary, 1998), 167, 169, 170, 172, 174, 182, 188, 191, 193

Edgerton, Robert, 150

Embodiment, 100, 104, 117, 124, 125, 131

Engerman, Stanley, 72

Eugenics, 9; feeblemindedness and, 143–147, 150; passing and, 151–152, 160

Feebleminded, 9; category of the, 142, 144, 145, 147; eugenics and the, 143–145, 150; social control of the, 145, 147; passing and the, 145–148, 150, 160; visibility of the, 146–147

Fernald, Walter, 146

Fett, Sharla, 75

Finger, Anne: passing techniques of, 25, 28; Roosevelt as role model for, 18, 22

Finn, Chester, 156

Fogel, Robert, 72

Forry, Samuel, 74

Frame-based knowledge, 178

Frank, Gelya, 4

Freud, Sigmund, 4

Gallagher, Hugh, 28–31

Gallaudet University, 188

Garcia, Juan M., III, 128

Garland-Thomson, Rosemarie, 47

Gender: disabled athletes and, 124, 130; passing and, 2, 102, 124; performativity and, 102–103, 105

Genesis, 65

Gerber, David, 48

Gill, Carol, 21–22, 154

Gimp (Zupan), 124–126

Gleeson, Brendan, 3

Goddard, Henry, 144–145

Goffman, Erving, 3–4

Govan, Archibald, 81–82

Green, Jacob D., 71–72

Grey-Thompson, Tanni, 115

Griffin, John Howard, 7–8; ableism and, 40; antiracism and, 48; *Black Like Me*, 37, 44, 46–54; passing as a black man,

44, 46–47; passing as a blind man, 36–42, 45, 47, 49; *Scattered Shadows* and blindness of, 37–38, 44, 53–54; stigma and, 38–41; suppression of disability, 49–50; vision regained, 43
Grimké, Archibald, 83
Gross, Anne, 29
Gross, Ariela J., 83
Guttmann, Ludwig, 120

Hackford, Heidi M., 73
Hahn, Harlan, 114–115
Hargreaves, Jennifer, 117
Harris, Marvin, 26
Hearing, passing as, 8–9, 172, 175, 183, 187, 189, 193
Hearing aids, 175, 188
Helping Others Perform with Excellence (HOPE), 133
Henderson, Victoria, 155
Hoover, Herbert, 17
Hostert, Anna Camaiti, 113
Houppert, Karen, 68–69
Huebner, Charlie, 127

Idealized cognitive models (ICMs), 178
Identity, passing and, 2, 39, 116, 117, 142, 190
Illinois, University of, 120, 121
Illness: feigned, 7, 73–74, 76, 79–80; female slaves and feigned, 75, 78
Image schema: container, 177; path, 177; source-path-goal, 177–178
Impairment, 116, 125, 131–132; feigned, 71–74, 78–79, 87–89; female slaves and feigned, 75, 78, 87–89; visible signs of, 113, 117, 131, 146–148
Individuals with Disabilities Education Act, 157
Insane, passing as, 107–108
Intellectual disabilities, 5, 9; passing with, 142, 145–148, 151–152, 156
International Coordinating Committee of the World Sports Organizations (ICC), 121
International Olympic Committee (IOC), 121

International Paralympic Committee (IPC), 121
Intersectionality, 2
Irvin, Cass, 31

Jacobs, Sadie, 45
Jastak, Joseph, 145
Johnson, Alexander, 144
Johnson, Barb, 24
Johnson, Mark, 176

Kaat, Jim, 119
Kenny, Elizabeth, 23
Kiner, Ralph, 119
Kleege, Georgina, 44, 53–54
Kotex, 61; advertising for, 61–64
Kroeger, Brooke, 114
Kunick, Linda, 155

Lakoff, George, 176
Leviticus, 65, 67
Lewin, Philip, 23
Lewis, Victoria, 52–53
Liddy, G. Gordon, 58–59
Liederman, Bill, 118–119
Linton, Simi, 60
Lipshultz, Stanley, 25, 28–29
Littleton, Charles, 157
Littleton v. Wal-Mart (2005), 157
Lomax, Louis, 50–52
Longmore, Paul, 60, 154

Mahoney, Helena, 15
Mainstreaming, 172, 183, 191
Manic depression, 101–102
Mantle, Mickey, 118–119
Marchand, Roland, 61
Marriage, passing and, 25–26
Martin, Emily, 101–102, 107
Masculinity, disability and, 40, 103, 119, 124–129
Mason, Marsha, 25
Masquerade, disability and, 68, 73, 87, 106–107, 114, 119
Mattilda (a.k.a. Matt Bernstein Sycamore), 113–114
Maus, Richard, 26–27

McCarver, Tim, 119
McElveen, A. J., 80
McLoud, Moses, 76
McRuer, Robert, 117
Mecir, Jim, 115
Mee, Charles, 23–24, 27, 29
Menstruation, 5; activism regarding, 68; advertising of products for, 60–64; denial of, 58, 64; disability and, 8; hiding, 62, 64, 66–67; Kotex and, 61–64; odor of, 63, 68; passing and, 59, 64; stigma of, 65–67; taboo of, 65–69; Tampax and, 69; technologies for, 60–61, 67
Mental illness, 5, 9, 104; cultural norms and, 101; passing and, 99–102, 103, 104, 107–108; performance and, 99–103, 105–106, 108; performativity and, 103, 105, 108
Mental retardation: normality and, 148–149, 151–152; parents and their children's, 149, 151–153; social services for, 149, 152–153
Metaphors, conceptual systems and, 176, 177, 178–179
Milam, Lorenzo, 26
Morgan, John H., 75
Moss, Marvin, 155
Mullen, Mike, 128
Mullins, Aimee, 6–7, 123; activism of, 133; athletic career of, 129; fashion modeling career of, 129–130; passing and, 130–131, 133, 134–135
Murderball (documentary, 2005), 124

National Association for Retarded Children (NARC), 148, 149
National Federation of the Blind (NFB), 4, 50
National Spinal Cord Injuries Unit (England), 120
National Wheelchair Basketball Association (NWBA), 120, 122
Nelis, Tia, 158, 159–160
Nepenthe, 63
Nirje, Bengt, 149
Normality: concepts of, 2; deafness and, 172, 176; mental retardation and, 148–149, 151–153; passing and, 25, 28, 41, 143, 148–149, 151–153, 160, 172, 176; social construction of, 3, 149, 160
Nudelman, Dorothea, 23–24, 26
Nugent, Timothy J., 120

Oakes, J. B., 80
Obama, Barack, 58
Oberkotter Foundation, films of the, 8, 167, 169, 170, 171–172, 175, 180, 181–182, 184, 185, 190, 193
Obermayer, Liz, 155
Olympic Games, 120–121
Oral method, deaf education and, 167–168, 170, 182, 184, 192, 193
Osteomyelitis, 118
Overcoming narrative, 127–128, 131–135
Owen, Richard, 21
Owens, Leslie Howard, 83–84

Paralympic Games, 7, 112, 115, 119, 120–123, 127, 129; hypermasculinity and, 122–123, 127; women and, 122–123
Paralympic Military Program, 127
Parton, Caitlyn, 192
Passing, 1–2, 113, 116, 130, 133–135; blindness and, 37–39; deafness and, 168, 172, 175, 183; disabled athletes and, 112, 114, 130, 133–135; family involvement in, 9, 27–28, 40–42, 150, 151–153, 174, 183, 189; feeblemindedness and, 145, 147–148, 150; hearing and, 8–9, 172, 175, 183, 187, 189, 193; historicized, 4; identity and, 2, 39, 116, 117, 142, 190; intellectual disabilities and, 142, 145, 147–148, 151–153, 156–157, 159–160; marginalization in literary texts, 8, 36–37, 49–54; marriage and, 25–26; meaning of, 5; menstruation and, 59; mental illness and, 99–102, 104, 107–108; normality and, 25, 28, 41, 148–149, 151–153, 160, 172, 176; parents and, 9, 151–153, 174, 176; performance and, 31–32, 41, 87–89, 99–103, 105, 117, 189; psychological toll of, 4, 20, 28–30, 39, 158–159, 191, 193; race and, 2, 5, 44, 46, 87–90, 189; Roosevelt, Franklin D., and, 6, 13–14, 18–19, 21, 30–31; sites of conflict and, 4; slavery and, 71–92; sports

and, 111, 115–125, 130, 133; staring
and, 47; temporary, 26–27, 116, 175
Paterson, Kenneth, 106–107
Performativity, 108; feminist accounts of,
100, 102–103
Physical impairments, 5
Poe, Edgar Allan, 63
Polio survivors: avoiding stigma and,
19–20; conceptions of normal and, 22,
25; passing and, 6, 13–14, 19–20, 22,
24–27; physical costs of passing and, 28,
30, 32; psychological costs of passing
and, 20, 28–30, 32; Roosevelt as model
for, 6, 13–14, 18–19, 21, 30–31; walking
and, 15–16, 21–22
Post-polio syndrome, passing and, 6,
13–14, 21, 30–31
Prince, Mary, 77–78

Quinn, Naomi, 176

Race, passing and, 2, 5, 44, 46, 87–90,
189
"Raven, The" (Poe), 63
Redpath, James, 84
Religion, passing and, 5
Renuart, Victor E., 127–128
Ritter, Bill, 128
Rosenstiel, Carol Greenfeld, 29
Roosevelt, Elliott, 16
Roosevelt, Franklin D.: accommodations
for, 17–18; deceptions of, 15–18; as governor of New York, 16–17; as inspiration for passing, 6, 13–14, 18–19, 21,
30–31; as president of the United States,
17–18; public image of, 6, 13–18; return
to political life of, 15–16; walking of,
15–17; wheelchair use of, 16–18

Samuels, Ellen, 87, 90
Sane, passing as, 99–101, 103, 105–106,
108
Scattered Shadows (Griffin), 37–38, 44,
53–54
Schafer, Judith K., 83
Schema, image: container, 177; path, 177;
source-path-goal, 177–178
Schlossberg, Linda, 5

Serotte, Brenda, 22–23, 27
Sexuality, passing and, 2, 5
Sheed, Wilfred, 13; passing and, 13, 24, 30;
post-polio syndrome and, 13, 30
Showgirls (movie, 1995), 59
Shriver, Eunice Kennedy, 150
Siebers, Tobin, 20, 24, 27, 30, 41, 101, 113;
theory of masquerade, 68, 73, 106–107,
114
Sign language, 169, 187
Slavery: disability and, 7; feigned disability
and, 71–81, 86, 87–92; fugitive narra-
tives, disability, and, 86, 87–92; malin-
gering and, 72, 74, 76, 78; masquerade
and, 73, 87; resistance to, 7, 72, 78–81,
84–86; self-mutilation and, 83–85;
stigma and, 7
Smith, Al, 15
Smith, Andrew, 115
Smith, James L., 78
Social Security Administration, 157
Society for Disability Studies, 51
Sotomayor, Sonia, 58–59
Southall, Monica, 128–129
Sports. See Disabled athletics
Stampp, Kenneth, 83
Staring, 47
Steinem, Gloria, 68
Sterilization, 9
Stigma, 2–5, 7, 9, 158, 169, 189; feeble-
mindedness and, 147, 150; John Howard
Griffin and, 38–41; menstruation and,
59; polio survivors and avoidance of,
19–20
Stigma (Goffman), 3–4
Stoke Mandeville, England, 120, 121
Stoke Mandeville Games, 120

Tait, Bacon, 81–82
Tampax, 69
Therapy, goals of, 9–10, 104–105
Thomas, Nigel, 115
Titchkosky, Tanya, 45
Today Show, The, 130
Training School (Vineland, New Jersey),
144
Trickster tales, 73, 75
Trollope, Frances, 84

United States Olympic Committee (USOC),
127

Vesey, Denmark, 82–83
Veterans, disabled, 127–129
Veterans Administration, 128
Virginia [slave], 81–82
Volta Review, 170
Vostral, Sharra L., 60, 67

Walking, passing and, 6, 15–16, 21–24
Warm Springs, Georgia, 15, 17
Warrior Games, 127–128

Wheelchair, 16–18
Wheelchair sports: basketball, 120; rugby,
7, 112, 124
Williams, Serena, 69
Wolfensberger, Wolf, 149
World War II, 67

Zigler, Edward, 148
Zola, Irving, 22, 24, 28, 31, 51–53
Zonite, 68
Zupan, Mark, 6–7, 123–124, 130, 132, 134,
135; *Gimp* and, 124–126; passing and,
125–126